Mother Love
Now and After I'm Gone

I0150360

"There is a Gift in Everything."

By the Award-Winning Best Mommy
Atlanta Jewish Times 1994
Adrian Meyer Mallin

AP Publishing

Dedication

This book is dedicated to G_d and My Soul. I just learned that while I thought I was dedicating this compilation of stories of my life to my sons, Ross and Andrew, the truth for me is that they are the greatest gifts that G_d has ever shared with me. YOU, ROSS and ANDREW are a gift from G_D. So, I take this time to share the joys that you have brought to my soul and how they continue to bless me.

I learned from studying at Unity Church that we children, select our parents in this incarnation, to learn what we are supposed to learn during our time here. There was something about that thought that always made sense. Now, if you think that is the most ridiculous thought, so be it; for me, it resonates loud and clear.

I am certain that YOU, whoever is reading this, have had some 'supernatural' events, observations and/or occurrences in your lives. And if you cannot imagine or recall any -- to ME -- just the cell phone, the radio and the shifting of weather patterns are all bizarre. Who woulda THUNK? ~Smile.

So, without further ado and you surfing your thinking of why we are here and what we came to learn, just imagine that my dear sweet sons have selected ME as their Mom and personally, VICE-VERSA! You boys -- as now the tears begin to 'well' -- are still teaching me EVERYDAY! NO, not just how to use my cell phone – eeerrrggghhh, my non techie mind -- more like LOVE, REAL LOVE, UNCONDITIONAL LOVE. I could go on and on, eyes all fogged up with tears and just thinking about you each and both of you. You move my heart - amazingly, joyfully, and sometimes fearfully -- and yet, MOVE MY HEART YOU DO.

Ross, you arrived after I literally had to take a course about CONSIDERING having a child. I was soooooooooooooooooooooo scared to conceive, as I believe my childhood was such that I was afraid to become a mom, and maybe have history repeat itself. I literally found a course, that by its end, I could not wait for the chance to become a MOM. OH MY G_D, it was the BEST choice I have ever made -- NOTHING even close, not even to become a dancing fool.

i

I just have ADORED this journey with you and trust me, it continues to get better and better. OH MY G_D, you would not believe the speed with which my fingers type. WOW, what energy to tell you how RIDICULOUSLY, hugely, amazingly I have loved this piece of my life! You arrived just as the saddest moments in my life were unfolding. MY mom died. What a contrast. Did you choose to be a PICK ME UP for a sad young lady? You surely were. Thank you.

I did not plan this piece of the book. I guess I didn't plan any of it; it just flowed. For some reason what is flowing to me now is the day that I raced home to watch "All My Children," a soap opera that I was addicted to in 1985. You were about -- I truly do not remember -- maybe 3 weeks, maybe 3 months old. Anyway, I was a new mom and it was almost 1 PM while we were driving down Mercer University Road and I was RACING -- to get home in time to watch Chandler and Erica and all the rest. I sat at the traffic light, determined to make the turn onto Happy Mill Road and get home quickly to watch the show. You must have been 3 weeks, because I cannot imagine being THIS stupid after being a mom for more than 3 weeks. Suffice it to say, I arrived to my parking spot and it dawned on me that going 45 miles per hour in a 25 MPH zone was NOT what good moms are made of. I slowed down, realized my stupidity and NEVER WATCHED THAT SHOW AGAIN -- NEVER! YOU meant that much to me. Perhaps I didn't mean that much to myself, but there was now a new responsibility and G_D only knows, I took it seriously! THANK YOU ROSS! What a gift you were and continue to be.

I can look back at all of the times we ENJOYED! There were the times that I wanted to give you away (16 year olds were no piece a cake in my experience), the times that we have traveled and the times we cried to one another on the phone. Perhaps I did more of the crying. ~Smile.

There are not words to express my journey with you and G_D, PLEASE G_D, let it be another 30-40 years with this child. I so pray G_d that you will listen to my desires. I cannot express my THANKS for you Ross; it goes hand in hand with my love.

One note here is something that I've observed just this year, perhaps maybe the last 2 or so. I have come to you and very often you've assisted me with raising Andrew, your delicious younger brother. You have been more like a dad to him and the "Go-to Guy" to me. You are more than a mere child and son, sometimes. I have come to you rather often these last few years and it astounds me how UNJEALOUS, how supportive of his volleyball career, how giving and wise, how protective and impartial and how amazing you are, to hear me complaining on one line while Andrew awaits your advice about me on the other line. IT is loving; it is. It has been kind; I commend you on your brilliance in negotiating success and love between Andrew and I. I could not have asked for a wiser, more compassionate son -- NOT IN A MILLION YEARS and 1000 lifetimes. THANK YOU MY FIRST CHILD GIFT FROM G_D!

Ahhhh and now a little bit of Andrew. I walked to the North Lake Mall one morning. It was about the 30th of April, a bright, sunshiny morning. I had a mission. It was to go to the bookstore and determine if I ought to have a baby, 2 or 3 years apart from my first son, Ross. I literally sat on the floor of Doubleday books and selected one particular book about the 'SPACING' of children's births. I was having a dilemma regarding how I ought to plan our lives - smile. So I wanted to get the answer as to spacing them 2 or 3 years apart. I was FERTILE MYRTLE with the conception of Ross -- first try -- and figured that, perhaps, the same blessing would be mine again for my NUMERO 2 child.

On my way home -- each way was 2.5 miles -- I thought about the pros and cons of each scenario; two years apart won my favor. I got home and began sharing all the info I had learned with your dad. At that moment the phone rang -- no cells in those days, no call waiting, no caller ID -- and so I picked up the phone and it was my dad. We chatted for a few minutes and he said, "So Adrian, anything cooking in the oven?"

Meaning -- am I making another baby? I giggled and said, "NO DAD."

Shortly thereafter I hung up the phone and said to your dad, "Wanna make a baby?"

We did. It was about noon time and you were born January 29th, exactly 9 months later. WOW, can you imagine how blessed I was to be THAT able to conceive? Some do not have such luck. DAD was a bit disappointed actually; he would have liked more ATTEMPTS at it. ~Smile.

SO, my pregnancy was amazingly PERFECT. I had a sweet little child already and knew that this was going to be another wonderful treat -- to bring into this world another sweet soul. I felt great. I was an experienced pregnant lady and I TOTALLY ADORED all of what being pregnant, giving birth and motherhood were all about -- NO FEAR. I could have been a brood mare. I TOTALLY LOVED being pregnant and THIS time, I set out to totally enjoy the newborn that I was about to have. The last birthing was so fraught with sadness, as my mom had passed away at the same time.

Andrew, I tell you there was no obstacle, no illness, no lack of money, love, or friends that were going to get in my way, as to ENJOYING you entering the world. I JUST LOVED EVERY MOMENT OF YOU. It was the most joyful time, as I had such a hard time experiencing it when Ross arrived -- of course, in no part due to ROSS.

We played, you nursed and we giggled. I swear there was a morning that we had a STARE-down contest. Here you were only 5 months old. We kept the smiles off our faces and stared at one another. I CAVED first and as I laughed, you broke out into this HUGE smiling -- a knowing; it was uncanny.

You presented challenges to me, with school and behavior and I even knew it then – you had COME to TEACH me UNCONDITIONAL love. What a gift that was. You were, to me, a TOTALLY EASY baby. I once called Dr. Veras and told him that you were sleeping until 11:30 am and I was AFRAID. He said, "Messes Malinnn (he was Greek), YOU are being blessed; just enjoy it!"

You used to wander off. We got a fence because of you. We even put you on a leash in Montana, to the horror of others watching, because you were 3 and wondered away from the store we were in. Holy MOTHER! What could have happened if we couldn't find you?

You always had your own mind -- oh my goodness -- from holding the telephone to squirreling away raisins in your mouth when you'd eat cereal. I just LOVED watching you. You were special and different in some regards and I loved that about you -- VERY amazingly aware. You used to walk through the mall with me and see different situations unfolding. You'd ask, "Mommy, was that a NICE man?"

You were literally evaluating behavior -- kind and not so. I recall putting Sweet n Low on my food and you asking me at 3 years old, "Mommy, why are YOU allowed to eat the pink stuff and I am not?"

Apparently it was because I loved you more than I loved myself. You gave me the inspiration to become a better person. There are still LOTS different about you and I LOVE it! You continue to inspire me. You are so discerning. You have shown me what TRUE passion is in the way of your love for and gift of volleyball. I was amazed, that first time that I saw you at a practice with Mike -- OH MY G_D! -- I don't think I could have done for 20 seconds, what you trained for literally 4 hours per day. It astounded me and it was that very day that I let go of my fear and came to support you, regarding volleyball. I finally had learned that THIS was your career -- your work -- that you were building. I had no idea. I was and, continue to be, so utterly impressed with your talent, your dedication and your determination.

Ross once shared with me that he wished you and he could be MORE in the way of all of the other mother's sons -- to be a lawyer, a doctor or something that I could tell my friends, while they show off about their children's successes. Do you recall that Ross?

NO FRICKIN WAY! My sons are MAGNIFICENT on the outside -- YES! And just as, if not more, loving and fun and healthy and joyful on the inside. I would NOT have it any other way! Talk about compassion and kindness.

I have to share a compassionate thought that comes to mind regarding each of you. First you, Ross -- when you were a little boy, perhaps 6 or 7 years old, we were at the mall. There was a blind man and you asked me if you could go and talk to him. "Of course!"

I watched you go to him. You shared that you were sorry that he didn't have sight and how you wished that he did. He thanked you, talked to you for a moment and told you that it was okay, as you told me what happened when you returned to me. We were in the FOOD COURT. If I could surmise what that meant to him, I know it meant the world.

And you, Andrew -- I will always cherish the memory of you being at one of our dances at the senior center. There was this 80 year old woman sitting there, in one of the chairs as the dancers twirled around the dance floor. I watched you, of your own volition go up to her and, at 12 years old, ask her to dance. OH MY G_D, thank you G_D for putting a soul on this earth to have such compassion and kindness. I think you made her year, let alone her day.

So, without further ado, I want you both to know that YOU have been the inspiration -- the love I have for each of you -- to have written this book. It has given me more joy, in the way of it having been quite challenging, and the greatest feelings of accomplishment, second to raising you boys. I have grown in self-esteem, I have grown in JOY and I have loved EVERY minute of writing. It has stirred my soul and given me comfort as nothing else ever has -- besides you two.

My intention for this mélange of stories is to FORTIFY you. I feel as if I have been most of your support -- emotionally, spiritually, positivity and lovingly -- thus far in your lifetime. And so, selfishly, I pray that if I'm here, you will continue to come to me. IF I'm not and you have a challenge or a need for HOW TO THINK, I want you to use this book to fortify you with a healthy way of looking at life -- KNOWING that there is a gift in everything -- the joys as well as the adversities. It will be your job to figure it out in a healthy way, surely not as a victim or in a pitiful way.

I want you to know that while I'm not leaving this planet, G_D willing anytime soon, that whatever unfolds, I adore you to the max and am grateful for you both and LOVE, LOVE, LOVE, that you adore one another. That is one of the greatest gifts that children can give to one another and their parents.

BLESS YOU BOTH and with heartfelt love ~XOXO Mom

Disclaimer - One Important Fact

When I set out boys to PEN this book - it was 100% for you two - entirely. I wanted to share some of my wisdom and looking back on my life and what life was teaching me - FAR REMOVED from the sting or the pain back then.

I shared my writing with friends and editors along the way - and heard an interest expressed in them wanting to read more and more stories and perhaps even GET what I set out to GIVE you - faith - and more mastery at life - as I have achieved a little.

It was suggested that I change the names of many of the characters in the story -

I so did NOT want to do that - as the book is about being AUTHENTIC - and my heart has been so open - with only my truth - good/ bad / indifferent.

I have been so determined in my life to let go of FEAR - and here I am changing names for FEAR sake - that doesn't feel good / HOWEVER - it feels wise.....

SO - ask me if you want to know who "so and so" is..............I love you both!~ x0Mom

---

Contents

Forgiveness   IV

Fate/Destiny   V

Believe in Yourself   VI

G_d Having Fun   VII

G_d Appearing Anonymously   VIII

Patience   IX

Signs   X

Wisdom   XI

Listen to your Gut   XII

Prayer   XIII

A Gift in Everything   XIV

Angels   XV

Faith

Where are We Moving? -- '97

I think this is close to about the time these unfoldings became very consistent. I had heard at Unity that just ASK and the answers are inside of us. I figured, OKAY!

Melvin and I had started packing. We knew we were moving; we just did not know where. Andrew could NOT attend that public school that I visited and still keep his self-esteem intact. He was in a special class and the demographics were just different from what I had hoped for him.

We were getting close to graduation from Vanderlyn and we had to be SOMEWHERE by the start of 6th grade for Andrew and 8th grade for Ross. Ross was also more than ready to move -- another story. Perhaps he will tell his own one day!

We were packing -- the breakfront, the glasses, the china – all the stuff we knew we would not need. It was March and while we had several months until school would begin again, we had LOTS to do, to plan a move and I am, surely, a planner.

The condos were up for sale, the house was up for sale, boxes were ready, internal repairs were done and we had taken several trips around the country. Would it be AUSTIN? HELL NO, we escaped the tornado of '98. Would it be Bakersfield, California or Orlando, Florida? Where were we moving? I WANTED an answer so badly. My faith was not as strong then, so I WORRIED.

I still do on occasion, but after having lived so many of life's experiences, it DOES grow your faith. You come to learn that it will all be okay and that goodness will prevail, even in the adversity and pain.

I was doing my walking at the mall and decided to close my eyes and ask G_D, "WHERE ARE WE MOVING?"

I decided at the moment I opened my eyes, there would be an answer. I was sort of playing and yet, trusting G_D, to see if what I had learned at Unity really worked. "Okay G_D," as I prayed; with eyes looking downward, sort of playing a game, "I will pray and look down at my feet while I walk and THEN when I look forward, upward and ahead, YOU will have my answer."

I prayed and walked...prayed and walked. As I looked up after the prayer, I immediately saw THE DISNEY STORE. Well, well, was this THE SIGN? THE DISNEY STORE...California...Orlando...Paris? ~Smile. Hmmmmmmmm, so... THE DISNEY STORE! I asked G_D to give me confirmation. I continued to walk and then saw a neat shirt in the window of a store I passed every day. But THIS day, I found myself going inside and having a look. Most of the time, my walks are TOTALLY focused. I have been walking since Durham in 1977 and when I go to walk, that is what I do – PERIOD -- USUALLY no shopping, perhaps stopping and chatting on occasion, but mostly focused, and there to do my exercise. This time I indulged and went in to check out the good looking shirt. I selected my size and, LO and BEHOLD, the label said "ORLANDO."

HOLY MOTHA! I left the mall, went home, walked in the door and yelled to Melvin, "I know where we're moving – ORLANDO!"

We did...that very July! ~Smile.

Yes, Not Now, I Have Something Better in Store For You -- Condo -- 1998

It was 1997 and we had our condo listed for rent, lease or sale. We were moving to Orlando and had to do SOMETHING with it. I was the one to show it, mostly, and within 12 months, I executed 4 different contracts -- all for sale. Each and every one of them could NOT get financing. Oh, we were upset. We were still humbled, regarding owning rental properties, and did not have the confidence that we could move and let someone else rent them. We were, quite frankly, distraught. We had listed the unit for $89,900 and THAT was a steal. WHY, oh WHY was it not selling?

We masterminded about it, asking for Rachel, Toni and Donna's help and prayers for us; it just stumped us all. "G_D, why can't you rent this unit, sell it or lease it. What is wrong? Have you lost our file?"

We were leaving, movers and all, on a Thursday. Here it was Saturday, ad prominently in the paper and doing EVERYTHING we could to find ourselves a buyer. The phone rang about 10 AM and this man introduced himself to me as Jay. He said that he wanted to rent our condo. I listened and he shared that his condo that WAS being built, was hit badly by the tornado in April (this was now July), totally lost it and needed something else quickly. I suggested that I show it to him immediately. I could be there at noon and he said, "NO, I don't need to see it; I want it! My office is down the block and it will be fine."

"Okay," I responded, thinking he might be delusional.

I continued the conversation, answering his questions and informing him that if he wanted to rent it, it would be $1K/month. He needed to be prepared to bring a check for $3K, for first month, last month and security. He mentioned that he might be interested in leasing it. I told him that he would need an additional $5K for the option. "Fine," he said and asked could he come to our house to close the deal.

"Surely!" and I gave him directions.

He was a little Jewish man, probably similar in age to Melvin and me. He had gone through a nasty divorce and had bad credit, yet wanted us to work with him. Shortly after his arrival to our home, he opened his brief case and had $8,000 in cash for the rental with the lease option. WOW! BIGGER WOW! We gave him the keys. He became an exemplary tenant. We met him 1 year later and made the option a permanent sale. He now owned the unit and paid US, as his monthly mortgage company. We had NO responsibility; we just collected checks with a 9.8% interest rate – NICE!

We enjoyed Jay as a tenant for over a decade and then when he decided to refinance, we were no longer able to keep him. He refinanced with another mortgage company. In the meantime, when we sold him the condo, I included a PREPAYMENT penalty of 20%. That translated into $14K. So added to what he had paid us over the 10+ years, it amounted to just under $200,000 – THIS, instead of $89,900…NOT bad, huh, -- a very sweet deal!

So I think back on this experience NOW, trying my best NOT to question -- just continuing to have faith in the universe. Actually, the only thing that is missing from my life at this time is a best friend, lover and partner in life. I am sure, just reflecting back on my doubts in 1998 and how the universe supplied HUGELY, that I no longer have ANY doubt. I, too, know that my right and perfect love partner is on his way to me, just as I am on my way to him. The seeds have been planted. The universe is conspiring to bless me. We will find one another in the perfect time.

G_D says either YES, NOT NOW or I HAVE SOMETHING BETTER IN STORE FOR YOU. And so it is! What a sweet, sweet, memory of TRUSTING in G_d and having that faith for things not yet seen!

Penny and CL -- 2/2000

It was difficult enough to lose my best friend. Couple that with having to constantly see her on TV and in the tabloids; oh what a tough time this was. AND THEN I realized that our children no longer had a viable guardian, as Theresa was the guardian for Ross and Andrew, if ever something were to happen to Melvin and me, in an untimely manner. Now there was fear coupled with loss.

You boys were about 12 and 14 years old. You were civil and mature, while still BOYS! I had to get to the lawyer, change the will and SLEEP at night; I cannot sleep when I do not know the fate of my children. Oh what a challenging time that was! I spent hours before sleep talking with your dad about Paula, Liz and Tony and every one of our friends and neighbors, family and co-workers. WHO would be decent enough, caring enough and loving enough to take GREAT care of our sons? We seemingly had no one to choose from and were almost at wits end. Now mind you, nothing was bad about our choices, but we were EXTREMELY selective. We needed someone with healthy parenting experience, no addictions and great role models for hard work and healthy values.

Would we consider our children growing up in another state -- uprooting them from their friends, in addition to 'if they also lost us?' There was MUCH to consider. My family was gone and Dad's family was not very close to you boys, so we had a HUGE and challenging decision to make. How about Penny and CL? They were neighbors just down the block and really sweet, caring, decent people. They raised great kids. Penny and CL were hard working, happily married, joyful people. So I figured perhaps they would consider taking you boys, just in case. We could specify that there would be money for them -- that whomever we selected would not be responsible for your financial welfare. We would make arrangements for you for college, your upkeep, getting your first cars and all of what would keep you going if something happened to Dad and me. We were responsible to the max.

One night Penny invited all four of us to dinner. Oh my, was she ever a cook. Speaking of plenty of food, I thought YES, YES, YES, the boys would LOVE being a part of their family! If everything went 'right," I would ask Penny about what I had been laboring over and see what she thought of me listing her and CL as Ross and Andrew's guardians. We were all sitting, eating hors d'oeuvres, when Penny called me into the kitchen. I excused myself, figuring she needed help. She called me aside and began, "Adrian, please don't think I'm silly or at all out of line, but CL and I were talking about how much we love your boys and we just thought we'd put it out there. If something ever happened to you and Melvin, we would be more than grateful to take the boys and raise them as our own. What do you think?"

"Did I hear you correctly? Are you asking me if you could be guardians, if ever something happened to Melvin and me?"

I was not sure if I was in a dream state. "You're never going to imagine what I was going to discuss with you tonight, Penny. OH MY G_D!"

YES, Oh My loving, gracious, generous and perfect G_D! Amen!

The Three Answers to All of Life's Desires -- 2012 and Eternity

God has 3 answers:

1. YES
2. Not Yet
3. I have something better in store for you.

Assign these, have faith and keep the faith!

A Call to Harold – I Know There's a Gift in This – 2005

I had to get my mail. I took out a PO Box when I first moved to South Florida, because I was not certain where I'd be settling. I went to the Coconut Creek site and opened my mailbox. OH MY! I am getting a visceral constriction, LITERALLY, as I write this. I think that the surprise I got was second, only to learning that someone had died.

I was being SUED to OVERTURN the divorce that had settled amicably well over a year prior. My heart dropped as if pulling on my tear ducts, causing the tears to run down my face. I looked up at the Heavens and babbled softly out loud, "Thank you G_d. I KNOW there's a gift in this. There's a gift in this." Then I reached for my phone and called Harold.

The story is in this book at greater length. Yet the point of this is that as soon as you TRUST that there is a gift in your adversity, the universe begins to agree with you. Actually, very soon, it will be revealed to you. The sooner you KNOW that, as has been my experience, the sooner the gift will be revealed. If you wait and suffer, being a victim, then that is what you will get -- WAITING and SUFFERING. Instead, if you have faith and KNOW that it is G_d's will for you, then you will be blessed. You will RICHLY learn something -- the universe positions itself and reveals lessons and blessings quickly.

For me, I heard the hard, HARD news towards the end of December and the incredibly RICH blessing revealed itself to me by late March of the following year. I just KNOW there was a connection.

Ring of Faith -- 2005

It was about 2005, August, and I had just put my house under contract. AMEN and Hallelujah, I was selling it 'for sale by owner' -- FSBO. Maxine said I could not. Dana was there to assist, if I needed help. Dad was gone, did not do a thing and what a challenging time it was. I was literally moving my life, enduring the ravages of divorce, no one even there to help me pack this HUGE house, with an attic that was 119 degrees and needed to be emptied. It was August in Orlando.

Still, I SOLD my house, and might add, for the HIGHEST square foot price in the neighborhood to date. Ta-Da! BUT, a house is NOT sold until the sale is CLOSED. This was under contract. All was moving along well. I had made the move to South Florida and was told by Luis that it is a big house and I ought to be there for the closing. UGH, and yet he was right.

So, you know how I detest long drives. Still I made the drive, quite pleased and happy. The best and only time, really, to sell a house in a good school system is either right after school is over or right before it begins; there is a small window. 4491 Lucky Lane was closing just as school was to begin, so the SELLING season was basically over for 2005. 2005 was also the beginning of the worst recession ever and the downturn in prices was HUGE. IT was just beginning and was not really OBVIOUS in August. I got the highest price! I wonder which angel masterminded THAT for me.

Anyway, I drove up to Orlando from South Florida, checked into my favorite Extended Stay and went to the closing at 10 AM. I was notified, upon arriving, that the paper work was not ready and that we would proceed later that afternoon – 6 PM to be exact -- so I left and returned at 6 PM...no biggie.

At 6 PM, on this particular Wednesday, I was told that the paper work was coming from Tampa and it had not arrived. We would reschedule for the next morning, Thursday, at 10 AM. I was a tad bit not well pleased and yet, blessedly, I could just stay another night in the hotel and see a few friends -- always a gift in everything.

The next morning, bright eyed and bushy tailed, I was prepared to sign the documents and sell the house. BUT, it still would not take place. Now I was getting a tad bit upset. This was the third time it was cancelled and something was not right. I called insurance and told them NOT to cancel the homeowners' policy, but to reinstate it, please. I called the utility companies, to keep the air conditioning on and in my name, and did all that I had to do to maintain this home; it was STILL mine. Oh dear, I was concerned.

Well, I returned at 6 PM, again on Thursday, and was informed that it would take place on Friday. OH MY GOODNESS, I did not sleep well that night. Talk about postponement, this was beyond! I stayed another night in the hotel and returned for the 5th visit to the mortgage office. All of my ducks were in a row and supposedly the same for the buyer. When we met there, for the 5th visit, we were turned away; it would not take place until Friday evening at 6 PM.

I met with Luis at Season's 52 at 4 PM that very afternoon. We talked. He had been a realtor in his PREVIOUS life; now he owned the ballroom, Dance Orlando. Anyway, I was teary. I was upset. I was now living in South Florida and there was no way that I could sell this home again, FSBO. I was calculating how much this would cost me -- perhaps to the tune of $38,000, more in commissions that I would have to pay a realtor AND what about the fact that the selling SEASON was over? Who would buy my house? All the little darlings were already in school. OH MY G_D, this was NOT GOOD. Luis tried to console me. I needed to go and wipe my face from my tears and headed off to the restroom. Just as I opened the door, there was this little silver circular "thing" on the floor. It called me, I picked it up and it was a small silver ring that fit right on my ring finger. It had an inscription as I held it up to the light, squinting to see what it said.

FAITH, "FAITH" was inscribed.

Like surrender around the high cliff roads in Colorado -- my heart, my head, my gut, and my soul relaxed into perfect faith. I felt as if it was a sign, a message, a signal from the almighty! I went back to the table BEAMING with exhilaration, as I showed my new found BEST friend to Luis. He too delighted in its message. Then again, HE, too, KNOWS.

I left and headed over to the mortgage company one more time. We closed at 6 PM. I reversed the ownership of insurance and utilities back again to my new buyer, gave MANY thanks to the above and have not taken this ring off since. I show it to many, share my story, and blessedly, it has vitalized me several times, reminded me, and fortified me when I most needed more...FAITH!

Andrew's Unfolding and My Finding HUGE FAITH in It
2012 July

Andrew is now 25 years old. He is excelling in the pursuit of his dream -- to be a Beach Volleyball Olympiad in Brazil, in 2016. He is THAT good; that intent is his focus. He is now playing tournaments ALL over the United States. He used to play locally, and then he branched out to all over Florida. He has driven to several tournaments in nearby states and now he gets on a plane and flies to a city, gets all settled and plays tournaments.

I want to share how far he's come. He was living in Orlando, some 4 years ago, maybe 5 and enjoyed playing volleyball. There was a memorable visit he paid to me over a Thanksgiving. I had lived here alone in South Florida and, "coincidentally," met a man at my gym who happened to be a Beach Volleyball player, as well as being the dad of a son who played. His name was Bill. We chatted one day while at the gym and he told me that if my son wanted to play, he had to EAT, SLEEP and BREATHE beach volleyball. I relayed this tidbit to Andrew.

In the meantime, Bill mentioned that there was a family called the Van Zwietens who have about 4 or 5, perhaps even 6 sons, ALL of whom play volleyball and are ranked number 1 in the state of Florida...something like that. Bill mentioned that if my son wanted to play with this family, that he could arrange it and he gave me their phone number before Andrew's visit to South Florida that November.

I recall asking Andrew if he had ever heard of the Van Zwieten family and it seemed as if his jaw dropped while over the phone. "OF COURSE MOM! They're amazing! They're the BEST!"

He was rather excited that there was the possibility of his playing with the Van Zwietens. I DID GOOD! ~Smile.

Well, Andrew arrived here and it was time to CALL them. Believe it or not, he was a bit afraid. He did not want to BOTHER them. Andrew is a humble man and did not think that he could ever play in THEIR league of talent.

So, I called and got Steve Van Zwieten, while he was in Ohio. I recall they were visiting their grandparents and he said that while they would love to meet Andrew and play with him, they were out of town. I almost think Andrew, WHILE DISAPPOINTED, was a bit relieved. They were THAT good and Andrew did not have nearly the confidence that he has today.

Anyway, I like to share from where he came, to show the contrast of how he is ranked today – HIGHLY! The recent trip that he was making to New Jersey, to play in a tournament, has added HUGELY to MY faith. It is probably the number one most recent reason as to my writing this book now, FINALLY! The experience I am about to share has inspired me in a faith-filled way -- like NO other. Several have been PRETTY inspirational, and that THIS one - took me over the top. So here goes!

Andrew located two tournaments – back-to-back weekends up in New Jersey. Boy, am I in the mood for a cigarette. NO, I don't smoke any longer. I gave it up 30 years ago and yet, this writing…this intensity…recalling these stories evokes such emotion in me, that, WHEW, a cigarette, IF I smoked, would be PERFECT just about now.

Lest I diverge, the story continues. So, he decided to go to Atlantic City and play a tournament near there and then the following weekend, play the Jose Cuervo tournament in Belmar, New Jersey.

He was NOT yet IN THE MONEY, so I was motherly and financially concerned about how he was going to miss 12 days of work, coaching and how he was going to pay for a flight, rental car, hotels, food, registration, etc. I discussed this with him, GINGERLY, so he did NOT get defensive. He even agreed that because the flight was so inexpensive, that he had decided to stay and play in both of the tournaments. He also agreed that it was a bit of a lengthy trip and so, he would learn for the next time.

MEANWHILE, I was concerned. I do not like him going deeper in the financial hole, and.............. I do NOT want to enable him.   I had agreed to pay for his flight with Spirit Airlines – an important detail. Yet, I did not want him NEEDING MORE MONEY! I agreed to take him and his volleyball partner, Dave, to the airport.

The night before, I lost sleep just WORRYING about him arriving in Atlantic City and, G_d forbid, sleeping in their car – thus, to save money.

We began the drive to the airport and I asked the boys, in a way that they would listen -- I BEGGED – "PLEASE boys, don't sleep in your car! Please! All I did was worry last night," I shared.

"Mom," Andrew responded, "NOT to worry! We are going to get a hotel room. We need our sleep and I promise, no sleeping in the car."

Whew! I was relieved. He would not lie to me. I kissed them -- LOTS – upon departure at the airport. I was just nervous. And off they went, with balls and duffle bags and lots of STUFF for 12 days.

I received a call at about 3 PM that afternoon, "Mom, we're fine, landed and get this, we were going to rent a car, BUT it was $500 and $100 additional for drop off! So, we hopped in a cab for $80 and just after about a mile or so, Shane calls and says, 'BRO, I can come to the airport and pick you up. I'll be there within the hour.'"

Andrew, Dave and the taxi turned around and headed back to the airport, where he told me they threw the driver a few tip dollars and waited for Shane. Shane arrived, picked them up and while driving toward their destination said, "You guys can stay with me and my parents thru Sunday…and this was Thursday!

WOW! I was soooooooooooooooooooooooo happy now…VERY relieved. And I continued to ask, "So what happened with the luggage?"

That was another thing that I worried about – Spirit --- nickel and diming them to death with baggage fees. "Oh, Tyler's girlfriend was on her shift at the Spirit counter and she let us on with no baggage fee," responded Andrew.

WOW! Now I am watching this scenario. My child…he does not worry, nor fret…he hands it over to G_d. He says, "Not to worry Mom," and most of the time, he is totally calm and I am the one who does the worrying. Hmmmmm, talk about manifesting GREAT STUFF, thinking creates life. Andrew's thinking is full of positivity and no worry.

I was such a happy girl and so tickled to share this story with a few friends. The weekend progressed. I was at dinner on a Saturday night,(when he usually calls to tell me how he did in the days competitions) and I sat there literally waiting for his call. The call came and he said, "MOM, we're in the finals - so pray for us! I'll call you tomorrow! G'night!"

Ahh joy, a toast and so with joy and thanksgiving in my heart, I prayed for him, went home from my date, went to sleep and received a call on Sunday. "Guess where I am Mom? I just got out of the shower in the penthouse apartment overlooking next weekend's volleyball courts and am standing on the balcony. We won the tournament this AM and met BIG MIKE on the beach."

"Who's BIG MIKE?" I inquired?

"A nice guy we met on the beach and he happens to own this penthouse where we're staying, right above the courts where this upcoming tournament is going to be, next weekend. It's about an hour from where THIS weekend's tournament was and he told Dave and I, that we could be his guests for the week."

"OH MY G_D!" I exclaimed, "YOU'RE amazing! Tell me more!"

He was pretty happy, pretty high, having won $500 for the tournament...and so the week progressed and I am watching this faith-filled young man just skate through the gifts and blessings of this trip. It was as if – NO, it was surely -- G_D paved his path, with NO worry, no angst, just faith!

17

He was to arrive home on Tuesday PM and I was scheduled to pick them up about 9 PM. I received a call that their plane was going to be about 4 hours late and I told Andrew that I did NOT want to get out of bed at 1 AM to go to the airport and to please figure out another way home.

By the way, he placed 13th in the Belmar tournament, earning $375. This was the Cuervo and the tournament was a huge invitational tournament, so even 13th place was quite wonderful! Back to the airport and his arrival home.

I went to sleep, knowing/praying that Andrew would find an easy, NOT too expensive way home. I looked forward to him arriving safely back in Ft. Lauderdale and then staying at my home for the night. At about 2 AM, I had to get up to go to the bathroom and I whistled "the mommy whistle" from when you boys were younger and, in one moment, who comes into the darkness of my bedroom standing in the shadow, but this big tall guy in his boxers! ~Smile.

"Hi Honey!" (big hugs) "So how did you get home?"

"Well Mom, we were playing with this cute little puppy dog in the airport, while the plane was delayed, and this lovely lady suggested that she take Dave and me home. So, she dropped Dave off on Sample and then brought me up here to Boca to you!"

Are you smiling? I am! What a perfect trip! I hope that in some way this restores, replenishes or gives you faith. It surely did, does and is giving it to me! If you just have faith, no worry! Know it will turn out just fine. Give it up and let it go. Do your best and have the courage to go after your dream. ALL will be well! And so, this was a HUGELY significant demonstration for ME! I literally do not remember when I LEARNED so much in the way of NOT worrying by letting it go and having faith.

I took Andrew to dinner the next night, for us to catch up. I sat there, getting the feeling that it was time to PASS THE BATON. This child knows and demonstrates more than I do. He KNOWS...he believes...he sets this HIGH example for me to follow and, BLESSEDLY, I truly give credit as my inspiration for the writing of this book, is in great part what and how Andrew manifested. What Joy! Thank you G_d! Amen, and so it is!

Honesty

PEANUT BUTTER SANDWICHES tossed behind the washing machine - remember??

Mom Had Just Died and I Had Just Given Birth -- 1985

Mom had just died and I had just given birth. Melvin, Ross, Olivia, and I came to Florida to have Mom's gravestone unveiling. It was a very sad occasion. I do not think we ever get over our loved ones' deaths. Ross was the joy, and quite frankly, I remember VIVIDLY he had his first SOLID food. Oh my goodness, this child was STARVING; he ate as if it would be the LAST meal he would ever ingest. We could not get that spoonful of cereal into his mouth quickly enough. I did not realize it, but I was literally starving this child. My milk had apparently dried up, but I did not know it. He would grab onto a breast, and here, I thought he was getting fed...NOT! He was starved! Sorry, Ross, I was a new mom and did not know I was supposed to drink lots of water. I learned.

It was literally HYSTERICAL watching you grab the cereal and be ready for the next spoonful before we could even LOAD IT ON THE SPOON. I am sure your dad would remember; it was so funny. What was NOT so funny was when my sister, in front of YOU, Dad and OLIVIA, accused me of stealing Mom's table cloths. WHAT? ME steal from my own Mother? Table cloths, here I was a caterer, why would I steal table cloths? I had dozens of my own, belonging to "A Catered Affair." This was sooooooooooooooooo hurtful and so unnecessary, I could not believe it; nor could I believe that my dad believed her. There was nothing I could do to convince anyone that I had not taken them. Of course Melvin knew that I had not, yet WHERE DID THEY GO?

THIS is one of the less pleasant emotional stories I have written, yet there is a reason. I do try and I am determined to REMAIN positive, NO MATTER what the situation is, in life. WELL, this too has a positive. It turned out that almost 13 years later, the truth and the mystery of where those tablecloths went was revealed. It was at your bar mitzvah, Ross, and Cousin Estelle was there. Out of her mouth, during some conversation came, "I couldn't believe that your mom, Irma, CHARGED me for her tablecloths, when she had her garage sale and was moving to Florida!"

What? My ears perked up, TABLECLOTHS? Here is the scoop. YES, it was VERY unfair and very inappropriate to be accused of something I did not do, and the only one that knew the truth was ME! ... ME and my G_D! Sometimes, I have found that life will be truly UNFAIR; it surely was in this instance. Yet the only person -- entity -- you have to comfort you and 'know what you know,' is yourself. I do not believe I ever even told Berniece. I truly do NOT care what she thinks; she did her damage.

What matters, to me, is to do MY best, to be the BEST ME I can be and even then, others will find fault. I guess that is the meaning of having to turn the other cheek. It is what it is and I was grateful to have the truth revealed, even if it was some 13 years later. AMEN and thank you G_D!

The Truth and Nothing But the Truth -- The Today Show -- 1990

It was 1990, I THINK. What I recall most was that it was a recession. Businesses were struggling, people were paying big time at the gas pumps and here I was a CATERER, with only other peoples' indulgences that FED us. I spent a great part of late November and early December COMPLAINING. There was little on my books in the way of December turning out to be a great month financially. The month of December usually earned more than all of the other months put together. It was HUGE and I was usually busy from Thanksgiving Day until the 24th of December and then again on the 31st. It was the time of year that financial joy was found and bodily exhaustion was expected.

I was at my catering friends, Rob and Steve's location, Art of Catering. They were the number 1, best in town. I got food prepared by them, equipment loaned to me and everything that one could possibly ask for with them as my mentors. I loved them; they were so good to me and we were friends as well. I sat there and we all kvetched; their business was HUGELY off and they were feeling the pinch, to the point where it was more like a major pressure squeeze. They had hundreds of employees. They had a multi-million dollar business and while they earned fabulously YEAR round, this December was surely putting a crimp in their style and the worries were huge.

I went home and did what I could to summons up business. A day or so later after complaining a bunch but feeling a tad bit better in the 'misery needs company department,' I received a phone call. It was a Sunday night; I remember it vividly. The four of us had all finished dinner, it was time to wash the dishes and then have dessert. The caller was a man who said he was working for the Creative Loafing Newspaper and he wanted to do a story on me and my catering businesses -- A Catered Affair and Breakfast N Bed. I got out of doing the dishes and attended to the interview. ~Smile. I chatted with him for about a half hour and he asked all kinds of questions as to how business was. Specifically, he asked if the recession was affecting me. "Oh My G_D, yes!"

He fired away with dozens of questions. He mentioned that he had chatted with several other caterers in town, Perfect Cuisine, HIGH END, Art of Catering and a few others. He was surprised at what I told him; as the others said, business was GOOD. "WHAT?" I said, "GOOD? We're all starving, I just chatted with the others on Friday. Did they really tell you that business was good? They're liars!"

We laughed and I hung up. "The article would appear in next week's paper," he said. The following Tuesday, I was sitting in my office when the phone rang. "Hi this is Susan, from the Today Show, NBC Live."

"Yeah sure," I responded, "who is this?"

"It's Susan, I'm not kidding. Is there an Adrian Mallin there?"

"Speaking, come on stop kidding, who is this?"

"My name is Susan and I am from the Today Show. I'm wanting to talk to an Adrian Mallin about being on the show this Friday, December 14th."

"Oh my goodness," I responded, now feeling the sincerity of this woman on the other end of the line. "How can I help you?" I asked.

Then she began to tell me that the interview I gave on Sunday night was sent to The Today Show and they wanted to do a story on how the recession was affecting the country and if I would consent, they would send their crews to me in Atlanta and film me for the 7 AM show on Friday. OH MY G_D, OH MY G_D! I could hardly contain the excitement and enthusiasm over the next 4 days.

I recall doing my walking around Perimeter Mall that day, feeling like a celebrity. I'd pass stores, wave and think, "YOU DON'T KNOW IT, but I, Adrian Mallin, am going to be on television this Friday, with something like 40 million people watching me -- ME! The week unfolded. I shared my enthusiasm with several friends and Friday AM arrived.

It was 5 AM when the crew and the BIGGEST camera truck I had ever seen would be parked in front of 828 Misty Lane, our home. It was a satellite truck. Remember this was 1990, almost 22 years ago, and so clearly not as techie as life is now.

So, the truck arrived and shortly thereafter, a knock at the door. A few guys entered our home to set up the camera, shoot and film me. I was all dressed up in my black pants, white shirt, bow tie and catering apron...A Catered Affair. My Hair was in place and someone did a little makeup enhancement, hair and then camera taping in my office. You boys were upstairs with Irene, our nanny, and she would come downstairs with you guys, every 20 minutes or so to let you come into Mommy's office and see what all was going on. You were 3 and 5 years old at the time. Daddy was behind the scenes. He was there MUCH for moral support. Oh my goodness, I was nervous, yet it was such a thrilling nervousness. They did a run-through, telling me how Katie Couric would conduct the interview and shortly thereafter, I would meet her over the phone. First I was told that it would be a countdown – 10, 9, 8, 7, 6, 5, 4, 3, 2, 1...and then the interview would begin.

The ear plugs were affixed in my ears. We got down to business, office arranged, you boys up stairs watching the Today Show and Mommy in the office with my heart BEATING out of my chest...how many million?

And the countdown began 10, 9, 8, 7, 6 and OH MY G_D, my ear piece fell out of my ear. I almost had a heart attack, talk about hysteria and nervousness. I grabbed it in time, PLUGGED in back in my right ear and 2, 1..."HI THERE, Adrian, so tell me about your Christmas Catering Season this year," Katie began.

I shared how we were serving more meatballs than shrimp this year, how tonight, the second Friday in the month and usually a HUGELY busy evening, was totally slow. In the past, the second weekend of December -- both Friday and Saturday nights -- were the busiest nights of the month. NOT SO this approaching weekend, I normally would have had 2 or 3 parties each night and, instead, had only one for the entire weekend. We chatted for quite a while and then I mentioned that I WILL SURVIVE and that of all the catering companies, I will still be around -- that this recession will be what separates the "men from the boys." Katie chimed in, "NO Adrian, this will be the recession that separates the GIRLS from the GUYS!"

We laughed and the interview was over. Ahhhhhhhhhhhhhhhhhhhh, relief. I did it and just as it was over and the crew left, the phone starting ringing for the next 3 hours. They called from Colorado, Las Vegas, NY, Florida and California. Even our neighbors from behind our house, Walt and Shirley, called to say they were in a hotel room on a vacation and while Shirley was in the shower, Walt was screaming, "SHIRLEY, IT'S ADRIAN! SHE'S ON THE TODAY SHOW!"

~Smile. They were all watching. I got lots of business out of this taping and yet, what I got, DEEP inside, was that it was the TRUTH that enabled me to be on the Today Show. I told that interviewer the truth! What a gift that turned out to be!

The Cadillac and Sean Hannity -- 1997

When I was 23 years old, I had my Maverick, CLEO. I used to get it serviced by O'Neil Ford on Northern Boulevard. I think I was a CHARACTER even then. I went in for a service and the mechanic told me that I needed new brakes. Oh dear, I was supposedly driving into Manhattan, some 26 miles away. They told me that it would take 2 days and cost $110. They added that I wouldn't make it across the viaduct without losing my brakes and that I had better leave it there now or SUFFER the horrible consequences. Talk about NERVOUS, I was rather upset. While deciding how I was going to give them two days to repair the car, this sweet black guy named Eddie, who had been my friend from having services performed there prior, came over to me. "Ms. Meyer," he said on the sly, "you don't have to worry; you have brake pads left. You're not going to be in danger if you don't have it done now."

"THANK YOU EDDIE; you're clearly an angel." I was grateful AND mad. I left the dealership and headed across the viaduct to a brake shop in Great Neck. I walked in, wearing a business-like outfit, approached the guys and LIED! I said I was a reporter for a local station and we were doing an expose on getting BRAKES repaired and what was THE best that they could do for me? Perhaps lying DID PAY! I was told, "For $68 dollars, we'll have you good as new in 1 hour!"

Amen and Hallelujah, I got my brakes repaired! ~Smile.

I am a little embarrassed to write here that I did it again. It was some 20 years later and I was purchasing my second Cadillac. It is a rather interesting story. I detest looking for new cars. It is survival of the fittest, in endurance and patience, as the car salesman makes the deals, breaks the deals and then some. NOW, there are easier ways of purchasing, but back then it was still the bait and switch along with all sorts of shenanigans. I did not want to drive all over and be treated like a stupid woman, so I got on the phone, knowing exactly what I wanted in a new car, and proceeded to call each of the 5 dealerships around Dunwoody.

Long story short, I told them that I was a reporter -- SORT OF THE SAME STORY, yet a BIGGER lie. I told them that I was seeking to determine the BEST dealership and best price that a dealer in the Atlanta area could accommodate me with. They would get advertising mention on the radio. Oh my goodness, the guilt is now pouring out of my fingertips as I write this, while at the same time, I am thinking, "Pretty clever and pretty much fun." ~Smile.

I selected the dealership over near the Galleria and the time came to pick up the new car. I went with check in hand, did the transaction, got my gorgeous new red shiny Cadillac Sedan de Ville and proceeded on my way. The manager never said anything about the free advertising. Still I felt guilty. I am certain he included commission, so HE was happy and I was happy.

I truly do not recall, but there was some meeting or telephone call with Sean Hannity; he was a radio guy at the time. He was NOT very well known, yet he and I had a conversation. He had heard what I had done. He said, UNEQUIVOCALLY, I must go back to that dealer and make good. I must confess and suffer the consequences. I KNEW he was correct.

While it was difficult, and surely embarrassing, I was totally blessed. I made an appointment to go and see the dealership manager. He was rather kind and cordial. I told him EXACTLY what I had done -- how I had lied, how badly I felt and how I wanted to make good on my transgression. He completely excused me, found no harm and let me go with my dignity intact. Still, I was so, so, so, so, grateful to get this off of my conscience and fess up. Life is good when you play by the rules. I did. ~Smile.

KARMA -- '09

I think that karma happens QUICKER as you age. It could also be that YOU know you are responsible for your life and choices. For instance, if you KNOW something that you ought to not do and you do it, YOU ARE RESPONSIBLE. If you did not know that it was bad or inappropriate, you are not responsible -- not until you do learn that it is NOT right. I think it happens MUCH quicker as you age. A case in point, I tossed something out of my car window one day. I KNEW I should not have. I do not even recall what it was, but I felt guilty afterward. GUILT says you know better.

Anyway, I was driving home and just when I got to my street, I could see GARBAGE strewn all over my lawn. Someone's garbage pail was emptied on my lawn. I knew IMMEDIATELY, KARMA!

One more experience, I am embarrassed to say, but it is true and it surely was Karma. I do care about my neighbor Stacy and I received an alarming call from her one afternoon. She was frantic. "Can you help me get a snake out of my house?" she screamed.

"Oh my G_d, No!" I responded. "I'm PETRIFIED of snakes. I'll call the fire department or do what I can, but NO, I cannot come over."

I was literally so afraid of snakes and spiders that as a child, when reading the encyclopedias, I could not even TOUCH the S book, for fear that the photos would show me Snakes and Spiders...MAJOR scared. Anyway, what went through my mind during that conversation was, "Better YOU than me."

Not nice - but it's how I thought. Lo and behold, not a month later, I was walking out of my bedroom and noticed something under that desk in the living room, HOLY SHIT! OH MY G_D, it was a snake. I was frantic and, blessedly, after the gate guard could not come to help me, I called ANGELA, our neighborhood, tiny 5'2" president. She bravely came over and swept him out of my house. Thank G_d for wooden slippery floors...KARMA!

👍 Let Go/Let G_d 👍

Cleo and the Courtroom Charade – 1973
"Appearances aren't always what they seem to be"

It was a balmy August evening. I had just turned 21 and had gotten my first car. I got into my new blue Ford Maverick -- 1973 -- and was all excited to take my first drive into Queens. Driving on the Long Island Expressway was a rite of passage.

I got to Steven Goodman's house at 8 PM. We had a lovely dinner and listened to music. Then, at 11 PM, it was time to leave. We took the elevator down, walked to the front door and then exited the building for him to walk me to my car. I even had a name for this wonderful new car – CLEO!

Cleo was nowhere in sight. Steven thought that I had forgotten where I parked. "Are you kidding?" Of course I knew where I parked - it was my maiden voyage in my very first car. And it was obvious the car was NOT there. Oh my broken sad heart.

When Steven was finally convinced that the car was not where I had parked it - we called the police - surely not the way we'd intended for this fun evening to end. The police arrived, put me in the back seat and questioned me as they wrote up a report of car theft. "VALUE OF THE CAR?" the officer asked.

I responded, "$3400, $1700 that I personally contributed. My parents afforded me the remainder. "

The police officer wrote, in the 'value of car' box, $1700. "NO OFFICER," I said. "We paid $3400."

"Sorry Ma'am," he responded. "The minute you walked out of the car dealership, it lost half its value."

HOLY SHIT! NOW I was upset.

Steven drove me home. The night turned out wayyyyy longer than the plan we had made. There were no cell phones and so I got home as soon as I could - my mom and dad were up awaiting my arrival. They'd NEVER had a car stolen and so none of us knew anything about such an event - and went to sleep a bit distraught - the evening / my first voyage - what a mess.

The next morning my mom called her friend Doris Kroll to tell her what had happened and she suggested that we needed to go out ourselves and LOOK for the car, because the police in Queens surely would not.

So, my dad and I, unbeknownst to us what kind of adventure we would take, took off for Queens. We drove here and there…left and right…traffic lights…streets. We didn't have a clue where we were - just drove around, looking for Cleo and honestly hardly expecting to find him.................yes - my Cleo was a man. All of a sudden dad said - with a 'knowing' - "go left - go right and there was Cleo -

OH MY GOODNESS! There was Cleo…just sitting there…MY CAR! The police told us NEVER to enter the car if we found it. We were instructed to call the police department first.

We set out to look for a pay phone. Remember, this was 1973 and no cells. We drove up the block, scouring the residential streets and NO pay phone. A young man was walking down the street. I pulled over, as I was driving, and my dad leaned out and asked where we could locate a pay phone. I think we even told him that we had found OUR car and needed to notify the police.

He responded to go left, then first right, drive down Queens Boulevard and about a mile, on the left, after an immediate right there would be a pay phone. We drove away and my dad said, "NO WAY! We're not driving THAT far and leaving Cleo!"

He suggested we knock on someone's door and see if we could use their phone. We did. A lovely lady came to the door. I told her our tale. She invited us in -- even allowed my dad in…a much more trusting society back then. We called the police from her house and then asked permission to call my mom. "Surely," she said.

Mom was working at the travel agency. As my dad dialed the number, I went to the front door to await the police. Mom picked up the phone. "JET SET TRAVEL, MAY I HELP YOU?"

Dad joyfully chimed into the phone, "IRMA, we found the car!"

"Oh my G_d! Hey everybody, Arnold and Adrian found the car!"

Whooping and hollering ensued, but just then -- OH MY G_D! -- with my own eyes, while awaiting the police, I watched that guy who gave us directions to the closest telephone get in MY CAR -- MY CLEO -- and drive off again! No kidding, I ran out the door and literally, like in the movies, ran down the middle of the street yelling, "THAT'S MY CAR! THAT"S MY CAR!

Dad, in the meantime, was yelling into the phone, "OH MY G_D, IRMA! They stole the car again!"

It was out of a horror story and at the same time, looking back, it was rather hysterical. Well, the same young man, who told Dad and me where to find a phone booth, apparently stole the car AGAIN! We were distraught. We called Mom, "Mom, they stole the car AGAIN!"

Dad described to her what had happened, while I sat there at the screen door, looking out and awaiting the police. The police arrived and boy, did we have an earful for them. We were all sitting there, this being WAYYYYYYYYY more adventure than this sweet lady/homeowner anticipated, when she just ALLOWED us to borrow her phone. Just as the report was being taken, this kid – yes, the car thief -- showed up at the front door. He walked in and explained that he was not going to 'take the rap' for his cousin JOHNNY, who stole the car on Saturday night...NO WAY!

He gave a report, told us where the car was and that he had gotten in touch with Johnny, when we asked him directions to a telephone, and Johnny had asked him to MOVE the car. Well, the story continued. The car was impounded in some lot. We were told where to go to get it. It was in fine condition, with a bat, a joint, and a kung foo poster inside. Sweet CLEO...came home...he 'd been through a rough time.

So, it was now August and Mom and I were told to be at the Queens Courthouse on August 8th...yup, for any of you history buffs, that was the night that NIXON was resigning. I was rather PISSED... no TIVO to record it. It was history and I truly wanted to watch it being made. Instead, I was in a courtroom sitting with Mom , having to watch these 16 year olds be arraigned.

It was a sweet night with Mom though. Aside from THIS particular story, we watched and observed several other interesting cases in the courthouse. Mom told me that while growing up, she and her brother and friends would often just go to court to hang out and watch -- the evenings were totally fascinating. Well, this was no different.

Here we were in the rest room, taking a break, and I was in a stall when I heard Mom talking to this gal from the courtroom where we had previously been. She was RANTING and RAVING, "Isn't he BEAUTIFUL? Isn't he GORGEOUS? Isn't he the MOST magnificent man you've ever laid eyes on?"

And I am thinking, "Who are we talking about?"

I got out of the stall and there is this somewhat disheveled gal talking to Mom, about how she is engaged to this man, who is up on rape charges. "Oh my!" my mom exclaimed. "How awful. What happened?"

G_d bless Mom. She knew how to find out the 'scoop.' ~Smile. It turns out this gal, about 27 years old, was HITCH HIKING down Northern Boulevard on Saturday. This guy stopped and picked her up. Within hours, he proposed to her. He was an Italian Adonis -- ravishing for all to see. She told us of his plight and here they were in court, with him being arraigned on rape charges. "Your Honor," the attorney for the defendant said, "My client, Anthony blah, blah, blah, Italian name, is here with his parents -- his grandmother, his younger sister, his brother and his fiancée! Your Honor, Anthony is a GOOD boy. He is surrounded by his wonderful family and here, alongside him, the love of his life -- his fiancée. There would be no reason for MY client to ever have raped this girl. He is happily engaged to be MARRIED!"

Oh my G_d! Is this for real? Is this what truthful, honest attorneys do? Is this what women, who are so needy to be loved, settle for and believe? OH MY G_D! OH MY G_D! OH MY G_D! What an awakening this was? OH MY G_D! Blessedly, I received my car back and a WHOLE lot more.

Nadia -- 1975

It was 1975 and I was living in Manhattan with my best friend Debbie, on 54th street. I introduced her to her soon to be husband. She moved out and I was left with this great apartment, in need of someone to help pay the rent. I ran an ad in the VILLAGE VOICE and described whom I wanted to share my apartment with, listed the rent and began to collect telephone calls. I interviewed them over the phone, finding those that I wanted to meet in person and those that I did not. I cut to the quick, asking EVERY question and telling them every truth.

I found several roommates over the next 4 years: a gal from England, a super-model spoiled brat from Long Island, an overweight, sweet Jewish smart gal who became a dear friend and NADIA, an Arabic gal from Kuwait.

Yes, your mom and Nadia became dear, dear, roommates. We double-dated with my boyfriend from Argentina and her boyfriend from Ecuador. We were a literal United Nations. We cooked every imaginable food together and exchanged Aleichem Salaam's (Arabic) and Shalom Aleichem's (Hebrew). ~Smile.

We were so similar, in every way -- just decent loving kind spirited human beings who were raised Arabic and Jewish -- and who cared? I was grateful for the experience and sad that it so seldom exists today!

The Yellow Pages -- '84 - '85

It amazes me. I just thought of the way that I think G_D was paving my path. It was 1984 and my catering business was doing rather well. I was as busy as one could hope and pray for. The money was flowing, the marriage was flowing, I was pregnant with my first delicious child, Ross, and all was well. I planned for 1985 and part of the plan, a very LARGE part, was putting my catering advertisement into the Yellow Pages. The yellow book was the greatest source of my marketing dollars and along with the coverage on TV shows and interviews on radio; I got GREAT business from my 1 inch ad. I was always VERY vigilant about how I ran the ad and made 100% certain that it was a perfect fit. The copy detail was exactly as I wished it to be and the paper work and signatures, all perfectly signed off with my rep from the Yellow Pages. The yellow book had been known to make mistakes and so I took EVERY precaution.

I awakened one morning in early February, EXTREMELY pregnant and anticipating the birth of my first son, as well as a visit from my Mom who would come to visit me and help me be totally ready for Ross/Rory's birth. I had no clue if I was carrying a HE or a SHE. ~Smile.

I opened the front door to the condo and there sat my Yellow Pages for 1985 -- so excited. I went right to the Catering section. I wish daddy and I were on speaking terms now; he would remember that morning, I'm certain. Anyway, I opened the book, saw 'C,' then Catering, then scrolled the A's. The business was A CATERED AFFAIR, Inc. and Oh My God, NO entry. I was FREAKED out...Upset...Mad...in full total anguish...disappointed ...hysterical...totally distraught and yelling for daddy, "OH NO! My ad is not in the book!"

I was so upset, literally for days. I did not really know the mantra, "There is a gift in EVERYTHING." All I knew was what I saw and this RANG out -- that I would not have much business this year. Such anguish...I know you can already FEEL how I was feeling and more.

Only days later, Mom came for a visit. Never in a million years did I think she would say goodbye to me on Saturday night and I would never see her again. She was only 66 years old. Blessedly - because of my earlier experience - Lily leaving me surprisingly - I kissed my Mom goodbye as if I would never see her again.

She traveled down the 3 steps upon departing the condo for the airport - and I called her back. "Mom, come give me another kiss!" We met on the flat level of the stairwell and I kissed her goodbye having no clue that, in fact, this would be our last hug and kiss. Can you imagine that? I always did that - leftover fear from Lily's departure from my life. I do that often - but am not nearly as neurotic as I used to be. Smile. I kissed her goodbye not knowing in a million years that in fact - I would never see her alive again.

Ross arrived -- my sweet, sweet, first baby boy -- only a couple of weeks later. He was late; my 'uterus was irritable,' I had been told. If you think I had business on MY mind, I would think you were crazy, because I had NOTHING on my mind except holding on for dear life. My mom died; it was and remains the very worst day of my life. I believe it will hold THAT place in my life's history forever. My darling son was born and if ever there were a conflict of joy and sadness, this was the one!

I would go for walks with my baby boy in a snuggly, like a back pack, holding him in front of my body. I would cry and walk, walk and cry, until he would begin crying; and then I would stop the tears. I would drive on 285, the main highway around Atlanta and feel fear that I would purposely crash my car into one of the tunnel overpass walls. I was on thin ice, mentally and emotionally. Daddy was still a traveling salesman and gone fairly much during the week and here I was a new mom. I am biting my lip as I write this, trying to hold back the tears, as if I am feeling the fear from 27 years ago. It is still locked in me – that and the sadness.

I went to the psychologist and he had me put a rubber band around my wrist. Each time I had that scary thought, that I would purposely crash my car into the overhead on the highway - I would SNAP the rubber band and bring my wits back to the reality, instead of the fear that was oozing out of me.

The fear of going it alone without my mom, raising my child sometimes solo and always without my mom was horrific, actually. I have mostly put it out of my mind and gone on with life. Time does heal. Thank you G_D.

Suffice it to say, I was rather blessed that the Yellow Pages neglected to put my ad in the phone book. Need I say more?

I took Andrew to the plane this AM -- here we are in August 2012. He is my baby, my second born son, and he is on his way to a MAJOR volleyball tournament in California. He has practiced, trained and then some for this tournament. Then, all of a sudden, just days before this coming Saturday's competition, he hurt his back. Of course, I wish he did not go. He could hardly maneuver his way into and out of my car when I took him to the airport this AM. He is hurting that much and still, he went. "Why?" I asked, "Why are you even going?"

He responded, "Because you won't believe it, Mom. Are you sure you want to know my truth? "

"Of course," I responded in the car as we drove to the airport.

"Because the guys are counting on me. Because what will they think of me if I don't come, and instead leave my partner high and dry?"

Oh my darling child, as my heart went out to him, suffering through the anguish of his choice, not knowing how to proceed but doing the best that he can. I have left my fears and worries up to G_D. HE/SHE has a plan. I do not know it. Andrew does not know it, but whatever it is, it is our choice to accept it, to learn from it, to be blessed by it, to surrender to it, as we truly have no control…much as we would like to think we do.

Why do things happen? Why do we do the things we do? 'G_d only knows' is such a true statement. So I leave my fears in HIS hands, knowing that Andrew will be very fine, fine indeed, no matter how it turns out. He knows more and more how to surrender and I am learning as well. Actually, I was VERY blessed when the Yellow Pages left my ad out, very blessed indeed!

G_d Isn't Ready to Take Us Yet -- 1990

We used to go on States' trips. Each year our family would fly to a destination, then rent a van and tootle around the country to see 2, 3 or 4 states over a 2-3 week period. We started this marvelous undertaking when the boys were 3 1/2 and 5 1/2 years old. Amazing!

Our first trip was in and around Colorado, Idaho, New Mexico and Utah. Remember boys, when we arrived in Salt Lake City and YOU, Andrew, upon watching a square dance convention said, "Look at all the PRETTYS!"

You were referring to all the ladies in their square dance skirts. So cute you were.

We were in Silverton, Colorado, a very hilly and mountainous town with HUGE overhangs, mountains and valleys. Melvin did ALL the driving. I am wayyyyyyyyyyyyyyyyy too nervous to drive slowly around those bends and curves. So Melvin did a magnificent job of taking the turns slowly and with great caution, while I felt huge comfort in his ability. In Silverton, Melvin began looking to the right and looking to the left. I was in the passenger seat, spreading peanut butter and jelly for our EVERYDAY fare. Not only was it inexpensive and did not need refrigeration, but it gave me something to do to assuage my fears. I literally would turn from the window and get involved in peanut buttering to avoid looking down at the, what seemed like, mile-long drops.

On this one occasion, Melvin was checking out the beauty and I, with an elevated voice said, "THEY'RE SILVER...all the buildings are silver. Now pay attention to the road. I'll look for you."

I was PETRIFIED. I did NOT do well around those steep drops...absolutely HORROR-filled. In the rear of the van, Andrew, who had a major NY intonation said, "Mommy, are you sccccaaaaard?"

Not wanting him to pick up MY fears, I responded, "Well, maybe a little bit, Andrew."

Out of Andrew's mouth came, "GOD ISN"T READY to TAKE US YET!"

Oh my God! What did he say?

Melvin and I looked at one another, shocked to say the least, totally SURRENDERED. I do not believe I have ever felt so calm. I just let go and listened to this prophetic spiritual child. "How did he ever come up with that?!"

Melvin and I had NO clue. We were not religious. We hardly took the boys to temple. WHERE DID HE GET THAT? Regardless of where or how, we relaxed and never forgot those spiritual words of wisdom. Wow, Andrew was literally almost 4 years old.

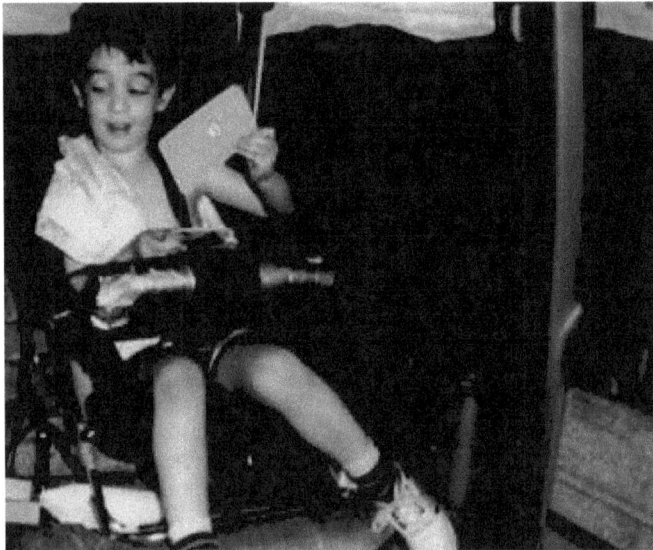

FAST forward about 6 years. Andrew was now about 10 years old, Ross 12. I went to a chiropractor for the first time and he checked me out, as well as my blood pressure, which was 80 / 50. He was VERY concerned. I have always run low, but he felt like my life was in jeopardy. He suggested we get to the ER at Northside. I was totally nervous now. I called Melvin. He came and met me there with the boys. I was crying...remember, my mom died when her blood pressure dropped and never elevated or came back.

So here I was crying and Andrew, Ross and Melvin walked in. I was on a table after triage and after a teary hello, I looked at Andrew and asked, "Andrew, is G_d ready to take me yet?"

I could not have been more serious. I was almost begging for some wisdom from him to comfort me. His response was basically looking at me like I was a deer caught in headlights, "HOW SHOULD I KNOW?"

We all got hysterical. Remember, he was not yet 10 years old. I once heard a story about a little boy who was about 2 years old and his mommy had just brought home a new baby brother. The big brother asked his mom and dad, could he go and talk to the baby by himself. Being concerned that perhaps he could harm the newborn, they purchased a video camera and set it up for the big brother to talk to the baby. They left the room with the two little children inside and listened from outside the room. What they heard was, "Baby, can you remind me about G_D? I've forgotten"

So, I THINK that Andrew must have known something, as you still have G_D so prevalent when you first incarnate, as well as when it is time to go or make your transition. It is in the middle that we haven't a clue and so, basically, do not recall. Wow! Interesting! Let Go Let G_d.

Tanya -- I Knew You Didn't Want Me to Come – 5/94

I was at the Perimeter Mall, back in the early 90's. I was waiting for a new friend to come, have a coffee and chat. I have always loved CHIT-CHAT dates. I love to just see friends and hang, have coffee or water and go for a walk.

THAT morning, I was full of anxiety. I had SOOOOOOOO many things to do and handle before I was to be home for you boys. I had made this date for 11AM. Here it was, 11:05, and no Tanya. I was tossing around the idea of how long I would wait for her. I did not have her phone number, but she had mine and I was exactly where we were supposed to meet. I waited, 11:10, and NOW I began thinking that I would wait another 10 minutes and then be GONE...abiding by the 20-minute rule. I learned in Manhattan, during a course with DAVID KING, that you wait 20 minutes for someone; that is mannerly. Then you have been appropriate and it is time to LEAVE!

I waited and waited. I began thinking -- THINKING -- that I hope she does not come. This way I can get to my chores and all I have to do, and not sit here schmoozing for the next 2 hours, when I could be home for you guys. It was 11:15. I thought, "I hope she doesn't come." I was watching the clock, getting more relieved by the minute that she was going to be a NO SHOW and I was going to get my chores handled. "Don't come; don't come," went thru my mind. "Five more minutes and THEN I'M OUTTA HERE. No call...no nothing...11:20. GOOD, I did what I agreed to; where was Tanya?"

I never heard from her. It was rather surprising -- not a phone call, nothing and we did not have email at the time. It must have been a couple of years later when I saw her at a Unity Concert – yes, she too was a UNITY gal who owned a vitamin health food store. We greeted one another. It was a NICE greeting. I said to her, "WHAT HAPPENED TO YOU, that day when we were supposed to meet at the mall?"

She responded, "I just got a feeling that you didn't want me to come."

WHOA! Does everyone know what I am thinking? How amazing is that? Scary, almost, it has to be an energy!

Hot Dogs and Potatoes on the Highway -- 1996

Oh what fun this story was. I owned the COFFEE GROUND, over at the galleria. It was a small coffee house, very avant-garde. The coffee craze was JUST getting started and we built a shop. It was across the hall from the movie theatre in the Galleria Mall, in Atlanta, Georgia. What a location! When the business was first started, February '94 or '96, we decided that we could make more money selling something for lunch, that there might have been those that wanted more than coffees and ice creams. We decided to serve baked potatoes and hot dogs.

Well, we did not find a following, hardly AT ALL. It was not a destination, like the movie theatre, so at the end of each day, there were many potatoes and hot dogs that we had prepared, but no one purchased. NEVER wanting to waste food, I would take them home.

In the beginning, it was NIRVANA. What child or hubby doesn't like hot dogs with all the trimmings? They loved the ease with which we dined, as well as getting away with HOT DOGS, rather than something healthy like veggies, fish or some such offering. After a week or so, they were getting a little bored, so I MIXED it up a little. This time I cut the hot dogs into little pieces and added Gates and Sons Bar-B-Q Sauce and fried the potatoes. I did what I could to keep their interest, while NEVER throwing away food.

I would go to visit the Coffee Ground. I did not work there, but would go almost daily to see what was happening. Day after day, there would be the left over hot dogs and potatoes. Eventually, I had run out of diced, scrambled, fried, toasted, roasted and pickled hot dogs and potatoes and the men were now COMPLAINING, "NOT another hot dog or potato is to enter this house MOM. Do you hear us?"

I did and yet it hurt my heart to throw away food. I took the dogs and the taters once again, wrapped in a bag, and headed home on 285. I was thinking the entire time, if I should give 'em to my neighbors or what to do with 'em, because Melvin and the boys would NOT eat them.

I thought and thought and thought and just as I was approaching the exit traffic light at Ashford Dunwoody, there was this STREET person with a sign, "WILL WORK FOR FOOD. JUST NEED A MEAL TO EAT."

OH MY G_D, an answered prayer, I thought. I wonder what his reaction will be when I open my car window and hand him all the food he has been praying for? So I did. He came over to the car, with the traffic light still red, and I handed him all of the Coffee Ground potatoes and hot dogs and said, "Here ya go, lots of food to eat. Enjoy!"

I do not know if MY joy or his shock was more palpable, but for me, it was perfect! He was expecting cash. Instead, he got JUST WHAT HE ASKED FOR. I never brought home another dog or tater again. Amen, Momma!

Tahoe and the Earthquake -- '89

Wow, we were SOOOOOOOOOOOOOOOO excited. Melvin and I were finally getting away on a romantic, terrifically planned, for 6 months in advance, trip to Lake Tahoe. You boys were 2 and 4 years old and we were ESCAPING for some much needed and desired romance. We even went so far as to IMPORT Linette from Boston. She had been MY nanny for years, working for my parents and helping me after Mom died to take care of you boys. She also assisted us in finding a nanny for the two of you.

She was living in Boston and we flew her down to Atlanta to help us care for you. She was the only one we trusted. She was so excited and thrilled to be with us for over a week. We picked her up at the airport the afternoon before our AM departure the next morning -- so excited. We brought her home to our SWEET little boys and where I might normally feel nervous leaving them with anyone, LINETTE was the MOST qualified person in our lives to leave with our precious children.

We played away the afternoon, ate dinner and went over the myriad of instructions -- what to give you boys to eat -- EVERY detail…everything to the max. We said goodnight and hugged and squeezed you guys. Oh I remember that like it was yesterday -- the anticipation, fear and emotion of leaving my sons for a week. Wow! We retired FINALLY, turned on the 11 PM news and there in front of us was "MAJOR EARTHQUAKE hits California!"

"Isn't California sort of REALLY close to Lake Tahoe?" I asked Melvin.

OH MY G_D! With that, I was on the phone to the hotel where we were SUPPOSED to visit. "Yes," the front desk reservationist said, "we certainly have felt the earthquake. We're still getting aftershocks. It's merely a 4 hour drive from where the quake took place."

"Forget it Melvin," I said; "I'm not going to Lake Tahoe -- NO WAY! Promise me you will not try to convince me to go!"

We were both sooooooooooooo bummed out. We called Delta, with no resolution. We packed the van with pillows and blankets, but we were not sure if we would just hike on down to Florida or get on a plane to SOMEWHERE. Talk about stress, here we went and hired Linette all the way from Boston. "Shucks" was not the only word we had for our frustration!

We left in the AM. Melvin was so kind. Knowing I was upset, he allowed me to be the GPS. "Let's try the airport," I suggested.

He responded that he thought I did not want to go to California. I assured him that perhaps we would find somewhere else to go. It had to be sort of warm! We arrived at the airport, where it was MANIACAL with others scurrying around, because of their trips too; their plans had changed. We talked to a Red Cap and Melvin said, "Figure out where we're going. I'll park the car and then you can let me know."

I was given the choice of Seattle or Denver. "What movies are playing on each?" I asked the Red Cap.

He was so polite and determined to accommodate. I liked the Denver movie best, so that was my choice. Melvin arrived, "WHERE ARE WE GOING?"

"In a hurry…the 9:35 to Denver. I'll do the tickets; you do the luggage."

And we did, with NO time to waste.

This was MANY, MANY years prior to the OJ incident, joyfully RUNNING thru the airport to get to the gate on time, I ran past other passengers, like OJ ran through the airport in that commercial…remember it? We made it to the gate, got onboard and set out for one of THE most awesome, amazing, and fabulous vacations we had ever taken.

We arrived in Denver and high-tailed it to Colorado Springs. I had friends there who were amazing to us; they treated us royally. It was a Jewish Holiday, as I recall. And Judy and Frank, our friends, invited us to celebrate with them. It was a spontaneously joyful evening.

Frank, Frank Aries, was a man who, believe it or not, OWNED most of the real estate in Colorado. I met him in Durham years earlier while dieting. While there, he flew me on his Lear Jet to Atlantic City. WOW! Anyhow, they were just wonderful to us. We stayed at the swanky Broadmoor Hotel on their recommendation. Later, we headed to Vail, where NO ONE, other than electricians and carpenters, dwelled. It was October and not quite ski season, so we were LITERALLY alone in an entire hotel. WE had the MARK hotel to ourselves at 1/5 the rate. It was a fireplace room, with every amenity. We were the ONLY guests in the hotel. It was FABULOUS! We had THE best time imaginable.

You boys had a great week, too! Tia Linette had a wonderful time with Ross and Andrew! So we learned to be grateful for an 'UNASKED for ANSWERED prayer.' What a vacation it was. Let Go and Let G_D. ~Smile.

THE Peak Experience -- California -- 1990

I was having a HARD time in life. Ross was about 5 and Andrew was about 3. Olivia, our housekeeper/nanny had left. She worked for us, lived with us and was part of our family for 4 years. We sponsored her into this country. That too is a story on how she was detained. I went to the Senator, Wyche Fowler. It is not what you know, but who you know and we were directed to him. Anyway, she was no longer with us and replacing her was VERY NOT easy. She did not quit; she became depressed. You, Ross, wondered if you had caused it. It was a terrible responsibility for a child to endure, but we no longer felt as though she could do a good job. Still, I am in touch with her and so the parting of the ways was loving. I just wanted you to know. You named her 'E.A.,' remember? 'OLIV EA.'

Anyway, we went through several live-in nannies. One of them was CONNIE. Oh my G_D, talk about ADD, Connie was the queen. She did EVERYTHING crazy and nuts. My intention is to not insult anyone, yet I can only describe Connie as major, major, ADD. For instance, I told her, "PLEASE help yourself to everything in the refrigerator, just please don't eat the pickles."

They were the green ones that I loved...MINE! She ate the pickles, because in an ADD fashion, she heard 'eat the pickles;' she did not hear 'please DON'T eat the pickles.'

Okay -- not okay -- she used to get the food out of the oven with a dishrag – yes, the pot holder was there, but she consistently used a dishrag, even after I warned her dozens of times. Even YOU, Andrew, said -- at 3 years old, "Connie, don't use the dishrag."

Connie still did. She was certifiable and I was having a really hard time. Melvin was traveling a bunch, coming home stressed. Connie was messing up, Andrew was behaving poorly and Ross, well, I am not sure that he did anything challenging; he was probably my right arm! I was stressed to the max. I needed to get away. I did not have a moment to myself. I was teary all the time. I went to the psychiatrist, not knowing what to do with myself.

I was a mess. The lady psychiatrist gave me a script for Xanax. Blessedly, I took only a few, calmed down, stopped the crying and decided to go to California BY MYSELF. Blessedly, I did NOT get addicted to Xanax; it is a VERY addictive drug; do not take it.

I was petrified, yet I did not want to stay in that crazy house either. G_D bless you Connie; you were nuts! ~Smile.

I used to tell Melvin that I wanted to go to the Oscars -- that was one of my greatest desires in the world. If there was such a thing as a bucket list back then, it would have been first on my list. We even made some calls to people we knew, who were producers. My Cousin Stephen might have had some pull; I wanted to go to the Oscars BADLY. Little did I know that the universe had even BETTER plans for me.

I flew out to California with my family's blessings, but NOT my dad. He was pissed. Oh well, I preferred the trip to a rubber room. I arrived and each day settled down more and more. I even remember dying my hair in the middle of the night. I just had SPACE and TIME and could be me, for the moment not having to run a family. Oh how I needed to get away.

I went sight-seeing, talked to dad and you boys every night, put some healing on our marriage and deciphered habits that needed fine tuning. It was a trip from heaven. Little did I know that it would bless me with MY MOST favorite peak experience of my life...still, to this day, some 20 or more years later!

I found in the California paper, A SALUTE TO THE STARS. It was an evening celebration for all of those stars that had anything to do with police, sheriffs, FBI -- you name it -- law enforcement. EVERY star that ever played in a law enforcement role on TV, in MOVIES or in theatre was there. I went to gawk and watch the stars. Actually I do not know why I went, but I went. It was at the Beverly Wilshire. It was at 6 PM, 3 hours earlier than its scheduled Eastern Time. I wore a very classy beige silk pants and silk top to match. I inherited it from Aunt Ida. It was class personified, as that is all she wore and owned in her clothing store. I was blessed to get so many classy outfits from her store upon her death.

I had Oscar de la Renta's and every label of clothing from Chanel to Dior, and in between -- all compliments of Aunt Ida.

Anyway, I looked pretty good. There is that photo on top of my refrigerator – still, with Angie Dickinson and John Forsythe. Are these names that my sweet sons might even recall? If anyone else reads this, they will know. So, I went to the event, on a Tuesday night before I was to depart for home in the AM. As I walked into the hotel, something CHUTZPAH-ISH came over me and I so I went to security outside the GREEN room and mentioned, "Hi, I'm here to see ERIC in audio visual."

Are you saying WHO IS ERIC? I do not know, but I do recall in my own catering business, I would have to mention something like that from time to time...so I USED IT.

They pointed me in the direction of the next security and green room. My heart was beating a little faster. What did I have to lose if they said NO? Mom always told me, "It doesn't hurt to ask!"

I proceeded down a hallway -- next stop, the gate. "I'm here to see ERIC in audio Visual."

"GO THIS WAY," she responded.

NOW I was in. Oh my G_d! Oh my G_d! Oh my G_D! I walked into this small room. Every face was recognizable -- Phyllis Diller, James Arness, Jimmy Stewart and Donald O'Connor! Several were giving interviews – with long bright lights and cameras overhead. I went up to Phyllis Diller and said, "You look like a million!"

She was BEAUTIFUL. She responded, "It cost me two million!" ~Smile.

I then settled into a corner, just observing and staring without being bug-eyed. This gentleman, whom I did not recognize, came over to me and said, "How do you do; I'm Howard. Who are you?"

I responded, "Sshhhhhsssss...I 'm a housewife from Georgia and I'm crashing this event."

He let out a big grin, "My kinda gal!"

Then he invited me, in his wife's absence, to sit at the dais with him and several others. Oh my G_D!

His wife did NOT like these occasions and events and was home with their 14-month old baby, he shared. He also shared that HE was the one that put the event together. He was the PR guy and we would be sitting with the Mayors of Beverly Hills, as well as Sylvester Stallone, although he thought Sylvester did not show up -- that he was on location, filming some snow movie. Alongside the Mayor were a few other notables. I was told to wait for him and that we would walk the red carpet when he returned and to go into the ballroom. Oh my G_D! Who needed the Oscars? We literally walked within ropes and stanchions, past a huge mélange of gathered gawkers. They were pointing and screaming at all of us who walked past them. I heard, "Who is she? Isn't she on Dallas?"

I giggle now with my ego intact, as it must have gotten a major rub with that statement! So, we were all escorted to our seats, right up close to the stage. I sat with Howard on my right and the wife of the mayor of Beverly Hills on my left. I was cold and so she offered me her shawl. We began talking. I told her as well that I was crashing the party and was a housewife from Atlanta, Georgia. Humility and authenticity, ESPECIALLY among THIS crowd went a long way. ~Smile.

We enjoyed the $500/plate meal. I say that because I was hugely IMPRESSED! This was 1990. We saw a show and I wish I could remember all of the stars that I saw. I can see the MC in my mind's eye, but cannot recall his name at this time. When there was an intermission I got up and decided that, "WHO CARES?"

I am going to weave in and out of the tables and see all that I can. If there was ever a time to have guts and courage, this was it. Who cared what anyone thought. You know that feeling when all eyes are on you and you are walking around tables at a party? I find it intimidating and yet, intimidation be damned, THIS was a peak experience and I was going to milk it for every last drop. I weaved my way around and saw George Hamilton -- talk about TAN, talk about HANDSOME, said hello to Mannix - Mike Connors. Fred Dryer and I had a little conversation. Eric Estrada from "Chips" was there. Maybe they are showing reruns; he was a young man, MAJOR in his day!

Then there was BOB HOPE. Oh my G_D! He looked as if he was about 95 years old; he might have been, alongside his wife. There were about 300 persons there and I weaved my way in and out of all of the tables until I happened upon ANGIE DICKINSON. She was my dad's FAVORITE. So funny, Dad would be glued to the TV set watching her and Mom would be calling her a SLUT! ~Smile. She was this sexy, voluptuous, beautiful blonde cop and had a figure that did not stop. Now, some 30 years later, she was a big blonde lady, wearing a muumuu to the event, but still, no denying, Angie Dickinson. She was with her date for the evening, John Forsythe, who has since passed away, but was a major movie star. She was as friendly as could be with me. "SYLVIA, take a picture of us. This gal here is a housewife from Atlanta, Georgia, crashing the party."

So I placed my arms around John and Angie, as I stood above them, posing for the photo SYLVIA was taking. It is the one on my refrigerator. I asked Angie if she would consider coming to surprise my dad for his upcoming 70th birthday. She never did, but it did not hurt to ask. I went back to my seat, intermission over, and reveled in all of those that I had seen and communicated with. I did not need to go to the Oscars. I had my own award winning ceremony already. By the way, I was told when in making the effort to get to the Oscars, that even Barbra Streisand's MOTHER could not get a ticket. ~Smile.

It was a glorious event -- a magnificent evening, one that I still pinch myself about – and the cherry on top was when I arrived home. I pulled into Hartsfield Airport with Melvin, Ross and Andrew awaiting my homecoming. They were cordoned off with ropes as we all stepped off the escalators. NO ONE was to go past the rope and just as I was approaching my three men, Andrew slipped under the rope and came running to me. The tears are falling as I recall that DELICIOUS moment. My breath is heavy with delight, as my precious 3 year old said ROPES be darned -- not really, just his actions -- as he ran to hug and welcome his mommy, ME! Talk about heartfelt joy, what a life!

Letting Go -- Meeting Armando -- Surrender My Will --
8/22/09

I thought for sure he was a gift from G_D. I was in Spain and Portugal with Ross. Wow, just writing that makes me feel so especially blessed, not only the ability to travel and the exotic locations, but to be with my 24 year old -- AT THE TIME – son, is extraordinary. I do not know if I have given enough thanks! ANYWAY, I had taken Andrew to California that very same year and now Ross and I to Europe. Both of these trips took about 6 months to plan.

Being single has been joyful, to the degree that I could dance and find pleasure alone, which I surely did UNTIL I could not, due to an injured back. Day after day and NO dancing, I found joy in planning and executing these trips. They are a great deal of work and I would hang at the bookstore many nights. I was busy, occupied and anticipating great joy, first with my Andrew in California to play in the AVP. What a thrill! Then to return and be with Ross through Spain and Portugal, it does not get much better than that! The trip was great. My back was GREAT and we arrived home after 2 weeks away. It was 8/18 and as I said GOODBYE to Ross, my brain thought, "Oh dear, I could get depressed now. No companionship and no trips to plan."

AND with that thought, almost immediately, I just HANDED it over to G_D. It was as if the scary thoughts, of lack and fear, vanished and I sent them up to the heavens.

I returned home to my computer and my "flirting" online. I saw this guy who had found me on Plenty of Fish, a dating site that I had been on for AGES, and made plans for a date with him for the 22nd of August. I had been single and alone for quite a few years, lots of dating, a few short term connections, but nothing truly satisfying for almost 2 + years. I met Armando on the 22nd of August, just 4 days after my journey with Ross ended, 4 days after I had that fleeting thought and handed it over to G_D. AMEN and Hallelujah! I do think there was a major connection in having expressed the thought of lack, then surrendered it and had faith!

53

We met just 4 days later and here we are. It was a sweet 2 1/2 years. ~Smile. Thank you G_D! Perhaps when we totally surrender and believe in G_D's plan and give OUR will to Him/Her, we manifest more. Amen!

It Just Takes ONE -- A Double Story – Dad and Armando
4/98 - 11/09

This is a DOUBLE story. The title, "It only takes one," is profoundly true and has revealed itself a few times wonderfully! The first time was when Dad and I held a garage sale. We had tons of JUNK displayed in our garage in Dunwoody, including all of Dad's figurines from his gift-selling days. We were having a very unsuccessful morning. I was losing heart and losing steam. No one was coming to our sale! I was disappointed and decided to go take a nap after I expressed my dissatisfaction and disappointment to Dad.

He was POSITIVE! He said, "Bunny, it only takes one."

"Okay," I responded, wishing him good luck and kissing him, before heading upstairs to nap.

About an hour later, I returned to the garage. It was MY turn to be ON. I noticed one entire table was cleared. Where did all the figurines go? All the figurines -- Hummel, Beatrix Potter, Lilliput Lane and more -- were gone!

I think dad had about $1895 in his pocket. HOLY HAPPY! Oh my G_D, what happened? It turned out a collector came while I was sleeping and purchased ALL of Dad's samples. Wow! EVERY last one of 'em was gone. How exciting, it only took ONE! ~Smile.

Several years later Armando, my ex-boyfriend, had a house that was "UNDER WATER". That was a term for when you pay a mortgage based on the original cost of the house when you mortgaged it, versus enduring a recession, where the house is worth MUCH less. He decided to sell it.

I came over to his house for a visit and he was a bit down. He was frustrated, as NOT ONE PERSON had shown interest in the house for the almost 2 months that it was listed…no one.

I told him what I had learned and stated, "It only takes one!"

As the words came out of my mouth, the second I said them, the phone rang. Armando answered and said, "Hey Jackie!" Jackie was the realtor.

The next thing I heard was Armando saying, "Yes, you can show it at 1:45!"

With that, Armando looked away from the phone and mumbled quietly, so as not to have Jackie hear, "WOMAN, YOU'RE SCARING ME!"

Jackie came by, showed the house that day and returned with an offer that night. The HOUSE was sold! It only takes one!

Daisy, Coincidence and Armando -- 9/09

THIS was the first time that I had decided to go visit the home of a man that I was dating, BEFORE he came to visit me in MY home. I had been dating Armando for probably only a couple of weeks and I was invited, upon my request, to come to HIS house. He had not yet been to mine.

I was greeted by this beautiful, BIG slobbering St. Bernard. She was a gorgeous specimen of DOG, yet a major slobberer.

Having liked Armando thus far, I was thinking about how this dog would ever FIT in my home, if we progressed that far in our relationship.

It did not take a great deal of thought to feel as if there was NO way that a slobbering huge animal like Daisy was going to fit well in my home...Oh Dear! I let it go, figuring there was NO reason to put ANY energy into that -- wayyyyyyyyyyyyy too premature and just no reason to even go there...let go, let G_d is what I thought and dismissed the concern completely. I did not give it another thought.

A few days later, Armando and I met at the mall. He called and arranged a nice spur of the moment 'let's get together.' We were sitting in the food court having a lite bite and conversation, so enamored with one another -- NEW LIKE -- when Armando had an announcement to make. I listened up as he began explaining that he had come to the decision, in light of our making a plan to get away for a weekend, that he wanted to GIVE Daisy away. My ears perked up. GIVE DAISY AWAY? This was his DOG, man's best friend, give Daisy away? I could not help but wonder, "Was this a connection in our unfolding? Give away the SLOBBERING dog?"

Armando was planning on giving her to Richard, a friend of his, to care for her in his absence while we would be away. Instead, he decided since Richard's St. Bernard had recently died and Armando's St. Bernard was now so lonely with his late wife's death, that it would be a blessing to GIVE her to Richard -- not just for a weekend, but for good.

Richard was still distraught over the loss of HIS dog, so he would be thrilled and delighted to get Daisy, love her and give her the attention and time she needed. "Wow," I thought, "What an answered prayer this was.

I have to say it astounded me how quickly this manifested, from my thought to its reality. WOW! Perhaps a connection in having the thought, handing it over to G_d and, VOILA, manifestation! I shared with Armando how amazing, that it had been on my mind and here, all of the pieces were falling into place. G_d has a plan and so it is.

👍 Forgiveness 👍

"Forgiveness is For Giving to Yourself"

Merle Kalish -- 1962

My best friend in 4th and 5th grade was Merle Kalish. We slept over at one another's houses, spent every moment in school that we could, exchanged sandwiches at lunch time and gossiped about the boys and more. I loved her as a little kid. We were all BRATTY, gossipy and mean-spirited girls from time to time. I was no different, so when it came time to go to Jr. High, my mom suggested that I no longer be friends with the group that were my main friends in elementary school. I listened and literally ignored these good friends the first day of Jr. High. They hated me and dissed me for the remainder of Jr. High and High school. It was rather unpleasant, to say the least, but that is not the juice of this story.

I felt badly over the years about the dislike and hatred that spewed within my soul, regarding Merle. I know I am sensitive and I do NOT like unfinished business. I like life tidy, neat, orderly and closure on whatever is gone. I did not have that with Merle in my heart and mind. I wanted it.

I attended a reunion back in 2005, I believe my 35th (NOT sure), but I literally looked for Merle. I wanted to apologize for MY part in the "mess." Sadly and disappointingly, she was not an attendee. Oh well, I WAS prepared to ask for forgiveness and clear the bit of angst out of my heart. I went to the duck pond -- a visit with a bunch of other kids, professors and teachers after the big reunion party. Merle was not there either. Instead, there was this gal from a grade ahead of us, CINDY, who knew Merle. So I walked up to her randomly to ask her about Merle. LO AND BEHOLD, who should she be on her cell phone with, but MERLE?

"May I have your phone?" I inquired.

"Surely, here she is."

With heart racing, I began. "Merle, this is Adrian Mallin, was Adrian Meyer. How are you?"

She responded kindly and I continued. "I just wanted you to know that I apologize for any and all angst between us over the years. It has bothered me and I wanted to share with you and clear the air!"

"Oh that is not necessary, how are you?"

We spent the next 10 minutes catching up. It was lovely, seemingly inconsequential, and yet there was a resting and comforted place in my heart that replaced the angst. I felt so much better. Forgiveness is for the one who is blessed enough to ask for it! It is FORGIVING yourself -- the comfort of releasing any and all hostility. I think that it makes life richer with blessings, in the space that you let go of the angst that once resided there.

Patricia and the Skip Tracer -- 1995

We were living in Dunwoody and renting out the condos in Chamblee. We had the sweetest, classiest tenants -- both stock brokers – a fine black couple. They had two adorable young sons and were prospering hugely. I even recall you boys wondering why THEIR sons got this big candy cane FILLED with sweet treats -- almost as tall as you were - and you guys never got something like that. They would arrive in their big beautiful BMW and come to pay us the rent, ALWAYS on time, until it was not.

We had not heard from them. We called and called, but to no avail. A less than comfortable feeling arose in the pit of our stomachs, until we went to the condo. Not only did we NOT find them there, but found a pile of debris, as well as punched in walls and slammed off the hinge door wells. It was a nightmare before our very eyes. The condo was in shambles. This was worse than all of the 16 years that I had been renting out real estate, including in New York.

I assessed the damage and eventually, after looking high and low for them, I went to the Dekalb County Courthouse and sued them. And while the suit was victorious, it was a rather shallow victory. We could not find them. How do you get money out of someone you cannot find? So, upon exiting the courtroom, after winning a settlement of over $1500, a SKIP TRACER came up to me. I learned that day that there is such an occupation as one who searches and locates someone who has SKIPPED -- either skipped bail, skipped bond, skipped a law judgment, SKIPPED -- left town and cannot be located. I thought about it, learned of this man's terms and came to the conclusion that these poor people who had apparently 'fallen apart' needed the money surely more than we did. I elected to just skip it and not seek these tenants. I received calls after the court hearing from the skip tracer telling me that he had located them. They were in Philadelphia. Still, I wanted no part of it. They were pathetic to have lived as they did and ruined property as they did. I wanted no part.

A couple of years passed and we moved from Dunwoody to Orlando. It was shortly thereafter that I received one of those letters with the yellow strip on the address. It was forwarded from Misty Lane to Lucky Lane, our new address. I saw that it was from the Dekalb County Courthouse and opened it immediately. It asked me if I was ADRIAN MALLIN from the former address, Misty Lane and if so, to please notify the court as they had a check for me in the amount of $1539 and a notice that P. H. had elected to make good on her debt to us. WOW, was there a connection between me NOT pursuing and my 'good' finding me anyway? I think for sure.

I believe that the universe rewards us when we do the "right thing." Call it karma, but whatever it is, I truly believe what goes around comes around -- either quickly or even in another lifetime. Sometimes I see people's lives so tarnished and twisted. While it seems as if they are living a good and decent life, I cannot help but wonder if it is their THINKING or a debt from another lifetime? I do not know. I do know that there are rich rewards in living a life that has me follow my inner guidance. While I am not always so clear and sometimes push the envelope, I continue to strive for the most GODLY way. I am a work in progress. I think in THIS case, I did the right thing. AMEN!

Fate/Destiny

Lily – 1959 and Beyond

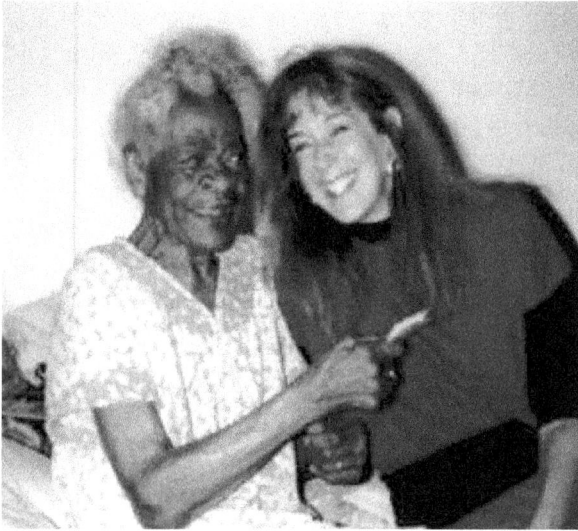

So why would this story have waited 'til last? Obviously, because I knew I would experience more pain than pleasure when writing it. I have held off and held off. Now, after tea and coffee, snacks and email letters, IT IS TIME! Here goes...

I was a normal, healthy, happy and joyful little LEO child. ~Smile. I recall a few early memories in the house in which I was born in Malverne, NY. It was a very middle class neighborhood. Perhaps, we had 1 or 2 bathrooms, I am not certain, but there was a great deal of calm, comfort, peace and love, I do recall. As I said, I do not have a great deal of memories. The few that I do have are Lily teaching me how to chew gum – no, not cracking it -- just chewing it and blowing bubbles! She taught me how to tie my shoe laces. I do remember that vividly -- on the driveway or some porch. I recall us having a rabbit and then finding out that the cat ate it. We tried again and the cat ate it again.

There once was a fire and I remember Lily taking me in her arms out into the street, while the firemen showed up. The TV had burned up in a fire in the living room. I was in her arms while the other neighbors had come outside to see what all was happening.

Oh, and yes, there was the time I locked MYSELF in the bathroom and, once again, Lily called the fire department. JUST as they were arriving, little Adin walked out of the bathroom. That was my nickname. I think I was creating a little drama, quite frankly. But, there she was, there they were, and all was well. Oh yes, and MANY other memories -- of Lily cooking, my goodness, could she cook and bake! This writing at the moment is rather pleasant, all of the sweet memories of me as a little girl. All of these took place before I was 6½ years old.

Lily cooked a MAGNIFICENT Arroz Con Pollo, rice and chicken. Every time she went on her day off, I was excited for her return as she would bring me a Planters Peanut Bar. Oh how I LOVED them! Sometimes she brought back avocados and sometimes even her native foods.

Once I was kissing her goodnight, standing tall on my bed to reach up to her. She had brought back FISH from her day off and she ATE the head, the brains and the eyes. "OH MY G_D, I'm NOT KISSING YOU!"

That was disgusting! I will never forget. Yet we laughed. She ate some CRAZY stuff.

You know boys, I wrote the LILY story once before, when I was first setting out to write this book, but I lost it. I sent it to Laurie. She read it and loved it. Then I do not know what happened. I lost it, on the computer of course -- MS NON TECH. At that time, I did not write about the good stuff. G_D only knows why I lost it and why I had to be writing it again now. But I do believe there is a reason, perhaps to be grateful for all of the above that I am sharing. Anyway, I guess there were more memories than I thought and here is another, one so DISGUSTING!

I was sitting outside on the curb with my sister and a cousin. I think it was Cathy, who lives in California now. There was dog poop on the street, so we sat a bit down from it, Yes, poop; there were no laws about cleaning up after pets.

Anyway, Mom had given us chocolates…you know, those chocolates with the marshmallow inside? Anyway, we were all sitting there and eating the chocolate off the marshmallows when I looked down on my pants. I think they were corduroys and there was chocolate on my pant leg. I NAILED it with my pointer finger, scooped it up and put it in my mouth. UH OH, it had NO taste! Could it have been the dog doo? Methinks YES! Ugh, gross, disgusting!

Life went on. Lily would call me in at night to get me showered, off to sleep and awaken me in the AM to get me brushed and off to school. Even if it was only kindergarten, there was lunch to be made, flowers or apples sometimes to take to my teacher and a walk to the bus stop just down the street. Lily was there. Her days off were only on Saturday and she would return on Sunday.

May 29th, 1959 arrived and that was the BIG day, the day we moved to the BIG house. It was in Roslyn, Long Island and it was a fancy, schmancy, bigger house. Sadly enough, it was so far from Malverne, at least 35 minutes. I was no longer allowed to take dance lessons. Yes, 'yo' momma' took dance lessons with June Taylor. She was famous. She was the choreographer/dancer on the weekly Jackie Gleason show and here she was, MY dance teacher. Mostly it was ballet but we did a little bit of tap. I LOVED dance and decided I would grow up and become a dancer. Mom took me each week. I don't know where she went while we were learning how to dance, but she brought me and took me home. Now, living in Roslyn, I was told that I could no longer dance, as it was too far. I think it disturbed me, but I do not truly recall. Life went on. We moved into this schnazy house. Dad was so excited about 4 bathrooms. Both Berniece and I had our own separate rooms and a HUGE kitchen, as well as a basement. That is where Lily slept. Everything was new including an entire bunch of new neighbors.

Well, perhaps that is where I became a nice person. ~Smile. In contrast to the new neighbors, who were rather SNOBBY and unfriendly, we were just grateful, excited kids moving on up. ~Smile.

Naomi Banpf and Sally Brown -- they hardly looked at me, surely no talking to me on the bus to school. I remember the Erlichs and the Schwartzs; none of them had anything to do with me. It was VERY different from the sweet, nice neighbors we had in Malverne. It seemed as if NO ONE talked to anyone, here in Roslyn. It seemed as if no one cared. I finished out school at the new school, even though there was only one month to go. It was uncomfortable and yet I do not think it bothered me all, that much, as I came home to Lily and the new house. Perhaps even then, I LOVED change and the non-mundane.

I used to ride my bicycle and flip baseball cards. I was literally the champion. I had thousands of baseball cards. I still remember having the Phil Neikro card, lots of Cub cards and several that were prestigious. Dougie Black, Jeffrey Tolken and all my buds LOST their cards to me. Jeffrey's mom did not like me, because I basically won ALL of Jeffrey's cards. I was a major tomboy. I even had my own basketball hoop. This in 1959 and GIRLS did not play hoops then. The net was compliments of Dad. I was his 'son.' So, here I was, never really close to my sister -- NEVER at all. I was hanging out, getting the lay of the land, watching my P's and Q's with the snobby neighbors and coming home daily to Lily and love. It was just peachy, a piece of cake.

It was a Saturday, in the afternoon and I was riding my bicycle. I do not recall knowing why Lily was still there. She had not left for her day off and yet, I do not think I paid that one speck of thought. I was riding and having FUN! Mom called me inside, I rode up the driveway and was told to say goodbye to Lily. She was crying for some reason. I do not recall ever seeing her cry before.

But there she was rather hysterical. I kissed her goodbye. I did not have a clue why she was crying and after a big hug, she left. I would see her in the AM. I left to go back to my riding. Honestly, I was not at all compassionate. I only recall wanting to get back on my bicycle and go, go, go...self-centered kid.

Uh oh, the tears are beginning to fall. WHY? Am I crying over the story I just wrote? Am I recalling the little girl, as I sob, knowing that I WAS selfish.

66

I did not stop and concern myself with Lily. Perhaps I did, I do not recall. All I know is that which was about to unfold would change my life forever.

I am turning 60 years old in 10 days – Ssssssshhhhh, hush, don't tell. Still, I learn the why, how, and not to take it personally. I have not gotten it yet -- how to just FLOW with life and take it moment by moment. I PLAN, I make myself secure, I fear loss, I still cry while writing this and yet, it is what it is. G_D only knows I do my best, best, best! ... Always! Do I wish it happened differently? I think not! I would not have you boys!

So, to continue, Mom called me inside. "WHAT NOW?" was my thinking. "I wanna ride my bike!"

I went into the den -- real wooden floors. Mr. Hartley used to come each month and wax 'em. He was this big black man and my friend -- Lily's too. So, there they were, Mom, Dad and Berniece all seated awaiting MY presence. "Hmmmmmmmm?" Dad spoke. "Lily is not coming back."

"Yes she is."

"No, she is not."

"YES SHE IS!!"

"NO, SHE IS NOT. SHE IS NEVER COMING BACK!"

And with that, I cried and with THAT, Dad pointed his finger at me and said, "WE DO NOT CRY ABOUT ANYONE WHO IS NOT OUR FAMILY."

END OF STORY. He did not say that -- end of story. I am just telling you now, that when Dad spoke and told me not to cry – my, my -- you listened and I no longer cried. As if I zipped up my heart and soul and listened to his instruction, it was a closed chapter.

I only recall feeling lonely. I do not really know what I felt. I do not remember much after that 'meeting,' except that I do recall going to the refrigerator. I would stare in there. If I could gather the thoughts NOW, with the memory I have, I would say that I thought perhaps I could find LOVE in there. Yes, ridiculous, but I was looking for something -- maybe pleasure. Fortunately, I was a skinny string bean and I exercised as much as there was daylight. I had energy BEYOND beyond. It is in your genes boys. ~Smile. I think of you guys working out.

So, here I am, ALMOST 7 years old, my birthday around the corner, and I have very few memories after that day. I do recall missing Lily. I do recall trying to fall in love, and I did with the next black nanny and the next and the next, on down through the ages of Edna, Alice, Linnette and Doris. Oh, how I loved the nannies. They were my best friends and made life okay. One by one they would leave. It never hurt so badly. Never again, Edna must have stayed for 3 years, Alice for another 3, Doris only for a year -- she was a hoot. She had a blond wig and she was a glitzy young gal, surely not cut out to be a MAMMY and clean houses and cook. But clean and cook she did.

THEN, there was a respite. I do not know if Dad had a lean year or if Mom just could not find good HELP. But I do recall cleaning the downstairs bathrooms. Mom gave me such positive reinforcement, "You're the best cleaner in the world Adrian."

I felt so proud. WE did without help for a few years and life went on. Somewhere along the line, I made a decision that no one would EVER leave me again.

I turned 23 years old. I had been a binge eater for several years. I do not recall if I did that before I turned 14, but at 14 the weight started to increase. Oh, this is getting tough to write, I so want to escape and yet, I truly want to write this story. I shall...perhaps another trip to the fridge or maybe something more to drink. If I could only smoke NOW, I would have lit one 10 minutes ago, but I will refrain; yes I will. So, the weight began accumulating. I began dieting. I would binge my guts out. Yup, you are ready for that word, GUTS out. After school every day, I would go to Marge's and Molly's houses. They had the best food. Their mom probably detested me. I ate them out of house and home. You could almost say that after school, I went where there was good food. I truly did not feel any comfort among these friends and whatever I was stuffing down -- sadness, loneliness, etc. -- FOOD was the best medicine, rich, creamy, fattening and sugary food. My stomach TURNS today to just think of what I used to put in my body.

Ya know, I write this and the person THEN – MOI -- is so alien, so different from this ADRIAN now, it is uncanny. Wow, what a metamorphosis. I do know that I started binging, eating away my feelings VERY early on. It is just that I exercised it away and remained skinny until I started to become a WOMAN. Then everything changed. So, I would eat, eat, eat and hang with the girls and then go home and be forced to eat again. I was so not hungry, but Mom told me I had to eat everything that she was serving. I hated dinner. I was stuffed, but I obeyed. I wonder what would have happened had I refused to eat; I did not dare.

Sip sip, drink drink, the beverage NOW calms me. I did the above behavior all of my growing up, NEVER purged, nor any of THAT stuff and then went off to college. I did NOT love me; I did NOT even LIKE me. I was so messed up, I wanted to see a therapist WITH Mom. She refused. Mom used to tell me that I was crazy and it was ALWAYS MY fault, whatever happened. I learned that I was responsible and I would often be sent to my room to do some SOUL SEARCHING. I giggle now. Is it not interesting how soul-connected I feel? I guess all that searching got me results. ~Smile. Anyway, I went off to college and loved the escape -- LOVE, LOVE, LOVED the escape of summer camp each July and August. We had spoken on the telephone from time to time with Lily and I would always be her 'baby.' ~Smile.

College was blessed with new friends, new experiences, new everything. Yet I binged at least weekly and what a perfect place to binge. I was on the dining plan. I could go back for 15 pieces of cake, if I so desired, 12 sundaes and everything in between. I used to diet almost every week of my life and I would be perfect with every morsel that I ate on the diet until the next binge. I once had soooooooooooooo much salad -- least amount of calories -- that I ate it morning, noon and night until the fiber began eating a hole in my intestines. I stopped.

The memories are flooding. I think there is another book in this one that could be the story of HEALING and perhaps help others. I know there is. Whether I can write it is the question.

So, here I am at college and my girlfriend Barb took me to the rest room one night and tried -- THANK YOU G-_D -- TRIED to teach me how to throw up after I had eaten too much. I just could not do it. Trust me, I tried, but I could not do it. Gratitude at this moment is a mere word for what I feel -- such a blessing and a gift that I was not able to do that. It would have totally wrecked my life. I graduated college with honors and did most things well. I had to find ways to like myself, because every time I binged, I hated, detested and could not stand myself. And so, with each A, with each accolade, and with each success, it made living for me more tolerable. It was just the core that was f----d up. Why oh why did I binge? Too funny, having tried EVERYTHING to figure out why I was binging. I even once purchased a baby pacifier. Perhaps that would be put in my mouth and I would not want to eat food...IT DID NOT WORK!

I will save the rest of the story and just get to the time I was 23. I went on a major diet. Nah, I am gonna save that too, and just stick to the story. I will share that I went for help; life had become intolerable. I was out of control -- NEVER really fat -- just not living a full life...out of whack. I went to the dietary rehabilitation center in Durham, North Carolina when I was 25 years old, right before my move to Atlanta. No one knew at the time about binging. It was not vogue as it is now to share all the stuff about addictions, etc. I was perhaps a pioneer? ~Smile.

I went for help, paying for it MYSELF, and met THE most ANGEL of angels in my life. His name was Joe Kertesz and he was the MOST significant healing part of my life, bar none. The tears of gratitude are rushing down my cheeks as if he saved my life. He did! I will be ETERNALLY grateful! Together we discovered, the day Lily left, I needed to process feelings of loss, anger and sadness, since I never got the opportunity to do so. I was SHAMED by feeling sad and never allowed to do so. It was inappropriate, as I was taught, to feel sad when I had "NOTHING TO FEEL SAD ABOUT." So said my parents. It was as if sadness was a weakness and we were SOOOOOOOOO blessed and so lucky that there was no reason to feel sad. Look at all of the starving and unfortunate people in the world, "I'll give you something to feel sad about young lady!"

70

Oh how those words haunted me. I never felt sad. I never felt angry. All I felt was a need to cover up my feelings, then stuff 'em real good and then HATE myself for doing so. In Durham, I learned how to recognize perhaps that I wanted to feel angry. YES, this is another book. ~Smile.

So, at this time, with new skills, a new life, a journey into myself and support, I moved to Atlanta and continued to heal. Why should this be a story of EXTRAORDINARY experiences that I live? Well, because it has shaped me into who I am. Still growing and still challenged by sadness and yet for the very first time, I grieved in a healthy manner over the loss of Armando. I did not eat it away, I did not dance it away and I never attempted to stuff it at all. I only FELT it – cried and learned – as it dissipated.

I feel so, so, SO grateful. I have met angels along the way. G_D and I have gotten closer. I am writing this book and all is well. Surely there are tough times. It is not fun being alone without a significant mate to love and yet, just from writing I can see the tapestry of my life, what I came here for and how I have always been blessed. Even the tough times felt GOOD, eventually. This time is no different. THIS story has been a LONG journey. It is the foundation of my entire life and it continues to play a part. It is only now that I can see the myriad of all the blessings.

While Lily was the most painful experience, it has also blessed me, shaped me, made me sensitive and carved me into who I am. Blessedly, I can finally say that I LOVE ME! I am grateful beyond the words I can write here. I am so fortunate to have lived a life raising you two guys, that I truly NEVER thought it would be possible that I could. I feel more blessed and grateful for the experience of what I believe is THE richest experience any woman could ever have -- that of giving birth and loving and growing two HEALTHY souls. Oh, how my heart is full with my love for you two! Thank you G_d!

DEPARTED -- 1974 - 2001

I have lost many in my life. I recall the first person who ever died was Aunt Inga's mom. I must have been around 7 or 8 years old and my mom told me what had happened to Aunt Inga's mom -- Death. She tried to describe it and while I hardly knew her, I still felt sad. Interestingly, I sit here and ponder which is harder, which hurts worse, losing a loved one -- a romantic love due to our inability to grow together -- OR losing a loved one to death. They are both, for me, hugely difficult. I love deeply, and yet, I guess what has not killed me, has made me stronger.

The next death I recall was that of my beloved cousin Edward. Oh, how I loved this guy. He was my first cousin -- Aunt Inga and Uncle Harvey's eldest son. With due respect, HE WAS MY FAVORITE! Oh my G_d! Whenever we went to Aunt Inga and Uncle Harvey's house, it was Edward that I would want to be with, sit next to and just adore. He was tall and handsome. He was the eldest of the 4 cousins – Berniece, next eldest, then Samuel, then little Adin. Yes, Adin…what my family called me from time to time. I would vie for the seat next to him, at every Jewish religious dinner at the club. I adored him. I was like a little girl to him, he being 7 years older than I. He was handsome – oh, I said that. It deserved a second mention.

He and I became closer as we grew older. The age gap narrowed. He even began to date my friend, my best friend at the time, EDITH. He had been in the National Guard and, apparently, he got into drugs -- not just the garden variety -- but heroin. He was messed up. Once when his mom and dad traveled on a buying trip to England and France, he came to our house to stay for a while. It was, maybe, only a week. Yet I got to spend quality time with him. We went on walks and talked at great length.

He was on a program to help him get off of the drugs; it was methadone. It is so weird to even be writing this, as it was never mentioned. Anyway, he and I would go for walks and talks in Roslyn, around my house, and I learned of the struggle he was having.

72

He began dating my girlfriend, but no one knew of his issue. I surely did not tell her. He was my blood, a deeper allegiance than a friend. This was not to be shared with ANYONE. Why do I find the ability now to tell you? Because TRUTH prevails...that's why. Edith and Edward dated for months, maybe even a year, when he began drinking too much -- a side effect from letting go of the drugs, where the user SWITCHES addictions. Edith told him clearly, one night, that she would no longer go out with him if he continued drinking. She cancelled their Saturday night date.

I was up in Athol, Massachusetts on a farm, with friends, after college -- another story. Anyway, there were no phones, no cells...nothing -- just a wall phone in the main house. At about 5 AM, I was sleeping in a barn when a LOUD horn went off -- a car, of sorts. We awakened, wondering, "What is THAT all about?"

I heard someone yelling for me. Oh my G_d! I was at this far-away farm in Athol, Massachusetts, where hardly anyone knew where I was, yet someone was screaming MY name, "ADRIAN MEYER! ADRIAN MEYER!" -- Screaming!

Apparently my mom had called the sheriff and informed him of important news to get to me. She knew I was on a farm where people were building boats. I opened up a window from the barn where I was sleeping and responded, "I am "Adrian Meyer."

It was the sheriff and he had come to tell me, "CALL HOME!"

I immediately went to the farm house, where the phone was, and dialed 516-621-2586. I still recall the number. My mom picked up the phone and before I could even think, she screamed into the phone, "EDWARD is DEAD!"

Later, she told me that she did that so I would not think it was my dad, hearing my mom pick up the phone. Hmmm. Oh my G_d, it was 38 years ago, yet the tears still fall as I write this...he was gone. I do not know if it was an overdose, a suicide -- I think not -- but no matter. It does not matter, because he was gone. My dear, darling, beloved Edward -- Oh my G_d! Sadness does not describe one of THE darkest periods of my life.

I was on a plane from Boston within hours, heading home by myself, to LaGuardia Airport. It was a 2-hour trip from Athol to the airport. My girlfriend Abby and her boyfriend Steve took me to Logan airport. I cried the entire way. They consoled me best as they could. I had been traveling around the northeastern United States and Canada with my girlfriend Abby. We had just graduated college and had been to Ontario, Toronto, Quebec, Montreal and the entire northeastern portion of Canada and the U.S. Yes, I had the travel bug way back then too. We used Athol, Massachusetts as a home base, as Abby's boyfriend, Samuel, was there building a boat, along with several other guys and a couple of families, all building sailboats. It was like a Noah's Ark kind of backyard -- in preparation to be less dependent on government, NOT pay electric bills and just be free to sail the waters of the world. All of the people up there were very educated and rather radical in their dislike of government and bills. They were all planning on escaping with their individual sailboats. I met a man, Alan, and he, too, was building a boat.

I LOVED being up there. I did everything differently up on the farm - different from my life in CONCRETE Manhattan, where I would eventually dress in heels, wear nail polish and go to work for the largest ad agency in the world, ON MADISON AVENUE, Doyle Dane Bernbach. On the farm, we picked berries and made jam. We cooked for dinner whatever we had caught during the day. We drank dandelion wine. OH MY G_D! While I had never taken LSD, I surely felt OUT OF MY MIND drinking dandelion wine. It was a high different from all the rest that I have ever had -- even since. Actually it was great fun~ smile.

I recall trying to be helpful and generous, so I decided to bake peanut butter cookies -- from scratch -- for all to enjoy. They were all working on their boats and I was figuring a way to use the wood burning stove to surprise them all with these yummy cookies. So, I baked them. They were delicious and I was soooooooooooooooooooo proud until the first person came into the HOT kitchen and roared, "WHY is it so damn HOT IN HERE?"

I proudly announced that I had made peanut butter cookies. If he could have, he might have strangled me for heating up the main house, where there was no a/c, "YOU DON"T BAKE IN THE SUMMER!"

OOPS - I didn't know that. I learned so much. I swam in a quarry, skinny dipped as a matter of fact, and not just with my friends, but even with the entire families of the inhabitants on the farm. It was a marble quarry and the water was about 40 degrees. I kid you not! It was FREEZING and this, during the summer. OH, how refreshing and awesome it was. There were about 15 of us from the ages of 3 – 35 and all in between. There was nothing sexual about it, just joyful and natural. I became as NATURAL as I had ever been. I lost weight -- a GREAT thing. I didn't wear a stitch of makeup. I was a NATURAL WOMAN! ~Smile. I recall the song, "YOU MAKE ME FEEL LIKE A NATURAL WOMAN," my theme for the summer. Anyway, feel free boys to ask me anything about that time. It was glorious. At the same time, my mom and dad were CRAZED that their smart graduate daughter that they had spent hugely on to put through college was now living on a farm in Massachusetts. This was NOT what they had intended for me. I think this was one of the MOST major times when they disowned me. They were for real THIS time.

I recall after Edward's funeral that I was instructed by Mom and Dad to either go back to DC and get a job, or live at home and get a job in Manhattan. I had planned on going right back to the farm, to be a farm girl some more. Just because Edward died, did not mean that I had to change MY life as well. Anyway, I arrived home to Long Island that day, in plenty of time to mourn with the family and endure a funeral. THAT was my first sad death. I knew and adored this departed soul. So many have been lost to me ever since.

What is weird is that most of my loved ones departed in the order of my love for them. Yes -- very weird -- so odd, that I noticed what I will share with you. First, there was my mom in '85. I adored her - I missed her - I still do. There was such a void in my life and so I got REALLY close to my Aunt Inga. She became like a mom to me.

Here I was pregnant and no mom, so   I went to her for my MOTHERLY needs and wants. Shockingly and sadly, she was next. We were having the SWEETEST relationship. She never had a daughter. We adored one another and I needed a mom! It was totally shocking when she announced that she had been diagnosed with lung cancer.

Oh my horrified heart! I was on a plane to see her at the finest cancer hospital, I think, in the world -- Sloan Kettering. And still, they couldn't save her. By the way Andrew, she was the first one to give you a taste of ice cream. I was so, so stingy with sugar for both of you guys and she decided to give you ice cream, regardless of my choice on your first birthday. Do you recall that YOU and Ross called her your "LOVEY DOVEY?" ~Tears.

She departed almost, exactly to the day, 2 years after my mom died. More grief, within 2 years than I'd known in my entire lifetime. She had lost her fight with lung cancer and departed on 2/17…Mom two years prior, on 2/15.

Each time I endured a loss, I got closer with those still ALIVE. It came to me when I was feuding with Arnold, my dad, that G_d or something seemed to be taking those that I LOVE MOST away from me, in the order of my love for them. This did not make sense until the formula continued. I would get closer and closer with those that still were alive and well...

After Aunt Inga made her transition, I got closer with Grandpa Fred, Uncle Harvey and Aunt Jeanie. Without getting too detailed, I started to think about those that I truly LOVED and those whom I rather did not. I felt my mother-in-law never liked me -- not from the beginning of time when she first met me. My dad and I were feuding, as you know, after my mom died and so those two souls were my least favorites. Yet shockingly, perhaps as if an order to it, they were the last to go. Myrtle is still alive. Of course, we have nothing to do with one another. It is not important – it is what it is. ~Smile.

And lo and behold, the only ones left were Fred, Myrtle, Aunt Jeanie and Dad. I got sooooooooooooooooooooooo close with Aunt Jeanie. My goodness, there was no one else.

I did adore Fred. He was a sweet, sweet man. We had great talks and GREAT love from the very first time we met. He was a dear man.

I noticed that G_d took those that I adored and left those that I was challenged by. I can only ascertain, in a spiritual way, that the EASY ones, the ones that I loved, and those with whom we shared pleasure, were taken first. Yes, there was sadness when they departed, but they did NOT grow my soul. Surely, the ones that were challenging, that I remained in relation to, THEY grew my soul. I evolved, as to getting along with them. Of course, you have more of a desire to get along with those that you do not particularly like, because there is no one else. And so, in order to get along, you must give thought and care as to HOW to do that. It is not easy! You become more humbled. You tread lightly. You do what it takes to not get in a fight, debate or to piss one another off. I got along with Myrtle, just not as easily or as joyfully as Mom, Aunt Inga and those that were so easy to love.

THEREFORE, I believe for my life -- a life that is constantly evolving, constantly growing, constantly looking at myself -- I believe that in order for me to grow and evolve as I mention, the ones that I was challenged with remained the longest in my life. Interestingly, Fred died, then Uncle Harvey, Aunt Jeanie and then Dad. It was almost a hierarchy of the favorites first and then the most challenging last. You might say, as you have, "MOM, you think too much." And yet - it makes perfect sense to me.

Perhaps there is a way to be grateful, even in light of the pain. Are we here to GROW our souls?

Kansas City -- MY Dad and YOUR Dad -- 1981

"YES DAD!" I responded, "IF I fell in love with a man from Kansas City, YES DAD, I'd move to Kansas City, OKAY? Now leave me alone!" I said under my breath.

It was 10/16/1981 and Mom and Dad were visiting me from Florida. We were in Atlanta -- I was single -- NOT married and NO signs of hope on the way. I was 29 years old and while Dad never liked most any of my boyfriends, he was getting HARD UP, I think, worrying that I would be a spinster. I, too, had my doubts (~Smile), BUT there was no way I would ever marry, if not for love!

I was dating this well-to-do man who worked on Wall Street and he came down to Atlanta to see me, to WOO me, and Dad asked me how things were progressing with Mark. I said, "He's a great guy. I like him a bunch and yet, he'd never leave Wall Street and I certainly would never move back to New York...NO way!"

That is when Dad said to me, in the tone that I had to agree with whatever he said. "So, if you happen to fall in love with a man from let's say Kansas City, would you move there?"

"YES DAD," I responded, just to give him lip service. "If I fell in love with a man from Kansas City, YES DAD, I would move to Kansas City."

My patience was wearing thin. That was 10/16/1981. I met your dad on 12/16/1981, a mere two months later, and we danced, we dined and then I asked him where he came from. "Kansas City."

~Smile. We were married 6 1/2 months later and, blessedly, we remained in Georgia, NEVER to move back to Kansas City. Thanks Dad!

Was It Fate? -- 1470E-1471B -- 1981

Of course it was. I went to the Sporting Club to meet my girlfriend Mary Jane. She and I were to meet in the Jacob G. Maroone Bar, and so we did. While there, we noticed that there was FREE food in the gym. THEY were having a Christmas party; it was 12/16/81. I was NOT looking for or at men, just interested in meeting my girlfriend and getting munchies.

I saw this LONG line queuing up for the buffet and thought, "My goodness, why are they just on one side of the table getting their food? Why not go on the other side of the table as well, have two lines?"

I surveyed the crowd, had a LITTLE bit of courage and decided to venture past about 100 persons to start another line for helping oneself to the buffet. I somewhat meekly walked over and felt about 100 daggers of those who had been PATIENTLY waiting in line, now wanting to stab me -- make ME into chopped LIVER! All of a sudden, standing there a bit shyly, but at least doing something wisely to move the line along, I showed I was not a caterer for nothing. This big, tall guy comes over and says, "Are you thinking about doing what I'm thinking about doing?"

I looked up, saw his face, smiled and said, "Yes, but these people are going to KILL us!"

He responded, "Ahhhh, go for it!"

I did; and that was the start of a 23-year marriage. Here's how the evening continued. He had a crush on me. I just wanted to eat. ~Smile. WE sat down, Mary Jane and I. I was truly starved. When Melvin started asking me questions from across our table, "What do you do?" I was so not in the mood to have a major conversation, so MJ answered the questions for me. Dad and she began a conversation about me, my business, Errands Accomplished and such. I was not really at my most INTERESTED. They continued to talk while I sat there and ate. The truth is that LOTS of people would ask me about my business. "Aren't YOU 'the errand lady'?'"

I had gotten lots of press, was in several TV shows and 'ins and outs' on the news, so I sort of had my 15 minutes of fame. It had come to the point where it was a bit annoying; I liked my anonymity. Anyway, they talked about me, the music was playing, NOT a soul on the dance floor and this big, tall guy asked me to dance -- yup, Daddy. What went through my rather fairly good dancing brain was, "IS HE CRAZY? There are so many people here. I wonder if he can even dance."

I accepted and OH MY GOD, he could SURELY dance – woo-hoo! He was terrific and we had a ball. All the while, I was thinking, "Hmmmmmmm. He's tall, he's nice-looking, he can dance, he's a nice guy and my interest was piqued."

I left him and went into another party room, flirted and did not really think much about him. MJ went home and then I followed. I did not see him, left and went home to 1470E Crystal Lake Drive. I had a recording on my answering machine – recall, no cells in 1981. It said, "Hi, this is the guy you met tonight and I just wanted to tell you that it was a great pleasure meeting you and dancing with you and I wanted to thank you!"

WOW! Smooth, mannerly -- how lovely, it surely was special. I do not recall when HE called back, but I was impressed when he did and I was a bit eager to know more of him. He asked to see me, we made a plan and then he asked where I lived. "Destiny Valley," I responded.

"Oh," he said, "me too! Really, where in Destiny Valley do you live?"

I responded, "1470 E, why? Where do you live?"

"1471 B," he responded.

WHOA, that was pretty amazing. It turns out there was a street divide between odd and even numbers, so Dad lived on the ODD side. ~Smile. I lived on the even side. He came one day to JOG with me. YES, I was a consistent jogger during those days. I would awaken at 6 AM and go jogging with my neighbor Lisa, around the lake. This time Dad joined me and while we were jogging, I asked him how hold he was. I was 29. He said that his birthday was approaching and that he was 23 years old.

In that moment, I was disappointed. NOPE, your mom was NOT a cougar, THEN! ~Smile. So I just remarked. "OKAY, so you'll become the big little brother I never had."

G_D had different plans for us. ~Smile.

Is There Premonition for All the Souls I Meet or Just MY Soulmates – 12/16/81

Melvin and I had just met. We had a sweet romance. I just knew right away that he was THE one. I used to ask my mom, "How will I know who the right man is to marry?"

She would respond, "You'll just know."

So, here I was, 29 years old and I met this man who was 23 years old. At first I thought he would be the BIG/LITTLE brother I never had. As time passed, we fell in love.

A rather short story -- he proposed to me on March 31, 1982 and before I could respond "YES," I had to mention that I thought he was rather young and perhaps he needed to LIVE LIFE MORE...have MORE experiences. We had only known one another for 3 1/2 months. He looked at me and responded, "When I see what I want, I KNOW IT!"

I heard him, gathered more confidence in HIS knowing and responded, "I hope this doesn't come back to haunt us when you're 45."

END of story -- we got engaged, married and had children. We were rather happy for the most part. We were a team, enduring every kind of experience and growth possible -- deaths, money challenges, health challenges...LIFE.

He changed. He went from a happy-go-lucky, sweet, loving, adorable man to an angry, frustrated, self-proclaimed out-of-control guy, having a nervous breakdown and all. I did not even realize he was sick. I took his moods and illness personally. It was very sad.

I guess in life you TAKE the TEST before you learn the lesson. Sad to say, we split up. He became ill -- when? -- at 45 years old. Was that another premonition? I suppose so. Perhaps our souls KNOW stuff that our conscious minds do not.

Two Marriages -- 2 Divorces – 7/2/82 - 11/6/82 – 4/22/04 - 4/22/06

I guess Daddy and I never did much that was totally typical. We had two wedding dates and, oddly enough, we had two divorce dates as well. The wedding was scheduled for 11/6/82 and then we found a condo that changed our plans-- the one you were both born in -- 4653 Happy Mill Road, Chamblee Georgia.

We decided a bit towards the old fashioned side to NOT live together and only move in when we were BETROTHED. The closing on the condo was scheduled for 7/16/82, so we ran off to the justice of the peace on 7/2/82. We were exactly the opposite of other young lovers. They all lied that they were married, when they decided to LIVE together. We lied that we were LIVING together and not married, when we were. Thank goodness we did it twice, as the first wedding was really a bit of a disaster. I am amazed that I remember it well, as it was a memory any normal gal would want to forget.

The 7-2 weddings happened so fast...there were flights to catch -- last minute -- get a dress, get flowers and find a restaurant. MY parents came to witness it and even my sister and her husband flew in. How lovely! HOW STRESSFUL, when it took us 2 days to put the entire thing together. The justice was a Jewish man that was as bland as rice pudding without the sweetener. The restaurant was THE FINEST IN TOWN, Hedgerose Heights, at my dad's insistence. Yet it was THE most horrible dinner I think all of us ever had, prior to and since! It took them about 2 hours – I am NOT exaggerating -- to get FOOD to us. I was having low blood sugar, your dad was trying to make everyone happy, Mom was so frustrated – bordering on angry and my dad was wondering where the Hell I found this horror. "If we were in New York," he said, "we'd be at the Rainbow Room. What kind of an establishment is this?"

I think the cook had a virus, went home and no one noticed except US, whose food he had not prepared. It was horrible! We were finally served and nothing could have comforted us.

We were beyond stress – exhaustion, joy and more. We finished and left. We then went to the Sheraton Hotel on 85 for our HONEYMOON night. We were guests, compliments of my parents for our first night. It was a lovely hotel, EXCEPT this was July 2 and there was NO a/c in our room. Dad was not the most assertive guy on the block, so I had to complain. It did not start our nuptials off well – no, not at all. ~Smile.

I laugh – ahhhhhhhhh, retrospect! Anyway, lest I digress, I flip to divorce. We had been separated for a year. During that time I went to New York to dance and I met with an old friend of mine. He was an attorney and while discussing my husband and catching up on 20 + years, he suggested to me that I get a divorce NOW. I was shocked. Why would I do THAT, when I still loved your dad and did not want to divorce him? It is just that he could not live with us; he felt out of control. It was uncharted territory. Anyway, it was strongly suggested to GET THE DIVORCE NOW, before Dad would take a girlfriend. Because then, Dad would not be as nice or fair, surely not be as nice of a guy. That is what I was told. And my response was, "NO WAY! I LOVE HIM and he will never get a girlfriend; he is so in love with me."

Phillip impressed upon me that I can always remarry him, but to trust Philip. "He IS going to find someone else". "Don't wait for that," Phillip urged.

I surely did not think so; still, I listened. This was October. I eventually went to court in January. First time I went, Dad was too depressed to attend. "DID WE GET DIVORCED? " he asked when I got home.

"No, I couldn't do it. When my case was called, I sat there blubbering and crying. The judge said to work it out or else come back in a few months. He stated that I was clearly not ready to end my rather lengthy marriage. I listened."

That was 1/12/04. I cried; I just could not do it. April 22, 2004 was a different story. I had given up hope. Led by the mantra, "If you live on a diet of HOPE, you will die of starvation."

I read that and coupled with the fact that I had a QUESTIONABLE mammogram a week prior, I lay in bed the night before court thinking, "IF I have cancer, I am getting divorced."

It dawned on me that the only way I could go through with the divorce was if I was dying, and I decided that was a HORRIBLE reason. I decided no matter what, I could not stand the depression. I could not stand his change of personality. With the angst directed at me then and now, all these years later, I realize that I took it personally. I truly did not think about HIM being sick. This was not about ME, yet that is how I processed it. NO ONE was going to leave me! I made that decision when Lily left me some 53 years prior. I felt as if Daddy already had. He truly did not care about himself, me or anything, but that is the reality about horrible depression. It was very sad; it was and still is.

Anyway, I went through with it on the 22nd of April, 2004. One hour in the courtroom and it was signed, sealed and delivered -- we were divorced. I still loved your dad and I thought vice-versa, so we decided NOT to tell anyone. Perhaps he would heal and we would make it. I was in counseling; he was in counseling. I truly thought he still loved me. Hmmm. I knew that MIND thought is huge and if the world knew that we were no longer married, our world would change and it would surely tear us apart. We kept the secret for a great many months, almost 5 I think.

Then one morning, the morning of our flight to California for a vacation together, I received an email. It was from Dad's sister, Babs. She wrote, "Is it true that my brother and you are divorced?"

WHAT? How in the HELL did she find out? I called Daddy. We were separated, even though heading out on vacation together. I was sure he told her. HOW ELSE would she know? He swore, "Bunny, I didn't say a word. I haven't a clue as to how she found out."

I wrote back and asked her without saying yes, WHAT MADE HER THINK THAT? She responded that she looked up the court records and found "dissolution of marriage."

What a piece of work. Melvin and I had more than those thoughts about her – did she not have anything better to do in her life than look into OUR business? Apparently not and with that, we learned that she told her brothers Seth and Howie. They apparently told their mom and like wild fire, it was spreading. Here, our children, you and you, Ross and Andrew, had no clue. "We had better tell them before someone else does. Can you imagine if you do not know that your own parents are divorced and you hear it through the grapevine?"

Surely it is a different scenario from most other couples, parents and children. Anyway, you guys were at camp; Daddy and I gave this much thought and decided as soon as you came home, we would share the news. Talk about lots of thought. Whew! It was not something that we looked forward to; our hearts hurt for you guys. I truly believe we were a happy family -- quite a strikingly fun, happy, family for over 2 decades. I abhorred the idea of sharing the news in our living room, where the energy of that discussion would hang in the air forever. I thought about a restaurant -- always a great idea to share ANYTHING with men -- over food. So the plan unfolded and we went to the Casselberry Park, where we all worked as a family, sponsoring Cajun dances – oh, the memories are bright. I prepared quiche, fruit salad and croissants. We had flowers -- and pastries for dessert, just like the breakfast in beds from several years back. We made a beautiful spread on a picnic table. You boys were joyful with camp behind you, stories to share and being with your Mom and Pop!

I began the 'event' and said, KNOWING what your responses would be, "ROSS, has there ever been ANYTHING in your life that you didn't have a clue what was coming and it just surprised you?"

"Oh yeah," Ross responded.

I KNEW what he would say. "What was that?" And he began, "Well, when I got my full scholarship and then didn't attend classes, I never dreamed in a million years that I would lose the scholarship and that you and Dad would decide that I was going to put MYSELF through college. I never saw THAT coming."

Hmmmmm, we both looked at one another, Daddy and I, and said, YEAH, we see -- Interesting, knowing exactly that he would say that. "What about you Andrew?"

"Oh yeah," he began, "I never thought I'd miss senior year at Lake Mary – NEVER, NEVER. I would have bet that I'd be there, and here I found myself going to military school."

Yup, we agreed; that too was a surprise. "Well, Mommy and I never saw THIS coming either," Daddy said, "but we've gotten divorced."

Andrew broke out into tears and Ross covered his face. The shock was palpable and yet, they had to know. We were a united front, Daddy and I. So I surmise the blow was not nearly as bad as it could have been. We talked, you guys asked questions and then I think it was Andrew who said, "Are you guys still having sex?"

Out of the mouths of babes, we were hysterical. The conversation now got quite funny – joyful, actually. We talked, we laughed, we strategized, we cleared the food and hiked out of the park. While it was a sad memory, it was a loving family unit. I am sorry those do not exist any longer -- more for the boys than for Melvin and I. Yes, the world helped to pull us apart. Even while Daddy wore his wedding ring, there were still gals at the ballroom that would look up at him and ask, "Is there a MRS. MALLIN?"

Like vultures -- it was only a matter of time. Such contrast -- in 1982 we were married and could not wear our wedding bands, because people would know we were married and perhaps would not attend the BIG wedding in Florida in November. In 2004, we were divorced and wore our bands, not wanting people to know we were no longer married. KOOKBALLS? For sure! ~ smile.

Having a Boy -- 1986 -- Amniocentesis

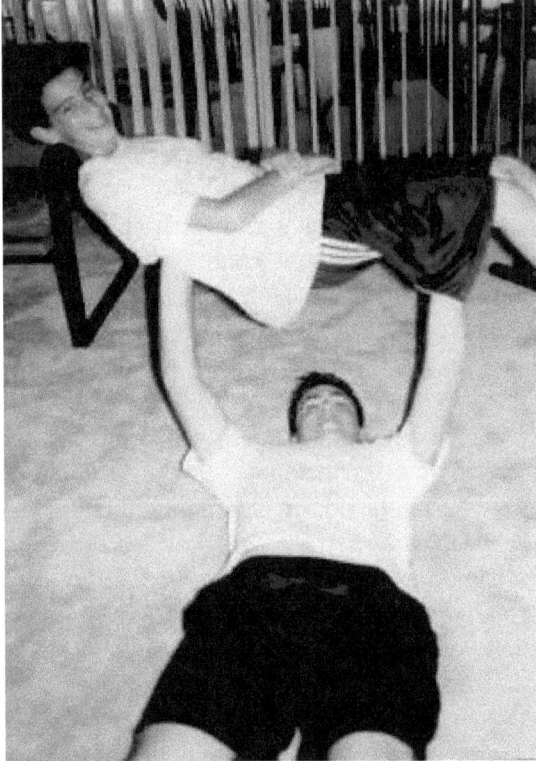

It was 1986 and I was about 4-5 months pregnant with Andrew, yet had NO idea if he was going to be an Andrew or an Amanda. Melvin and I had selected the names, based upon his grandma, Anne and my grandma, Blanche.

Aunt Ida was very much alive, Mom had passed and it was time to go for an amniocentesis. I did not determine the sex of my first child, YOU, Ross and was just surprised and delighted on March the 6th.

With this second pregnancy, it was different. We decided that we wanted to know the sex, in preparation for the room, the clothing and everything that goes into having a baby. I went to the doctors. They stuck the needle in my tummy. There was no pain, that I recall, in drawing out amniotic fluid.

In my heart, I wanted a baby girl, just for the contrast -- something different. I had been told that a GIRL will always be my child, whereas a boy will one day marry and not be as close with his mom. POOH! POOH!

We were all excited and, literally MORESO, just to determine if my baby was healthy. The sex REALLY did not mean as much, not even close. I received the report just a few days later and was THRILLED that it was a healthy child. I was then informed that the baby, growing inside of me, was a boy. Disappointed for a moment, I later called Aunt Ida, to share that the baby was FINE, healthy and was going to be a boy.

She was THRILLED, not only with my healthy report, but that I was having a boy. I shared that I was a tad bit disappointed. She shared that having Ricky and Stephen was wildly joyful and that their relationship with one another was worth all the baby girls in the world. They adored one another and to have two of the same sex, was a blessed treat. They would play and be best friends, so I was happily digesting the news. Thank you, Aunt Ida.

Fast-forward to about 1992. Andrew was about 5 years old and we went to visit my friend's new baby. Debbie had had a girl after her first son, Rusty.

I took Andrew with me for a visit and Andrew asked me, "Mommy, are you disappointed that you had ME instead of a baby girl?"

"OH MY G_D, NOT IN A MILLION, GAZILLION YEARS."

I do not think I could love this child any more than I do - or get the joy and lessons of unconditional love as I have received from Andrew. I honestly think he heard my conversation with Aunt Ida. Wow! Of course he did - from inside my tummy.

AND...even though my sons have not married, YET, I truly believe that you guys are THE greatest and I am thrilled to have each and both of you. When you marry, I just anticipate that I will adore your bride and, surely, not lose closeness with either of you. I will gain daughters. I have no doubts and so it is!

What is This Connection with Ross' Fractured Elbow and Broken Leg -- '92 - '12

Ross was about 7 years old. I was a caterer and I fractured my left arm while attending a Toastmasters' convention. It was rather challenging; it interfered with my livelihood in addition to the pain. I remember sitting out on the stoop in Dunwoody with my sweet little child and him telling me, "Mommy, I wish I could take your pain away. I wish it happened to me, instead."

Oh my sweet boy. My heart bled for his gesture, thinking and kindness. It was about 2 weeks later that I had my first job that I attended after the injury. I did not lift anything or work, but I had to be there. It was a BIG job with Dow Chemical. I had a REALLY hard time finding a babysitter and so my baker, Gina – boy, could she bake -- came and truly enjoying the boys, she was the babysitter for the afternoon and evening. She was so kind to babysit and help me out.

I received a call from her early in the evening that Ross was playing SPIDERMAN and was climbing the door frame, fell and did something to his left arm. "Meet me at the ER," she said.

Can you believe it? My child fractured his left arm. Watch out what you wish for and what your thinking is. BLESS you ROSS! Now years later and I do still think there is a connection. Ross and I were heading to China for a phenomenal visit to 8 countries and a super terrific cruise. A week prior to the trip, I was informed by a psychic that I was going to BREAK my leg and I should not go down the Great China Wall in a toboggan as we were scheduled to do. I told Ross and he understood; he would do it himself. Oh well, nothing even as exciting as the Great Wall and taking a toboggan is worth a broken leg.

We arrived atop the wall and it was just TOOOOOO, too difficult to pass up. I had come several THOUSAND miles. There was no way I was going to break MY leg. So blessedly and excitedly, Ross and I embarked on this adventure. It was great, safe and, TA-DA, we were all in one piece as we continued on our adventure. We arrived home, all in good stead, having had a marvelous trip.

Ross was supposed to begin a great new job on Monday of the following week and instead, he called me to share on Sunday night that he had broken his tibia, some bone in one's leg and ankle.

Oh my sad heart! Is there is a connection? I either get injured or warned and Ross manifests a similar injury. Personally, I think there is a connection. What could it be? I think after writing this months ago and pondering the above, I have an answer. It's a bit far-fetched, but still, for me it makes sense.

Ross was born very shortly after Mom died. He literally used to be in a snuggly against my chest. I would take him for walks. It was a VERY sad time and all I would do was cry. Mom was gone.

No sooner did I begin crying, Ross would start to cry and then I would stop. It was as if MY reaction to HIS crying made me stop. Perhaps he could heal my pain. What went on in his sweet little mind? I get tears now; it is so sad, Ross, that you had to endure my crying when all I wanted was for you to know how joyful I was in giving birth to YOU! It was a MARVELOUS pregnancy. You were so easy to conceive. All I was, was thrilled, BEYOND anything you would understand.

I never knew if I would get married. I thought not, and surely I did not anticipate having children. My childhood was NOT the greatest. I did not want to mess up my own children. So, to have conceived so easily, after taking the course to consider whether Daddy and I wanted children, was just so amazing. Anticipating you was beyond 'beyond.' Still unplanned for, the loss of my mom changed my joy. Whether or not on some level you could understand, I do not know. Still it seemed as if you must have decided that when MOMMY cried or had PAIN, you could take it away from me.

Remember how you WISHED you could take the pain that I endured from my fractured elbow and, lo and behold, you fractured yours? I think this too, the idea and suggestion that I would break my leg, as suggested by the psychic, might have, on SOME LEVEL, translated for you an unconscious desire to take MOMMY's pain. DO NOT DO THIS AGAIN! BREAK the CYCLE. MY pain is my pain and yours, G_D willing, will be minimal! I love you so much. I do not want to see you anguish; breaking your leg was horrible.

I do think there is a connection and NOW, we have broken it! AMEN! Perhaps there is forgiveness. Perhaps you were feeling as if YOU created my pain. GUILT seeks punishment, but YOU did nothing. Forgive yourself; my tears were NEVER your fault. MAYBE as a teen they were. ~Smile. ~Mom

Is It a Coincidence – Mr. Woodard and The Olympics – 1996 - 2016

Is it a coincidence? I don't believe it is. Instead, I believe that G_D paves the way for our destiny and we follow.

For instance, Andrew was now a student at Vanderlyn Elementary. He thrived academically and yet, even MORE so, with Physical Education. He just LOVED being active, was rather good at sports and had the gift of PLAYING at the 'Y' after school. Because of his having to go to Vanderlyn, it was a neat unfolding, due to changing schools.

One day I received a call from the PE teacher, Mr. Woodard. I went in to see him for our scheduled appointment and he told me that Andrew was THE best athlete he had ever had the privilege of teaching and coaching in all of his 17 years as a PE instructor. I was thankful that this appointment was not to tell me about BEHAVIORAL challenges about Andrew. THAT was a relief!

More importantly, he was so flattering, asking me if I knew how coordinated and skilled Andrew was at sports. I had no clue. I know he played Basketball well for the Church and I know that he LOVED to play, yet I had NO idea that he was as talented as Mr. Woodard made him out to be. He was merely in 4th grade. He asked me what 'plans' I had for Andrew. Quite frankly, I had NO plans, other than raising him with every morsel of love, responsibility and blessings that I could give him. I asked him what he meant and he responded that I could send him to a private school or find a coach to work with him. Quite honestly, while I was very impressed, I sort of let it go in one ear and out the other. I did not really know how RIGHT ON THIS EDUCATOR was. At some point I will find him and tell him where Andrew is TODAY.

TODAY, 8/25/2012, Andrew is in Los Angeles , California -- Huntington Beach specifically -- playing in the Jose Cuervo tournament, as a beach volleyball professional. He is ranked anywhere from 28th to 42nd in the nation in beach volleyball. He is a skilled athlete and has been training for the Olympics 2016, his goal for the last several years. He has sacrificed an education, he has sacrificed finances/riches and he has sacrificed GIRLS...plus, plus, plus, and let me tell you, he is a specimen of a man.

Interestingly enough, he went out to play this tournament and right before his departure date, he hurt his back. He could hardly walk to the gate, as I saw him entering the airport. I THOUGHT, as any mom would that he would change his mind, stay home and take care of his back. I drove him to the airport, suggesting that he stay home. I told him I would reimburse his partner for the frustration and expense of going all the way to California. No way! He was determined and could not let his partner down.

It is 6:50 PM at this moment, my time, and 3:50 PM, California time, so he is playing right at this very moment. I USED to worry and fret about how he would be feeling and what would be happening to my child. Instead, I have prayed, asking for others' prayers and putting confidence in G_D and the universe to bless him – to let him heal during these next 2 days and know that whatever the outcome, it would all be for the best.

Regardless of winning or losing -- NO matter -- he was being blessed...there is a plan.

This child is an athlete and what I have found and learned is that they are built differently. It is PHENOMENAL to watch. He is his own man and I support him 100 percent in knowing that he is going after his dream. Apparently Mr. Woodard knew something I didn't know.

In addition to PAVING the way as I have expressed, there is another INTERESTING coincidence. The Olympics were in Atlanta in 1996, so we had the rare opportunity to take our family to see many of the events. I chose 6 events. Four of them were for the Special Olympics -- blind goal ball, limbless swimming, etc. Additionally, we saw the closing ceremonies. The ONLY event that I selected, that was part of the regular Olympics was – YUP, you guessed it -- Beach Volleyball. How on earth did I choose that one particular sport, when there were literally hundreds of other events to choose from? The boys were 9 and 11 years old and I have no clue how I selected Beach Volleyball, but I have this GUT feeling that it was all part of the plan. I just love to see how the universe works and, blessedly, how I learn to follow its lead and riches. Amen and G_d Bless You, Andrew during this time. I am so grateful that you endured those challenging years in early elementary school.

I think that G_D makes us, some with more challenges than others, so that we can go forward and thrive in ways that are exemplary, especially for those that we never would have thought could be successful, i.e., Oprah. She surely came from adversity and was put on the planet to show others how THEY, TOO, can thrive, even in the midst of challenges like she faced. I believe that G_D has a purpose for each of us and is using Andrew, as well, to be a blessing to others. Would you believe it, his birthday is 1/29. Guess who else shares that birthday? Yup, OPRAH! ~Smile.

Andrew's Bar Mitzvah was April Fool's Day, 4/1/2000. We did a STRIPTEASE on the way out to the guests and YOU, Andrew, tripped and fell on your way out. We surely choreographed an amazingly fun time.

Then, do you recall how we handed out bills to our guests? MOST everyone either thought it was hysterical and GOT it, although there was the one that totally flipped out and balked -- your Grandma Myrtle. She was sooooooooo mad. When Seth came to pick her up in her room the next morning, AFTER she left the event early, she was as mad as could be saying, "Do you realize what Melvin and Adrian did? They CHARGED ME FOR MY DINNER! CAN YOU BELIEVE IT?"

Seth responded "Mom, look at the date."

She did...end of story...WOW! TOO funny!

Do you remember Ross, when Daddy went to your classroom and sat in the rear? You were so mortified. He wanted to see you behave as you had, without him there. Ya know where he got that idea? He and I listened to Dr. Laura and she gave her audience the idea, just at the very same time that you were "acting out." It was such perfect timing. Daddy went there and YOU never misbehaved again. TOUCHE!

Did you guys know that when I became pregnant with Ross, I was in Durham visiting, honing up on my diet skills and seeing Joe. I went to the DUKE lab to take the pregnancy test and found out – POSITIVE!

Daddy was arriving that weekend and I kept it a secret, until he arrived at the Downtowner Motel. On the billboard sign, in big bold letters was the following:

"CONGRATULATIONS DADDY MALLIN"

Oh my joyful heart, that was how he found out -- before we got out of the car from the airport...the hugs and kisses and joy in observing that billboard – happy, happy, joy, joy!

How did your mom become a coach? Do you remember Charlene? She used to come to me all the time and ask me questions about investing, home maintenance and relationships, etc., etc. I loved it and used to help her as best as I could. One day, SHE called me and said, "There is a NAME for what you do for me."

I wondered, "What are you talking about?"

"She responded, "There are 'coaches' that you literally pay to answer your questions or help you to get from where you are to where you want to go...and it's a PROFESSION."

I inquired that day and found the courses. I then began flying up to Atlanta, to learn and study! Amen and thank you Angel Charlene!

Ross, of course you recall our reading "HIRE THE HEAVENS" while we were in Spain. So, each time we did what they suggested, we let go. We believed in the outcome we desired, i.e.: Hired the Heavens and each time we manifested what we prayed on/for...only because I believed it? ~Smile. What do you think? How does it work?

Melvin Will Take Care of Me -- Our Words Hold Weight -- 2004

And so our words hold weight. Melvin told Irma before she died that he would always take care of me. I believe he surely meant it. When we divorced, he told me that he felt bad that he broke his agreement with Irma and would NOT be taking care of me. He felt really bad.

HOWEVER, unbeknownst to him, upon suing me and losing hugely, he, in reality, has been taking care of me -- somewhat more, financially. Amen to his agreement! While he is not doing so in this reality, his choices and decisions have blessed me in many ways – in ways that he did not know he was going to bless me. Thank you Melvin, thank you Irma, thank you my Angels and thank you G_D! Suffice it to say I am grateful!

Souls Going in Different Directions – 1/04 - 1/10

I do not know how this universe works, but it surely does amaze me. Daddy and I had been married almost 22 years, when that horrific depression hit. You witnessed it. Well, I awakened one morning; of course I still loved your dad, even though we were now living apart. I had this feeling. It was nothing like I had ever known or had before. There seemed no reason, no rhyme, just a feeling, and it scared me. It was a gnawing, a discomfort.

I called daddy and asked that he come over right away. It could not have been later than 9 AM and he arrived within the 1/2 hour. You know he was living at the condo, just down 434. He asked if I was okay and I was not sure. Anyway, he came over and I was crying. I asked him to lie down with me and we went into the bedroom. I began to cry that our souls were moving in different directions. He did not understand what I was saying; it came up in avalanches of tears. I told him that I just had this feeling, as we lay there lovingly wrapped in one another's arms. I told him that I felt as though his spirit, his soul, was going in THIS direction and mine was clearly going in THAT direction. I physically expressed my left arm to the left, where HIS soul was heading and my right arm to the right, directly opposed to his, where MY soul was heading. I had never felt, thought, or expressed ANYTHING like this before.

He started to cry. We both spent the next several moments just THINKING about WHY? How can this be? We still love one another. Why are we not going in the same direction? He asked question after question. Repeatedly he said, "Bunny, why is this happening?"

"Melvin, I don't know. I just don't know."

Several times he just continued asking, "WHY?"

"I JUST DON'T KNOW."

I literally didn't know what to say. "I don't know. Maybe you're supposed to become a Jew for Jesus (I said it with MORE question and hyperbole rather than a knowing statement)?"

I stammered and picked an idea kind of outta my hat, "I don't know. Maybe, Ummmmmmmmm, maybe, I'm supposed to SAVE SOMEONE"S LIFE and God needs me THERE, while YOU'RE here. I just don't know!"

Well, about a year later Daddy and I were divorced. A year after that, he met Ava, a minister's ex-wife. A year later they were married. Shortly thereafter, daddy became a major, radical zealot Jew For Jesus, or so I am told. You guys know; you told me. In the meantime, life went on, You boys and I noticed that daddy was really into Jesus -- sort of like the premonition I had. Yes, it was a bit odd, yes.

Some years later, I went off to Jamaica. I went with Brenda, a friend of mine, and we went for a week to dance ballroom in Montego Bay, Mon! What started out really joyful grew to be rather challenging. Brenda not only was a SNORER, but she would take a sleeping pill before bed and SNORE her friggin' brains out, while I lay there -- FRUSTRATED as all get up, literally taking my weary bones to the bath tub to get some sleep. It did not work. I lay in the tub with the pillow over my head, as uncomfortable as any other 5'12" person would be and finally decided, "I'm GOING home!! If it costs me $1000 to get out of here, I'm leaving. I cannot stand this any longer!"

I figured if I am going to be awake all night, I might as well skip this trip; I so detest not being able to sleep. There were no additional rooms in the hotel; all were booked up, sold out! I got on the phone and called the airlines. They would have charged me an additional $575 to depart on a different flight from my scheduled flight. OKAY, you know I do NOT like to throw money away. She literally sounded like a train. I recall lying there thinking perhaps this is what the warning of a tornado sounds like. She was peacefully sound asleep. I was MISERABLE! I then called the CAR transport to find out how much it would be for the 11/2 hour ride to the airport and they told me $150...FINE! I'm outta here! I called back the airline and was just about to book the flight when I learned the next flight available was for the following Thursday. This was Sunday night! HOLY CRAP! Maybe I said some other choice words as well. ~Smile.

So forget that, I am not going to stay until Thursday and endure this and spend that kind of money when the entire trip is complete on Saturday! I decided to get up, go about the day, dance a bit and put in my request for a PRIVATE room, if one opened up. I could not even take a nap, as they were doing construction on MY floor...NOT fun. Still I danced and had a good day.

That evening, I selected this LILY RESTAURANT, a supposedly YUMMY Asian restaurant, All of our meals were paid for and we were to visit each restaurant during the course of the week. I selected the Lily. I walked in, reservation and all, and they sat me on the side end of a rectangular table. There was a lady across from me, one to my right, one at the tip end of the table and then ladies and men down to my left. We ordered. When the appetizers arrived, we were engrossed in yummy food and good conversation. Then the main course was served and more conversation ensued. It was lively and fun!

My attention was on the gal in front of me and the one to my right, when, very gently, I felt a tap-tap-tap on my left shoulder. I turned around and there was this woman who had a major look of fright on her face. It was BEYOND fright; it was deathly fear. I do not know what drove me, but I immediately stood up, walked around behind her and applied the HEIMLICH maneuver. It was ALMOST as if I was waiting for this scenario to unfold. I did not miss a beat. One look at her face and I was in flight, wrapping my arms around her from behind and giving her that HEAVE HO, right to her sternum.

It worked! She projectile-vomited! I did it again, as she was a pale GREEN, and she vomited again. A piece of chicken flew out of her mouth. With that she hurriedly walked to the restroom. I broke out into HUGE tears. OH MY G_D, OH MY G_D, it was an intense moment; it was SURREAL!

She returned and I said to her, "DIXIE, did I just save your life?"

"HELL YEAH," she responded.

Then I explained why I had the hysteria that I did. No one could understand why I was SOOOOOOO hysterical. Melvin became a Jew For Jesus and I saved someone's life. How amazing was that?!

On the plane going home several days later, there was a minister in the aisle next to me. He was one of the ballroom dancers. We chatted during the flight and he knew what had happened; everyone knew! It's not often that someone saves someone else's life; it was drama! I asked Tom, the minister, why -- why this story occurred as it did? I shared my story regarding divorce and how I felt as though our souls were going in different directions. He responded that there are 12 'something's biblical,' I think 12 gifts. One is premonition, one is discernment, one - prophecy etc. -- something like that. He added nonchalantly, "YOU HAVE THE GIFT OF PREMONITION!"

Wow! Remember when I called you guys that very night that I saved Dixie's life? It was a rather amazing night; I was supposed to be there!

Adrian,

I am so thankful for your quick action in coming to my rescue in Jamaica. It was an emotionally charged event for both of us - one I will not soon forget. I can only say thank you and tell you I am forever grateful. You were an angel.

Dupe

Mom Died, Ross Was Born -- We All Went to Hong Kong

Do I believe in reincarnation? SURELY, I do. Here's what I think. Our souls are eternal, yes? Well then, either they remain UP there and hang or they get affixed to the next physical body that G_D and they choose. It really does not matter. For me, I take comfort in THINKING that I understand and WHY life happens. It comforts ME to believe what I have seen in my life. I like to attach meaning and figure it out if I can.

Some would say I was in the SPIRITUAL REALM line when G_D was giving out TECHNICAL smarts. I have not only lost seven chapters of this book from many years ago, but recently I lost one of the stories of this most recent 'writing'. Oh well, I like my life. ~Smile. Tech be darned.

SO, Mom came to visit me when I was 1 week shy of my due date with Ross. It was a MARVELOUS visit. She was totally the Mom that I always wanted her to be during that weekend – generous, fun and sweet -- like a girly weekend. With my mom, it was exceptional. We decided to PICK names for this about-to-be-born child. We grabbed the phone books and investigated all of our choices -- the names, first and middle had to begin with the letters R and B..."rhythm and blues?" ... Running Brooke? ... Ruby Begonia? So, we selected Ross Bradley in honor of my cousin Russell and Grandma Blanche. In Judaism, we name our newborns after our loving deceased relatives.

Mom mentioned, as we thumbed through, that she hoped -- "please G_D," she said -- that you will never have to name a child after Daddy or myself – surely, a desirable prayer. She had a toothache during her entire visit. It was uncomfortable, NOT painful, and so she did not want to go to the dentist; she just endured. We had a fabulous visit, actually -- the best we ever had. I had bronchitis and was rather uncomfortable. We laughed at what a bad influence she was on me, as we stayed up late and talked and talked and talked. She went grocery shopping for me, even paying, and was just the sweetest, most loving mom. It was the best time I had EVER spent with her. We laughed and we cried. We just had a marvelous few days and then it was time for her to go home, on a Saturday evening.

Mel had come home from the road and was taking Irma (Mom) to the airport. All packed and out the door, we hugged and kissed goodbye, knowing she would be back soon for the birth of my first child. By the way, boys, I LOVED, LOVED, LOVED, being pregnant. I was never as footloose and fancy free. No matter what the physical manifestation, I chalked it up to pregnancy, no longer worried that a headache meant a brain tumor. No fear, I was PREGNANT and I LOVED IT!

Actually from my challenges during childhood, I never thought, in a million years, that I would ever have a child. Daddy and I even attended a course at Emory University, "THINKING ABOUT HAVING A BABY AFTER 30." From the moment we graduated the course, we were GONERS. EVERY child we saw was adorable; we had the bug! We knew we were meant to be parents and passed the course with flying colors. Now it was just a matter of time. So these two pregnancies were the happiest of times, oh yes!

I kissed Mom and as she descended down the stairs, I called her back for one more kiss and hug. When Lily left me at 6 years old, I never fully recovered. So I had this FEAR that said, kiss your loved ones as if you will never see 'em again. Literally, every time Melvin went on the road, EVERYTIME I said goodbye to someone I loved, I kissed 'em and hugged 'em as if I would never see them again, JUST IN CASE!

So I will never forget that last embrace -- Mom and I, arms around one another, the energy of thanks for a WONDERFUL time. I never saw my mom again. Yes, tears come through my eyes as well, yet I got that last CONSCIOUS hug and kiss. NO automatic pilot here, she went home to Boca and my dad. That evening, so I later learned, the tooth ache traveled down into her glands. She was now uncomfortable and decided perhaps a doctor would be more in keeping than the dentist.

My dad called me on Monday and we chatted. It was very UNUSUAL as normally, my mom did all the calling and Dad and I did not speak, but maybe once per week. We paid for the long distance calls back then. I was a bit SUSPICIOUS of why HE was calling and not my mom. I asked for her and how she was. He said she could not come to the phone. Concern and a gut feeling that something was not right, he finally admitted she was in the hospital, resting and not able to chat at the moment. He was such a POOR liar. I hung up and called the hospital. Immediately I asked for the HEART ward. I just knew. Yes, she was in ICU and could not chat. I was not told her condition, until I called my aunt and uncle. They fessed up that she had endured a heart attack. The nightmare began.

I need not go into the worst time of my life -- worse than my divorce, far worse than losing Theresa and surely worse than my most recent breakup. IT was so, so, so, so, shocking! Dad did not tell me; he thought my pregnancy would be harmed. He did not know pregnancy is not a state of mind, as much as a state of stomach. I should have been told. Anguish…I was on the plane just days before my delivery, on my way to my mom's funeral. The letters on the keyboard hurt having typed the word funeral.

As I EDIT this story, I must add a line of INTEREST, sort of funny. I sat aboard Delta next to this man who was a GOLF course architect. He had a look of shock on his face when I mentioned that I was VERY pregnant. I did not carry that big, having had a LONG torso. So, when I informed him, he sort of QUIETLY freaked out. It turns out he had been on a flight the week prior to Houston. This gal sat next time him and literally was giving birth on the flight.

They had to land in some other city and she gave birth on the tarmac. He was rather FREAKED out, "Oh no, not again!"

From tears to giggle, just writing this. What are the chances of THAT?

Fast forward, Ross arrived. Oh my G_D, my beautiful, healthy, strong, amazing first-born child was long in arriving, yet I would do it again in a heartbeat; we are talking about a 36-hour labor, OMG! Could he have been Mom? I never really considered it then. Over the years, and observing life, Ross has truly become somewhat of my ROCK. I have not had a husband or life-long partner for most of the 8 years – wow, that long -- that I have been divorced. Yes, I have had short AND lengthy relationships, yet even still, Ross has been my GO-TO guy.

I recall when my heart was breaking. It was Ross I would call, to talk sense into me, to cry to him, to hear his views and help me. He, yes you Ross, were always there for me during the hard and needy times. I am so grateful NOW, even more so, as I recall you sometimes NOT answering the phone over the years and yet during the UPSET calls, you were always at the ready! The tears of happiness and gratitude flow. I would call Ross when I couldn't find Andrew, when I did not know how to reach Andrew, and was worried, etc. So Ross was literally a wise young man; he gave sound advice and never compromised his love for his dad or anyone else for that matter. He was rich in nurturing, understanding, listening and more.

IS he my Mom reincarnate? He surely LOVES food, as did Irma, even to the point where she DRESSED and prepped everything she ate. It had to be just so, and wow, so does Ross. Talk about HIS love for travel, why Mom was a travel agent as far back as in the 60's. Does a soul keep some of whom they were in their previous lives?

Ross became my most REGULAR travel companion. I have always had the travel bug and after the divorce, it was frustrating for me to not have a travel buddy. Melvin was supposed to be such and we did not make it. Anyway, Ross accompanied me on some AWESOME trips. We went to Prague, Vienna, Buda PESHT, Spain, Portugal, Egypt, Turkey and now this trip to Asia. I would have never taken this Asian cruise, save for the fact that it allowed us to visit SOOOOOOOOOO many countries. I was NOT the keenest on traveling around Asia; I had such an unpleasant experience with this Vietnam gal (back in '78) and yet, that was so long ago, I was determined to see as much of the world as I could. It was rather amazing that we did go on this trip, as it was during the major COLD months in China and Japan and you boys know how I am in the cold. So, I got the itinerary from Beth and it turned out that the trip was during Ross' birthday. Wow, perfect, it included HONG KONG.

You will not believe me when I tell you, BUT when Ross was a WEE, little boy, perhaps 18 months old, maybe 2 years old, he used to make us CRACK UP laughing.

He would say CCCHONG CKONG almost like a CHINAMAN -- VERY quickly, ccchhhong KONG! We would play with him and say, "Where are we going Rossy?"

He would respond with a nasal CCCCCHHHHH - HONG KONG, really fast, and we would all get hysterical. Where did he get that from? I have no clue. I do not EVER recall even mentioning the words Hong Kong, yet Ross would say it over and over again. That and PACI-FIA, as in pacifier, with that same Chinese sort of accent. We would just laugh.

Well, fast forward some 25 years later, and lo and behold, we headed to HONG KONG. The joy for me, in addition to it being another trip, was that as a world traveler and travel agent, my mom's FAVORITE city was HONG KONG! I could not wait to go there to see what she saw. Perusing the itinerary, I noticed that out of the 21 days of our trip, where were we going to be for Rossy's birthday? ... HONG KONG! Yup, March 6th was a PORT day and we were docking in Hong Kong, Irma's favorite city.

110

Was IRMA going there for HER birthday, her incarnation birthday as Ross? Was she 'sending' herself, her special grandson, her special daughter -- MOI? Like I said, we will never know.

What was the CCHHONG KONG funny expression about? I found it rather fascinating that we would be in Hong Kong, one of eight ports, during our 21 day stay on HIS birthday? I found it more than coincidence. It turns out that while it was NOT my favorite city/country, not even close. It was wayyyyyyyy too big and smoggy for me, but it was ROSS' number one, favorite city/country/port of the entire trip.

I cannot help but know that there are DOTS to be connected. WOWOWOWOWOW!

Oh what a fabulous unfolding, Why ever would I have any doubt of a G_D, a good benevolent G_D. Many, many years ago, and all through junior high and high school, I had a BEST friend. His name was Michael Meyerhoff and he sat behind me in homeroom. We said the Pledge of Allegiance every day. My last (maiden) name was MEYER. He was a brilliant young man and HIS best friend was David Marcus. We all hung out like the "Mod Squad." At that time, I much preferred my male friends. They were less gossipy and less catty; I just enjoyed them more.

My mom adored both Michael and David. She used to tell me that Michael had a crush on me. "NO WAY MOM, he's just my friend."

Our friendship continued for years and years, all through junior high school and high school and then some. I will never forget how we received our SAT scores. As soon as I read the one that was handed to me -- I did not let out a gasp, no enthusiasm, no excitement WHATSOEVER -- I knew it was Michael's. I think it was a 1575 out of 1600. NO question, no doubt, it was NOT mine. I just turned around and handed it to MEYERHOFF!

I must have hung with Michael every weekend – at the Roslyn Café, the duck pond, the movies, even when I was working as a waitress at the landmark diner. Michael would come in and visit, very often, to take up a seat in MY section. I was so overwhelmed and he would just sit over his coffee and grapefruit and allow me to concentrate on the other tables. He was so helpful and THEN, he would leave me a DOLLAR -- a $1 tip! That was HUGE! I think the entire grapefruit and coffee was less than a dollar; remember this was about 1969.

He was my best friend. I went off to Ohio University for my first year of college and he went off to Columbia University. See what I mean? ~Smile. He hitchhiked out to see me, even though he had a girlfriend. He told me, that he told HER, Adrian comes first! Oh my G_D, I had NO clue that he wanted to be more than friends, NO CLUE! He never went to kiss me, nothing! I was CRAZY about him, my best friend, but there was nothing romantic, or so I thought.

My mom used to tell me to "make it into a relationship, be more than friends." But I insisted that we were just friends. I had that effect on guys; they dated me and dated me and I waited and waited for them to kiss me and be the aggressor, but so seldom did it happen. I so wanted him to just KISS me. He NEVER did. I wonder if he did not want to ruin our friendship. Still, we remained FRIENDS.

Eventually, we went our separate ways, but stayed in touch. I married and I recall staying in touch with him. I especially remember him after I had children because I NEEDED his brilliance. Here I was, a new mom with no experience and no mom. I had a little boy who loved to touch girls'/women's feet. I thought perhaps I was raising a STRANGE child. Again, never will I forget when I wrote to Michael about my baby. We did not have email then, so I wrote long hand and waited for his LONG hand, snail-mail response. I told him that my child likes to touch the feet of mannequins, feet in magazines and even under the table at my dinner parties. He would crawl around at age three and touch the ladies' feet. OH MY G_D! I came to learn years later that he LOVED women's stockings and soft feet.

Michael, I recall, told me in a letter that I ought NOT to worry - - that he would grow out of it. He put my mind at rest. He even went on to make me laugh and told me a true story about a client that used to LOVE vacuum cleaners and even went to bed with the family Hoover. I will never forget; this child ended up going to YALE. Wow!

Well, skip to many years later, by this time Michael had met my children. I recall him coming to Atlanta. I do not think Melvin, my husband, was there. I think he was away on business. I met Michael, with both Ross and Andrew, and had a sweet visit. Somehow, along those lines, we decided to write and co-author a book together. So, business woman ADRIAN sent out a contract for Michael to sign -- some legalese. When he received it, he hit the roof! Never had I seen Michael mad in the decades of knowing him. OOPS! He was totally insulted that I would behave according to that level of distrust, as if he would ever steal or do anything NON-integrity packed, such as steal a co-authored book, especially from me.

I think in the divine sense, our friendship had to come to an end. I am not sure, but perhaps he was marrying then, or was already married and perhaps his feelings were inappropriate for me. I almost feel like he needed to escape our friendship -- and he did.

We never spoke again. I was just being wise and business minded. I never considered that he would be so offended. I apologize now. We, my ex-husband and I, attended my 30-year Roslyn HS reunion -- no Michael, no knowledge of him. That was that.

Recently, back online to date again, a man wrote to me. In his PROFILE, he mentioned jokingly how if you like Tennis, you get 5 points. If you like Golf, you get 10 points and if you like any of THESE masters, you get extra bonus points. He was just kidding and it added interest to his profile. Well, I read the names of these masters that he wrote about and read -- Maslow, Ellis, Jung and several exceptional 'scholars'. Then I read the name MEYERHOFF. My mind just went right to Michael. What a shock and what a major delight to see his name among these scholars. I was not at all surprised.

I wrote the man on the dating site back to inquire who this Meyerhoff was. Then I decided, before he got back to me, to do my own GOOGLE search. I found Michael, radiantly handsome, just like before, but GROWN INTO HIMSELF. I read his profile for his own professional site and company. He became a rather famous childhood psychologist in Chicago. He was married to a woman who founded the largest daycare center in Illinois. He counseled little children and wrote books, articles, and renowned scholarly pieces. In the meantime, the gentleman who wrote me from the online dating shared his information about Milton Meyerhoff. I had read it incorrectly.

Still, I wrote to Michael, asking that we be able to let bygones be bygones. He responded most willingly, even sharing that he so enjoyed my EMAIL address. HE was the one that took me to see the FIRST "Rocky" movie in December of 1976. My goodness, however did he remember that? Remember, he was BRILLIANT! Anyway, when I wrote back, I shared that I was planning a trip to Chicago this summer and wondered if he would meet with me? I had not heard back from him immediately, figuring it was due to the Memorial Day holiday. I mentioned how thrilled I was for him that he was happily married and with 7 grandchildren, as the article regarding his center expressed. IT was a wonderful and upbeat bio. I heard from him and he was more than delighted to begin a correspondence with me, sharing that his year had been rather difficult – hugely, as his wife died some 11 months ago and his dad had just died earlier that month. Oh my sad heart, I could hear the challenge in his email, yet the correspondence had begun.

He was excited to meet me, upon my arrival in Chicago, and was looking forward to catching up over these last several decades. G_d is good! All the pieces of the puzzle fit, for whatever reason. Time will tell. It is just so, so, so, so, so, so satisfying how G_D has divine planning. My ending with Armando would be the only reason why I chose to go to Chicago and dance. I had a choice of Philly, Michigan and Chicago and definitively decided Chicago; why I don't know. Perhaps it was to rekindle the connection with Michael -- surely one of the divine reasons. G_D before me had surely paved the way.

I wonder and do NOT question whether Michael would have seen me, had his wife been alive. I tend to think yes, but interesting was the timing of events.

I am so, so gratified with this unfolding. It only wreaks, shouts and blesses me with G_D's plan, at huge work in my life. Thank you G_D and AMEN! NOW, a couple of months later, I was blessed not only to see Michael, but he joined us for a birthday celebration. I spent my 60th birthday in Chicago with several of my favorite people. Who, in a million years, would have guessed that Michael would be sharing it with me! What a hugely DIVINE treat!

👍 Believe 👍
in Yourself

A Lesson Learned -- 1975 -- I Did It for Me!

I had been dating Philip -- the first LOVE OF MY LIFE -- for some time. I went out to Chicago to visit him in law school. He was the boyfriend that made me want to be a better person. He was smart and so I began reading the NY Times. What I'd do for love! ~Smile.

I was a smoker at this time, 23 years old and living and working in Manhattan -- a college grad, maybe smoking about 1/2 pack per day. Honestly. I smoked more to keep my mouth busy and NOT put food in it. I weighed about 160 pounds then and was almost 5'11"...you know I've grown in my 50's.

ANYWAY, I really wanted HIM to love me. I was young, had not much life experience and so I quit smoking for HIM. I was so excited to go out there, show him and have him be so proud of me – to be so excited and fall so much more for me. I arrived and, would you believe, I literally STILL recall what I was wearing! ~Smile.

Big hellos...he showed me his apartment. We went on a short tour. It was December 8th in Chicago and FREEZING! We hung out and about 5 hours into my visit, he had not said a word. SURELY by now, I would have had a cigarette...NOT A WORD.

I was getting frustrated, waiting for him to compliment me and FINALLY asked, "Do you notice anything about me?"

He responded, "No, should I?"

Actually he hardly gave it a second thought, and STILL did not see one thing different about me. Okay, I figured, with a little more time he will notice and be SOOOOOOOOOOOOOOOOO excited. I finally burst! He had not said ONE WORD! "Phillip," I said, "I quit smoking. Haven't you noticed?" And I threw in, "I did it for you!"

"No you didn't," he responded. "You did it for YOU!"

As much as the quitting smoking was healing my insides, what Philip said in those 5 words more drastically changed and began healing my life...I did it for me!

You've Reached Errands Accomplished, Follow YOUR Heart
– 1979

You've reached Errands Accomplished
and we do it all.

We'll arrange your promotion.
We'll cater your ball.

We'll sell your car
and rent your home.
We'll watch your kids,
so they're not alone.

Get rid of the pressure.
Thanks for your call.
Errands Accomplished,
we do it all.

Yes we're

Errands Accomplished
and we do it all.
Please leave your number
and we'll be glad to return your call.

The above was the poem that I recited on my answering machine. It answered calls for my business known as Errands Accomplished.

I graduated college, did rather well and moved back to New York during a HUGE recession – in 1974. There were NO jobs and here I thought I would BE somebody. I came to learn I was a NOBODY, however, at a HUGE, highly prestigious advertising agency. I got a job as a secretary in the radio/TV programming department. I worked on accounts such as Mobil Oil, Chivas Regal, American Airlines and I forgot the others.

I moved up to Traffic Coordinator, in the Traffic department, working on the Polaroid account and THEN started to write copy for the Polaroid Premium Trade Group. I quit for good reasons. I had experienced my first "Black Friday." About 85 employees were let go. One was my boss; another was his boss and on and on. I was promoted.

Everyone vied for the now vacant offices. There was pandemonium, as the employees that stayed on literally ransacked offices -- taking the lamps and whatever else left behind by those departed. I decided that I did not want to spend my career in a place such as this. I was so, so, so, so, totally idealistic and this was NOT the way it ought to have been.

I had a long list of short successes. I went to work for Macmillan Publishers, another good entry level position, but quit that as well. Then I went to work for the Greater New York Blood Program, as a blood consultant -- a fancy title for those who recruit blood donors. I had to do public speaking before rather large audiences and run blood drives. It was a MASTERFUL way to learn how to ORGANIZE. It seems as if all of my jobs CONTRIBUTED to whom I became when I opened Errands Accomplished.

Up until that time, there were HUGE disappointments and bouts of sadness. Primarily, I believed that I was a LOSER, as my mom and dad seemed to think. They called me a QUITTER. Dad even went so far as to disown me when I quit Doyle Dane Bernbach. It was truly the most prestigious ad agency. It is now known as Omnicom Group. Anyway, I felt like a loser, but it was more like I was lost. I did not want to stay in jobs that I did not respect and did not have a clue as to what I wanted to do.

My friends in Atlanta, after I had moved there, would ask me to help them. One doctor who took me out on a date asked if I would help him decorate his house, after he had seen MY apartment. Another friend asked me to help him cook for his boss and wife, as he had dined on my cooking. On and on, I received requests and was THRILLED at someone thinking I was good at something. So eventually, I realized that PERHAPS THERE WAS MONEY IN THESE REQUESTS!

I began Errands Accomplished, INC. in 1979, less than a year after moving to Atlanta. I started while working for the Red Cross, the company that eventually paid my expenses to move down there from New York. My boss was PISSED off at me, as I quit just shy of working there one year. Truth is I started my own business and thought I could do it "on the side" and continue with the security of a paycheck, while continuing to work for the Red Cross. HOWEVER, it was a mere 3 weeks and the business was taking off.

My philosophy is that you have to put your all into whatever you are doing or you will get so-so, diluted results – whether it is a career, a significant other, house shopping or job hunting. Give it your all or wait until you can give it all you've got - or you will get diluted results. I got ALL in the game.

Well the business took off. I was covered on every news station -- with Ins and Outs on TV and radio and you name it. It was a novel business idea and everyone wanted an interview and a story out of it. I found huge success and a decent clientele list. NOW I WAS A STAR. My parents could not show off enough about THEIR daughter, "the success" and they LOVED sharing my stories, Oh boy, there were many; that could have been another book. Perhaps it will be.

The lesson here is to LISTEN to YOUR gut; follow YOUR path, NO ONE else's. Still, life will hand you ups and downs, but do not sell YOURSELF short by "buying" someone else's dream for you. Listen and follow through with your own. I so love you boys!

My First Really Big Fantasy Catering Job -- 6/82

'A Catered Affair' was off and running. I was hired by BURT BRAUN to create a Fantasy Occasion for him and his wife. He owned this monster boat on Lake Louise as well as a nice little motor boat, maybe 30 feet – nice, but not the huge boat that he anchored up at the lake. He was supposedly a very well-to-do architectural supplier -- the guys who sell PF CHANGS those horses out in front. He had a huge location of artifacts on Sebastian Road. He might have been the guy to sell the original Jacob G. Maroone Bar to The Sporting House.

So, he called MOI...OH MY! He hired me to do this job and unbeknownst to me, that is the weekend that I was going out to meet my future Mother and Father-in-Law. CRAP! Well, priorities are priorities and so Kansas City HERE I COME! I had a few people working for me and decided this would be the time that I learn how to delegate, let go and leave my catering baby to Mike -- Mike McGrath.

He was clad in tux and tails. We had a masseur on board. Stephanie, my favorite flutist, was on board, as was some guitar player...I do not recall his name. Mike served Filet and Lobster, Stephanie served "Moon Dance" and the masseur just made Burt and his wife HAPPY! I even recall Mike asking me if he ought to secure 'LAND O' LAKES' special butter? Sounds silly, but we did EVERY detail in the highest fashion we knew how. Even the butter had to be THE BEST!

I went off to KC and Mike handled EVERY detail. During the course of the evening, or so I was told, Burt's son motor-boated over to see his parents, came on board, stayed for a short while, and then left. The evening went FABULOUSLY until at the very end, right before Burt was to pay the $1500 balance.. He ALERTED Mike that there had been a THEFT. This story was all HERESAY -- what I garnered from Mike, Stephanie, and Burt Braun and the Police up in Rocky Mount. Anyway, I received a frantic call from Mike that they were at the police precinct in this one horse town, Rocky Mount, North Carolina where Lake Louise is located, and that they were being released.

There was POT on the premises, there was a theft of jewelry, there were a host of complaints and it was up to me to determine what to do. The staff from 'A Catered Affair' was released. Burt decided to drop charges, as long as I dropped the $1500 charges that he owed me. In other words, SWALLOW the $1500 and call it a day. Now, I had known these employees for quite some time and I would have bet my ENGAGEMENT that they did NOT steal NOR get high -- NO WAY!!!~

I returned from KC and chatted at length with Burt, Mr. Braun. I requested a police report, but NONE was taken and between several calls to the police, as well as people that I personally knew, as well as others that I conferred with, it was suggested to me that everyone take a LIE DETECTOR test. ALL of this was FOREIGN to me, yet I surmise that is when we learn the most, when we are dropped into a situation that we know nothing about.

I got on the phone and called Burt Braun. "So Mr. Braun, I think it would be most wise for everyone to take a lie detector test."

As if it were yesterday, I heard him say the following, "Are you kidding," he exclaimed, "THE RICH DO NOT HAVE TO TAKE LIE DETECTOR TESTS!"

Yes, you heard me; that was his response. Had I known then, what I know now, and how it would eventually unfold, I would have been a VERY grateful lady. My Aunt Jeanie, a very clever and SMART lady, chatted with me and told me, "FROM HERE ON IN, NEVER do a job for anyone, unless they have paid FULLY IN ADVANCE. What motivation," she said, "do they have to pay for a MEAL or an event that has already taken place?"

From that moment on, I learned how to take a steep deposit, then payment in advance. If the count of people dropped, I refunded funds; if it increased, they paid more at the event. For 14 years this served me HUGELY. I never got stiffed again -- NEVER. Live and learn and blessedly, there was a HUGE GIFT in this; there always is. I ATE the $1500, a small price to pay for never having been cheated out of payment again. Trust me, there were many that I turned away because they did NOT wish to pay in advance; I learned my lesson well.

I did speak with 2 other caterers in town, as well as MARILYN, a very successful architectural supplier, much like Mr. Braun. I wonder if that is his REAL name or just a name that cannot be easily found, especially when one is trying to serve him with a legal suit. I have had THAT experience -- finding it difficult on one occasion to even serve someone -- because their name is hidden behind commonality. What a crook he was. I learned from Rob and Steve that he cheated people all over town; he would hire 'em and then NOT pay. I was just one of his many victims.

In addition, what was a rather interesting story is when I called Marilyn. I had known her from WOMEN BUSINESS OWNERS. Here is what he did to her. He literally went to North Carolina where there are a great many architectural supply places – HUGE, massive storages of amazing artifacts. He arrived at one, one day, and selected a great many fabulous pieces. When it came time to set up delivery and payment, he said that he was MARILYN's buyer and that the bill should be sent to her, down in Deer Run and that the delivery should be sent to the Sebastian Road location. The North Carolina wholesaler became suspicious and called MARILYN to inquire as to the legitimacy of this arrangement. It was NEWS to MARILYN that he was her buyer...END of STORY. This guy was a MAJOR CROOK. BEWARE…appearances are not always what they seem to be!

The Rolls Royce Facade -- 1989

Again a car story and façade ... I owned A Catered Affair and had my office in my home. I would have clients come to the house and work with them in my office, where there was a window overlooking the driveway. A man came in. He was MORE impressed with himself than I was. ~Smile. He wanted me to cater his daughter's engagement party. We discussed the entire menu, date, theme, etc. Then I drew up the contract and I requested a $500 deposit.

"No, you don't need to take a deposit from me," he said.

"Oh, but I do," I responded.

"No, you don't understand. I am very wealthy; I will have no problem paying you."

"I understand, but I will still need a $500 deposit to reserve the date."

"Come with me and let me show you something."

As we walked outside heading to the driveway, I just knew where he was going with this -- to have me EYEBALL his Rolls Royce and influence my decision. "I have LOTS of money," he said. "See the car that I drive. You're not to worry about collecting a deposit from me."

"Quite the contrary," I replied. "In order to pay all of your huge bills, I wanna make sure mine are first in line," was my response.

With a nasty smirk, he did not even shake my hand and never walked back into my office...END of STORY...end of contract...NO thanks.

Appearances are not always what they seem to be!

Be Discerning With Whom You Take Advice -- 2004

Just a quickie, boys. I laugh when I think of this story. It is about a friend of mine who mentioned a HOT STOCK TIP. I recall asking her, "WHO TOLD YOU?"

And she responded, "ROD!"

"Rod? ROD, the ROD who lives in the trailer park, who never has money?"

"Yup," she said, "he found this great stock. It's supposed to make LOTS and LOTS of money."

'NUFF said! If you want to excel at ANYTHING, go to those that already have. To those who are successful in business, take your business issues. THOSE who are married and HAPPY for a great, long time, listen to what THEY have to say about THEIR success. Those who are healthy and living a quality life into their 90's and those who have great love and great health, ask THEM! Listen to THEIR guidance. Be selective to the max! There are a great many charlatans out there. Beware! And if it seems too good to be true...YOU know the rest of that sentence. Listen to your gut and believe in yourself!~

I grew up as a cute little kid – friendly, smart and athletic. I sorta, kinda, basically had it all. And while I grew to be 5'10" by the time I was 18, my older sister only grew to 5'2 1/2". She was overweight, had a rather big nose that was eventually made more beautiful, she had bad skin, did not do real well in school and little, if any, athletic ability. We were the ODD siblings.

I guess people used to compliment me. I do not recall. Because anytime ANYONE said a thing about ADRIAN, there was a HUSH -- ssshhhhhhhh -- and a whisper of we do not want it to go to her head (ego), BUT, LOOK AT BERNIECE! They would proceed to BUILD her up. It was totally a case of building Berniece's confidence, yet it did not have to take place by neglecting or diminishing me; BUT IT DID!

I grew up literally thinking little of myself and whatever I did, it was NEVER enough. I could get a 98 on a report card and my mom would give me a SAD face, a frown and look at me with great disappointment while saying, "What happened to the other two points?"

It was never enough. Well, it is water under the bridge. I was now an adult and came to terms with my 'villains.' All the while, I NEVER felt pretty – EVER!

126

Surely, man after man told me I was gorgeous, beautiful and every compliment in the book. That still takes place. I never believe them. What I translated those compliments into was "He just wants to SLEEP with me." Partially, it is because when I LEFT Melvin, he warned me that EVERY man just wants to sleep with me. I shouldn't have listened.

Then a magical moment in time happened. Ross and I were in Prague. I met him at breakfast, as I was running late and we were to be on a bus tour that morning. I ran in and grabbed some food. A bit disheveled, we headed out of the dining room -- YUMMY BREAKFASTS in PRAGUE; that is for sure. I used to joke that I was the before and after poster child for makeup. I felt like I looked totally different before applying makeup and the AFTER results.

I arrived at breakfast, got my meal at the buffet and was gobbling up a little bit, while packaging up the rest to take with us. Rushing, rushing, rushing, as Ross looked up at me and said, "Mom, you're beautiful!"

"WHAT? Are you kidding?"

I was shocked. I surely did not know how to take THAT compliment graciously. Yet he sat there telling me that he is not a big fan of makeup and that I was beautiful, especially without the makeup. I had not applied any that morning because I was running so late. He said it again. I began to cry. I do not know if you remember this Ross, but I then, while shock was settling in and realization, I confessed that I had never felt pretty. I thought all the times I was told such, there was an ulterior motive.

HOWEVER, I would have to believe ROSS. He was my child, surely with no motive! WOW, live and learn. While I do look in the mirror now and see PRETTY, it is more of a MENTAL THOUGHT, rather than a cellular knowing. It is interesting.

I have even had boyfriends who NEVER complimented me. When asked WHY, they responded they did not want to make my head swell. Oh how we neglect to understand what comes from our own, very personal, experience...rather interesting. Thank you G_D and thank you ROSS! I FEEL PRETTY! ~Smile.

👍 G_d Having Fun 👍

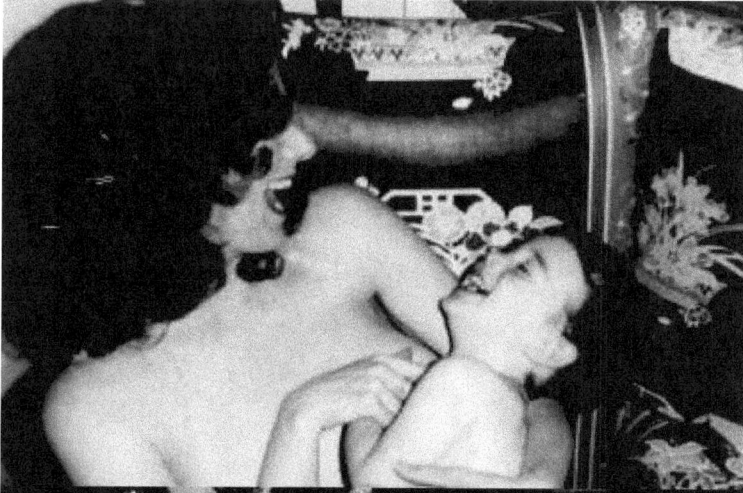

Wow, He Had the Power EARLY On -- Andrew -- '92

Andrew, you were about 5 years old when you came up to me -- very normal – and innocently and said, "MOMMY, your hair is sooooooooooooooooo shiny. It looks beautiful!"

"Thank you Andrew; how neat. Thank you. What a sweet thing to say!"

He then continued, "And your smile, your teeth are SOOOOOOOOOOO white!"

"WOW, thank YOU ANDREW!"

Now my head was swelling. Then he said, "Mommy, can I have $5?"

Andrew and the WAGINA --1992

I was always looking for additional ways to increase our income and provide different streams of money. My friend Mike McGrath came over one day and introduced me to the vending business. Shortly thereafter, Mel and I were placing vending machines and spending time either looking for more locations or filling the ones we already owned with more candy.

One day while downtown, I do not recall why we were there, we were heading home and I saw this GIRLIE club. I suggested that we go there to try to get them to allow us to have a machine in their club. We had already been successful with a girlie club, perhaps 'CHEETAH' on Cheshire Bridge Avenue. The strippers would MAKE LOVE to our M&M peanut offerings, Chiclets and Skittles. We did rather well, having placed a machine in the girl's locker room of the girlie club. Well, here we were downtown, when I saw this club and suggested to Mel to go in and see if we could place a machine. I remained in the van with the boys. Ross was about 7 years old and Andrew was about 5 years old. We sat in the parking lot while daddy went inside to ask if we could place a machine there. Ross, Andrew and I were hanging out. They had no idea where we were and what kind of a business this was. Yes, daddy had tried to place machines before; he did it often.

There happened to be a BIG picture of LIPS on the side of the building where we were parked. I surely knew what they were, but did not think, in my wildest dreams, that the boys would notice. Andrew spurted out, "Mommy! LOOK! That looks like a WAGINA."

I had to stifle my HYSTERIA. I was soooooooooooooooooooo needing to crack up, but did not. "Ya know Andrew, it surely does," laughing inside.

That was that and when Mel came out, I couldn't wait to tell him...too funny! Well, we did not get the placement, but we did continue to have the other location and every now and then, Ross would be with Mel and request, "Daddy, can I go in there with you?"

The machine was literally in the girl's locker room -- need I say more? It is so funny to be the MOM of two healthy all-American red-blooded males. ~Big Smile.

👍 G_d Appearing 👍
Anonymously

Silly Mom and the Spoon in the Pots -- Greece -- 1972

It was Greece, 1972. Edith and I went to Europe for 11 weeks during our sophomore summer. We went with knapsacks, sleeping bags and about $1500 that I had earned working during college as a waitress at the Watergate in DC. Yes, it was during the break-in, an amazing time in history and YOUR mom was there, literally, and yet I did not know how significant a role it would play in modern history.

Anyway, we went to a bunch of countries. Edith and I found this totally and thoroughly exciting. LOTS of kids were doing the same thing – traveling, knapsacking and backpacking through Europe -- and we were no different. It was one of the BEST experiences in my entire life and continues to be. We were free. We were going on 20 years old, had completed our sophomore year and tootled around Europe -- England, Netherlands, France, Monaco, Monte Carlo, Switzerland, Italy, Israel , Greece and then some. ~Smile. I wrote a diary; it was a THRILLING 11 weeks.

Your mom is apparently not influenced by what others think and Edith and I had a ball just being a bit crazy. She would laugh at my antics and even told her husband when they married and headed for Europe that she did not think it would be as much fun as the time she had with me. ~Smile. How do you like that? But it was her truth!

One of the boldest, most ridiculous stories and memories was when we were in Greece. The food is totally different and the language is rather difficult, totally different than ours, as in that saying, "it was as if he was speaking GREEK to me." It is just a saying that GREEK is so DIFFERENT...unique. So, in the restaurants, you cannot know what to order from reading the menus, so they take you into their kitchens and SHOW you the food choices, then you point and they bring it to you. Well here we were with these young, flirtatious waiters and invited into the back to see the food to make our selections.

Instead of LOOKING, I picked up a spoon and slllllllooowwwlly dipped it into a pot, with their looks of permission and slowwwwwllllyyyy put it up to my mouth. They all started to laugh, Edith hysterically, not believing the BALLS I had. The other 3 servers just chuckled along. I literally tasted all 5 of the choices, made my decision based on taste rather than looks. We went back into the restaurant, sat down and had a yummy, delicious dinner. I am sure Edith would laugh right now; it was rather bold. ~Smile.

Nail in the Quiche -- 1981

I owned the Breakfast n Bed company. I was preparing the quiche one day and, OH MY DEAR, I noticed that the LONG red nail that had broken earlier and was hanging on and was connected to my THUMB was no longer apparent. I was so, so, so, upset. I called a friend who told me not to worry - and that it wouldn't hurt anyone - so I left it in the 10 pies that I'd prepared.

Lo and Behold, several weeks later, I was serving breakfast in bed to JOE ADAMS, a partner in a major prestigious law firm. I had placed the tray on his lap while he was in bed and he motioned for me to stay and chat with him and his girlfriend. We were schmoozing along when he inadvertently removed a spec of SOMETHING from his mouth and placed it on the side of his plate. He must have thought it a piece of gristle or something. He had no expression and just continued on chatting and dining.

OH MY G_D, it was RED and about 1/8 inch; IT WAS MY NAIL! He never said a word. He even hired me to cater his Law Firm Holiday Party. ~Smile.

Myrtle Beach -- 1984

I am just in the mood to have FUN and this story was one of the most joyful, fun times. Daddy and I were in Myrtle Beach. I was a little bit pregnant, perhaps into my 4th month, not too far along. Myrtle Beach was a major beach resort with a one lane road that backed up traffic for the vacationers 24/7. There was always WHOOPING and HOLLERING and cars moving at 3 miles per hour.

Daddy and I had a movie that we wanted to see. We had planned our afternoon and evening around the 5pm show. The traffic was ridiculous and so we just did not know how to get to this theatre in time. How were we going to escape this crawling at a snail's pace traffic? I do not know where I got the nerve, but there was the median in between the traffic in our direction and the oncoming traffic in the other direction. I suggested to Daddy to climb onto the middle partition of the highway and make our own GET AWAY THERE! Was I crazy? As I write this, I cannot believe our nerve. Quite frankly, it does not even seem like nerve; it seems like a moronic thought. It seems like I must have been not only a little pregnant, but a bit CRAZY too. The clock was ticking and we had to get to the MOVIES! We were moving along, driving down the middle partition, when WOOO OOOH WOOO OOOH! That is alphabet for siren screaming behind us. UH oh, Oh dear, holy shit, now what are we going to do? Believe it or not, I was laughing soooooooooo hard that I had to put my hands over my face (I'm actually laughing now too -- did I do that? Did Daddy do that?). When the POLICE OFFICER arrived with a stern look on his face, I was hysterically laughing. Daddy, straight faced, said, "Officer, my WIFE IS HAVING A BABY!"

Yup, we lied through our teeth! It must have looked like I was crying, with my hands over my face sitting in the passenger seat, yet I was HYSTERICAL – laughing. I could NOT believe we were doing this! The officer literally jumped into his police car and said, "FOLLOW ME," as he turned on his siren, "GET OUT OF THE WAY," was the message the police car and our car were saying!

Little did anyone know we were being escorted to the movie theatre. Oh my G_D, I cannot believe as I am such an abiding person these days, that we did THAT! The officer told us, actually Daddy, that he could not take us ALL the way to the hospital, but that he could escort us out of this traffic. I am laughing now, as I LOVE the adventure and the caper in me/us. The finest Myrtle Beach police officer saw to it that we got out of traffic and he carved a path for us. I surmise that the way to the movies was similar to the way to the hospital. In any event, we made it in time, laughing the entire way there -- hearts beating, somewhat shocked at ourselves and somewhat impressed as well. We pulled it off -- a regular Bonnie and Clyde.

Okay, so the story does not end there and yes, we saw the movie. Now it was time for dinner. We had seen a WENDY's earlier and decided that after the movie, we would go and enjoy a salad bar dinner. Yup, loved those salads even then. I fed you boys healthy and well, while pregnant! Just as we were pulling up to the restaurant, Daddy decided to drop me off and have me wait for him to go in, while he parked the car. OH MY G_D, the POLICE OFFICER that escorted us was literally walking my way, as if on THE BEAT. I was wearing a bright pink dress, with only a LITTLE pouch in my tummy. Standing 5'11" no one could miss me. I HID! Holy Mother, he better not see me; I am supposed to be in the hospital giving birth to you, Ross. ~Smile. So, Daddy was walking up the street, on his way to the Wendy's and I was sorta hidden, while peering my head out and giving him a look that said, "DON'T BE NOTICED, stay away."

Daddy was looking at me, "WHAT?"

I gave him the 'TRUST ME, just don't be noticed look -- whatever THAT look looked like -- yeah RIGHT, all 6'7" of him. ~Giggle. Anyway, we made it into the Wendy's without drawing attention from the COP and laughed our way through Dave Thomas' finest!

137

Does the Universe Reward Us When We Behave Properly
Uncle Harold -- 1993

I'll never forget…even the details. You guys were about 6 and 8 years of age. We were living in Dunwoody and having breakfast -- all four of us -- before you left for the school bus. My dad, Arnold had called. He had been a major source of pain and anguish for me, as you knew. I chatted nicely with him before handing each of you the telephone. He spoke lovingly and caringly to each of you and then asked to speak with me again. I picked up the phone, in a sweet happy manner. Life was good.

He began being so critical about not receiving thanks for some baseball cards that he had sent to each of you. I told him that I had given both of you reminders to write PAPA his 'thank-you' note and it would be sent out imminently. He started to become very abusive as to why he had not received them yet. I told him to tell you boys -- AVOIDING triangulation (speak to them directly). I handed the phone back to you and, again, he spoke so lovingly and kind.

You finished conversing with him and, AGAIN, he asked to speak to your mom – ME -- AGAIN - and yet, THIS time, he became so caustic and abusive that I FINALLY, after several years of his cruelty, REALLY let him have it. "I'm sick and tired of being your receptacle for all the nastiness you have to spew! Don't ever call me again unless you have something nice to say to me!" I literally screamed and hung up.

WOW! Again, WOW! If I tell you, after years of this abuse, that I had finally had enough, I cannot describe how ENERGIZED I felt. I think I could have run a marathon. FINALLY, I stuck up for myself. No longer would I tolerate his bullying me.

It is rather funny at this very moment, as I take a break from my fingers hitting the keys, I have an ITCHY palm. They say that when your palm itches, it means that you are going to come into money. Well, the day that I am writing about held MUCH more in store for me than just the nasty phone call and my freedom from abuse.

138

You had now watched your mom reign 'supreme' and while I do not know how you felt watching this display, I felt RADIANT. You went off to school, Daddy went off to work and I felt so full and proud of myself for finally standing up to the bullying.

The morning progressed and I went out to the mailbox, pensive throughout the day and, thus far, thinking about ramifications of, perhaps, not talking to Arnold again. I was wondering if he would ever call me again, sad about what had occurred, yet grateful and happy that I finally had the courage to no longer take his nastiness. My dad had mostly been there for me, and yet he turned on me when Mom died. Now I knew, I was on my own -- no going to him for ANYTHING!

That was fine. I was proud and, surely, no money in the world would EVER be worth tolerating abuse -- NONE! I opened the mailbox -- deep in thought. As I flipped through the mail, I saw an envelope from Uncle Harold. Oh what a treat! I adored Aunt Ida and Uncle Harold, but seldom did I receive a written note from him. Eagerly, I opened his letter and as I did, checks fell out of the card.

"Oh my Goodness, what have we here?"

Yes, checks, large checks with a note that indicated that this money was to take care of you boys to the best of my ability – for, perhaps, camp, braces, college, you name it -- whatever I thought would be in your, and our, best interest. NEVER did I ever, up to that point, receive a gift like this from ANYONE. Never before had I ever had the courage to cease tolerating Arnold's bullying. Were they connected? I surely thought so. I lay down on the driveway -- speechless and wobbly-kneed -- and cried out thanks to the universe for supporting me and my courage. WOW!

Carl and the Car Sale -- 1996

I had a beautiful silver Cadillac, my first Cadillac. Not only did I take very good care of it, but I hardly drove it. I was NOT a long-distance driver, not at all. Daddy did most of the driving.

I had about 40,000 miles on this car and it was almost 9 years old. SO, it was time for a new car. I decided to sell the silver one myself. DEFINITELY boys, sell your own cars – you will get MUCH more money and it is not hard to do. SO, I placed the ad and had a stream of potential buyers, and then, Carl appeared. He wanted it! He was in love with this car.

I drew up a contract and took $3000 from him. However, I could not give him the car on the spot, as I had ordered a new car and it had not arrived yet. I was getting heated seats. ~Smile.

I told Carl that it could take up to 6 weeks for delivery and he was fine with that, and I also told him that he would forfeit his $3000, if HE chose not to purchase the car when the new one arrived. No problem…he wanted the car and he signed the contract.

I received the call some 5 weeks later that my car had arrived and I contacted Carl, only to learn that he had changed his mind. He knew that he would forfeit the $3000 and was totally okay with that…an agreement is an agreement.

I immediately placed another ad in the Auto Trader and newspaper. Within days, I received a visit from a man named Anthony, who fell in love with my silver car. He, too, agreed to purchase it -- ON THE SPOT -- as I had already received my new red one.

You guys remember: When the universe wants to give you a gift, it will find a way. Here I was being blessed by selling my car twice and making an additional $3000 – THREE THOUSAND DOLLARS! Perhaps the universe likes it when you put in the extra time, instead of trading it in. I surely liked the gift! Thank you G_d!

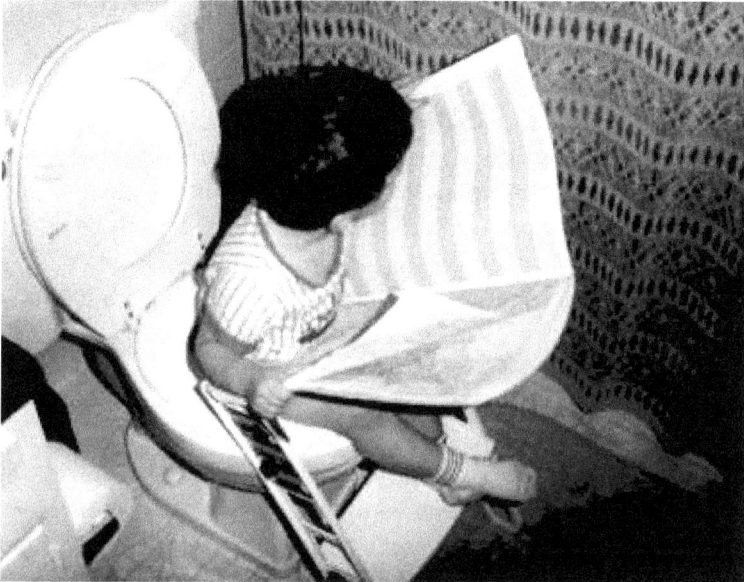

So, we were traveling around Buckhead, a wealthy area with miles and miles of beautiful homes -- one more majestic and magnificent than the next.

AND...I had to go to the bathroom! "Mel, can we drive out of here? I have to go to the bathroom!"

"Sure!"

As we rounded the corner, there sat a home under construction with a PORTA POTTY, right in front -- two seconds after I asked Mel to take me to a restroom.

THANK YOU G_D...UNIVERSE! ~Amen!

Aspartame is the Culprit -- 1998

It was November 1998. We had just moved to 4491 Lucky Lane in July and we took in our FIRST Disney Arts Festival. It was marvelous. You boys were 11 and 13. We were awaiting Andrew's Bar Mitzvah in April.

We were all walking through the exhibits and had decided to spend our FAMILY money to purchase something for the new house. Remember the glass/water piece of art?

It was a lovely afternoon as we strolled from exhibit to exhibit, vendor to vendor. Lo and behold, one of the exhibitors had only one eye...poor man. We continued to walk and just a bit further up was another ARTISTE. He, too, had only one eye.

Oh my, my, my, my! I started to see stars and flashes. A migraine was approaching. OH dear! Shucks! They did not happen often in my life and yet when they did, the pain was rather intense. I had to remove myself from life for a good day. I went to the ladies room, splashed some water on my face, regained my composure and announced to Dad, "We've gotta go!"

I do not know if, ever in my life, I had a migraine with Melvin. They really did not occur too often and so I explained further re: the auras. He understood, rounded us all up and drove us home.

I took a Darvon when we arrived home and slept the rest of the day. When I awakened, I felt headachey, groggy -- a tad bit different from previous migraines. Usually, it had been my experience that I felt rotten when they happened, took a Darvon and, blessedly, awakened with the headache gone and proceeding on with my life. This one was different.

The headache lasted for 48 days. It was only of migraine proportion for 2 days, but the remaining 46 were fraught with discomfort and a consistent hurt -- perhaps a 6 on the scale. You boys were 11 and 13 years of age and quite ADVENTUROUS and physically active, to say the least. And so, for the next month and a half, Daddy and I constantly kept saying, "Please talk low. MOMMY has a headache."

It was a most challenging time. Melvin took me to the neurologist, who ran all the tests. I had an MRI, discussed what foods I ate, but came up with NOTHING -- SO very frustrating and horrible. Each night before bed, I would pray to G_D to alleviate this headache and yet this one night - it was an extra intense prayer before going to sleep, "PLEASE DEAR G_D, tell me what to do! This headache was KILLING me!"

In the middle of the night, I awakened. I HEARD A VOICE! I was awakened by this voice and immediately reached over to Melvin, "I heard a voice!"

He was startled, but awakened, and I told him that the voice said, "Aspartame is the culprit."

"Oh my G_D! Was that G_D's voice?"

We got out of bed, hightailed it into the kitchen and began investigating all of the foods I was eating: Bran, Yup...Aspartame...Jell-O, Yup...Aspartame...Hot Chocolate, Yup...Aspartame...Diet Soda, Yup...Aspartame -- my daily fare! Talk about being HOPEFUL, we were THRILLED, knowing that we had found the answer to the now 45-day headache. I had most of the above EVERYDAY, so immediately, I gave all of them up. Within 3 days, the headache lifted. It is such an unhealthy product!

I proceeded to investigate on the internet and found an immediate batch of articles about how Aspartame does all kinds of nasty things to the body and the brain. Why it is on the market saddens me. Still, I was thrilled to finally have the answer. Thank you G_D! I do not know who else it could have been!

Harold and the Parking Lot -- 2005

I was newly divorced, on a dating site, and met this guy named Harold. We spoke for months and, finally one day, decided to meet. It was in February. I remember because he had shared that he was getting a new refrigerator. We had to schedule around that and some presidential birthday. We decided to meet at the Millennia Mall. He was driving all the way up from Boynton Beach and I was living a bit north of the mall in Orlando.

We met at about 11 AM and immediately felt a FUN, congenial connection. We dined, having lunch, and then went for a walk and talk around the mall. Then we continued to sit and chat. I think we had about 3 meals together. Before you knew it, it was 9:30 PM and the mall was closing. Harold had to drive back to Boynton Beach, a 2½ hour drive. He walked me out to the parking lot. BLESSEDLY, I remembered where I had parked. This mall was HUGE and had, at least, parking for some 2,000 cars -- NO exaggeration.

He walked me out and as we stood at my car he noticed a book on the passenger seat with the title, "ASK AND IT IS GIVEN." I had been reading it and mentioned how much I was totally taken by it. It was a GREAT book by Esther and Jerome Hicks.

"Guess what tape I was listening to for my drive up to see you?" Harold continued, "ASK AND IT IS GIVEN!"

"WOW, what a coincidence!"

We laughed as Harold said, "And guess where MY car is parked?"

Unknowingly, I said, "I hadn't a clue!"

He pointed to the NOSE of MY car, touching the NOSE of his car. "OH MY G_D, are you serious?"

Yes he was. His car, among 2000 possible spots, was parked exactly in front of my car. There had to be 12 exits and entrances to the mall and here, he selected THE very spot in front of my car. WOW! So, we said our goodnights and went on our individual ways. Next day, Harold called and we started chatting.

I told him that his name was a bit challenging for me to remember, although I had an Uncle named Harold. I used to call him "UNC" and had never met anyone else with the name Harold. Then Harold said, "YEAH, my name is Harold, but on my birth certificate Harold is crossed out and HERMAN is written in instead."

"OH NO, you're kidding! My Uncle Harold's last name was HERMAN!"

HAROLD HERMAN, whom I might add, was a MARVELOUS golfer, as is Harold Friedman! WOW, was this all coincidence or was there some supernatural power that brought Harold and I together? I think the latter. Harold is my DEAR, DEAR friend today, some 7 years later. I trust him enough to have made him the executor of my will. He is a decent, loving and wise, WISE man, to whom I go for help and smarts, whenever I have a challenge with you boys or any other reason. I love him dearly. Nope, NO coincidence. G_D gave us to one another to be dear, lifelong friends. Thank you G_D and thank you Harold, perhaps Unc Harold!

Unity and the Judge 1/06

Melvin had just sued me, perhaps within the last week. It was an intensely difficult and hugely busy time. I had just moved to South Florida. I did not even know my way around and was attending my first Unity service in my new location. It was the Unity Church of Delray Beach and this would become my Sunday morning place of worship.

It was my first time and as I was walking out of the service, this tall, nice, older gentleman came up to me and introduced himself. His name was John; he is still a friend. We were walking down the aisle to exit the church as he asked where I was from. "What do you do? Do you attend here regularly?"

It was all of the FIRST conversation, small talk, as one would typically have upon meeting someone new. We continued chatting and very casually he mentioned his dear friend, BOB -- 'the judge'...'THE JUDGE?' My ears perked up, "You have a friend who is a judge?"

Remember, I had just been SUED for the first time in my life and here I was hearing about a dear friend -- THE JUDGE! I look back now and realize that the universe was sending ME a judge. I was still in shock, hurt and in denial, yet relief was on its way. Judge BOB got in touch with me and became my friend. He was from Tampa, but just happened to be coming to preside over a case in Broward County the following week. He took ME out to dinner. My scared, delicate, humble heart was so HUGELY grateful to be in the company of this 76 year old, brilliant, man who befriended me. I hardly had ANY friends, let alone comfort from what was taking place in my life.

Judge Bob and I discussed the case; he knew lots about overturning a divorce. He shared what to expect, what to do and what my chances were in receiving a positive outcome. Was this an ACCIDENT? Interestingly enough, you have, more than likely, read those emails that mention that people come into your life for a season, a reason, and a lifetime. BOB surely appeared for a reason! Oh how the angels appear just when they are supposed to. Bob was a great blessing to me, explaining what I was going to have to 'travel through'...amazing, huh?!

I am not always so wise. I, too, worry bunches quite frankly, BUT I do see how G_d sends you Angels just when you need them.

Eric and the Motorcycle -- 2008

How bizarre this was. I do not know what category this should fall under -- perhaps NERVE...CHUTZPAH.

IT was a major COINCIDENCE to me, truly amazing. I was driving towards City Pub one night. My friend Mike suggested that I meet him there. There was dancing, etc. I had nothing to do and no one to do it with, so I drove over. Mike was just a friend. As soon as I walked into the pub, it was beyond smoky! No good, not at all, I spent about 12 seconds inside and quickly left.

I was chatting with Mike, outside, and went to sit down on "something" in the parking lot. There was no bench -- nothing -- and I spotted this motorcycle right in the front of the building. I seriously considered sitting on it...I would not hurt it. Mike said, "NOOOOOOOOOOOO," a resounding NO.

So I did not perch myself THERE, but down the aisle a bit, there was this car. It was not a fancy-schmancy car, so I got on top of it and sat. Mike did not say a word. We just continued chatting. Perhaps it was nervy, now that I know better, but then comfort called, more so than manners. I was sitting with one leg up -- bent -- and one leg stretched out very comfortably.

Out of the bar comes this RATHER HANDSOME, hugely handsome man and he heads for the motorcycle. He smiled at me and in a VERY flirtatious manner, I said, "I was almost going to sit on top of your bike, but..." then continued, "but I thought better of it. Would you have minded?"

He said, "No, not at all...why I think I know you!"

He proceeded to tell, me as he walked over to the car where I was sitting, that he happened to even have a PHOTO of me in his phone. I said, "Excuse me? YOU have a photo of ME...in YOUR phone?" I didn't know the guy from Adam. I would have remembered THIS guy - whew! ~

Disbelieving, I thought it was some kind of LINE. And with that, he presses a few buttons and shows me a photo of myself, sitting in a similar pose wearing an evening gown. "Oh my G_D, that IS my photo!"

It turns out he saved it from a dating site -- Match.com. He saw it over 4 months prior and decided that when he got a computer, he was going to write to THAT gal. He had a crush on her. And here she was manifested right before his very eyes. He said he almost went to his friend's place earlier, to borrow his computer and write to me. I was tall, lean and HIS type. Coincidence? What fun that was!

Patience 👍

Do You Boys Remember -- She Loves You -- 2001

Ross was heading out. He was 16 years old. I asked, "Ross, where are you going?"

He responded in a pithy tone, "OUT!"

I asked, "WHERE?"

He responded, "OUT!"

Eeerggggggghhhhhh! While Ross skipped the 'Terrible Twos,' he was making up for it -- big time -- with being a 16 year old. Andrew, sweet little Andrew chimed in, "Ross, Mom wants to know where you're going because she LOVES you."

Ahhhhhhhhhhhhhhhh! My sweet little child -- he so gets it!

Two years later, Andrew, now 16 years old, was on his way out of the door. "Where are you going honey?" I questioned.

"OUT!"

"WHERE?"

"OUT!"

Apparently the testosterone GOT to him, too! ~Smile. I threatened to put ESTROGEN in his cereal!

Waiting -- Looking Back -- 2012

So, what do all of my greatest blessings have in common? I am thinking that I desired each and every one of them and had to wait LONGER to receive 'my good,' longer than I would have liked. Yet, EVERY one of my greatest gifts in life and desires eventually became MINE. Why ever would I think that my desires, NOW, would be any different? Obviously I would not, so I do believe that the universe – GOD or call it what you may -- has so many riches in store for you, as it does for me. So I GIVE IT UP TO G_D, I let go and let G_D. I will wait. He/She knows best.

I waited to meet my husband, wayyyyyyyyyyyyyyyyyy later in life did I meet him than I thought I should, yet it was DELICIOUS when it happened. I waited to become a mom and each time I thought I was ready, the universe showed me that IT too, agreed. ~Smile. I waited for the condo to be sold. I waited for the right and perfect nannies to appear. I waited eagerly at times to make life long wonderful friends and I surely have. I waited for this amazing, marvelous, beautiful house to become mine – boy, did I wait for that one. I waited for a boyfriend after my marriage ended. I am waiting now for another love of my life – hopefully, my final and eternal one! And now - as I type away - I am waiting for the time when I can FINALLY deliver this book to you boys!~~

So, looking back, I see that patience, strength, faith and believing are all part of my life's journey and I surmise, perhaps, that you too will understand that so much of life is in the timing, as well as patiently waiting. The answers, seemingly to me, have always been: YES, Not now, or I have something better in store for you!

Amen and thank you Universe!

⌘ Signs ⌘

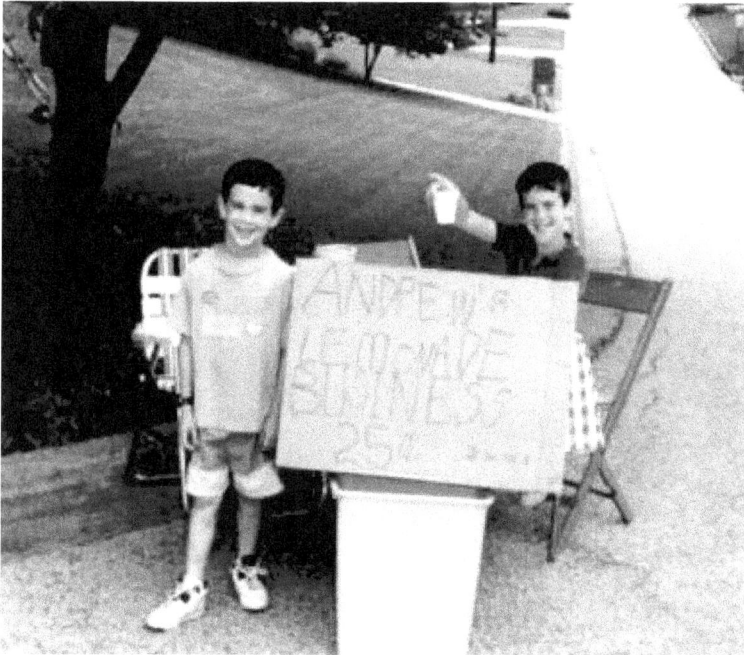

Queen Ida - '94

I found a weird looking plaque. It had the name IDA on it. I think it must have been from a garage sale. Having LOVED Aunt Ida soooooooo much, I purchased it. It said "QUEEN IDA" and so, we hung it...somewhere. ~Smile.

THEN, years later, Daddy and I became MAJOR Cajun and Zydeco dance aficionados and, lo and behold, I found out that QUEEN IDA was the "BOMB" -- Queen Bee Performer of Cajun Dance. Did her spirit call out to us to tell us to dance Cajun? That surely is NOT the most popular dance on the planet. It was coincidence, more than likely, or a message from my loving Aunt Ida to take up Cajun dance. That it would be great joy for us, which it was, an ANGEL, she was. Was this a SIGN? Perhaps...

Ted Dansen -- Highway 285 -- '96

Amazing, "Ask and you shall receive?" While driving around 285, the main highway in Atlanta, I was in the van, sitting in the passenger seat. When I was talking to Mel and the boys, I said questioningly, "WHO IS THAT GUY, you know, the actor on 'Cheers?'

Right smack above, on a billboard, "TED DANSEN - 7pm CHEERS – FOX."

THANK YOU! Most people think these are coincidences; I am here to SHARE with you that they are not; blessedly, they happen to me ALL the time! It kind of makes life more joyful!

Erma -- 2005

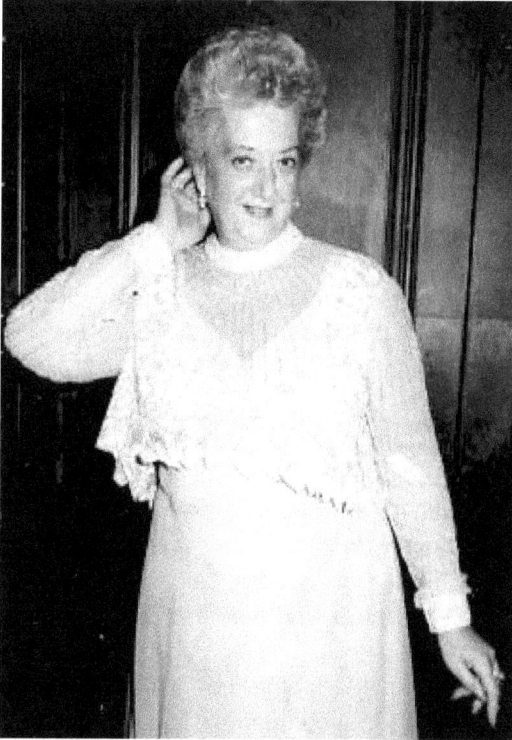

Have I ever told you about one of the GREATEST signs -- signals that I've ever received? I was moving from Orlando. It was a very sad time for me. I was leaving Andrew, my home, Melvin and all of my friends, my life. I was terribly distraught and full of anguish. Ross was in Tampa -- I wasn't leaving him.

I could no longer bear living in Orlando. I kept running into Melvin. I even once saw him making out with his beloved next wife, Ava...it stung. I could not go through a day without someone coming up to me and either asking how Dad was or sharing shock that we were divorced. We had taught dance together. We had held Cajun dances together, we were both rather friendly and we were a well-known couple around Orlando. I just could not shake the memories and sadness. I had to leave in order to begin a healthier life and get over the loss.

155

I was so sad and bewildered, making the move BY MYSELF to South Florida, that the night before, with 98 boxes packed and the house immaculate ready for closing the sale, I got down on my knees – the FIRST time ever -- to pray on my knees. That's how much I needed my prayers to be heard.

"MOM, where are you? Are you there? I have been praying to you and wondering WHERE YOU ARE? Please, PLEASE give me a demonstration -- something to tell me that you hear me!" I cried.

I was deeply sad and prayed my best. Then I went to sleep. The very next morning, I awakened and tended to a little preparation before the moving men were to arrive. Blessedly, Chrissy came over to bring me an Angel to hang in my NEW front yard. Yes it still adorns my entry walkway. Thank you Chrissy!

I went into my office to open up email. The only things that were NOT packed were the bridge table and the computer. I opened up my email and found a note from Naomi Harrison. It began with, "I usually don't send emails like these, but..."

And here is what the message said, "I just want you to know that the angels are alive and well and working on your behalf. Love, Erma"

WHAT? Say again? Mom? HOLY Mother, when did you change the spelling of your name? My mom hated her name. When she was single her name was IRMA HERMAN, said quickly, "Irmaherma" She detested it. It was also spelled with an I - and here I read Irma spelled with an E.

I read the message again and smiled -- cried actually -- what a message from MY mom. 'The angels are alive and well and working on YOUR behalf'. I get tears to this very moment - are you still there Mom? Please, please give me a sign! I love this life, although I wish it were less painful sometimes and yet, with REAL faith, there ought to be NO pain -- just Thanksgiving -- that it is all working on MY/OUR/YOUR behalf! Thank you G_d! ~Smile.

Dad and Chicago -- Arnold Was His Name -- 8/08

I was heading to Chicago, being trained in an insurance pursuit. At the airport, I could not help but think of my dad. He spent so much of his career in airports, traveling the Midwest. And here I was traveling to the Midwest, like Dad, for business as well. I sent a prayer up to him to bless me while I traveled. I felt akin to him strongly that morning, upon arriving at the airport.

We boarded the plane and made a stop-over in Atlanta. Just as I arrived in Atlanta, exiting the aircraft for my second leg, I walked into the terminal and there was this man whom I'd known from 15 years ago, while living in Atlanta. We gave one another a nice hello. He was in transit, as was I. "Excuse me, but I don't recall your name," I said.

"Arnie," he responded, "Arnold."

We made our salutations, spoke for a moment and then headed in our separate ways.

Hmmmmmmmmmm…interesting…ARNOLD…like Dad. I got onboard, arrived in Chicago and headed to the hotel. Upon check-in there was a problem with the reservation. I stood around, waiting to speak to the hotel manager and this lovely lady appeared, with her hand out to shake my hand and clear up all confusion.

"How do you do?" she shook my hand, "Madelyn Arnold,"

I almost giggled out loud, "Okay Arnold, I see you are here. THANK YOU!"

Ms. Arnold handled the 'snafu' and UPGRADED my room, compliments of the hotel. WOW, THANK YOU DAD!

The seminar progressed and on the second night, we had a fancy-schmancy cocktail party and dinner. I went with my business partner (at the time), snacked on hors d'oeuvres, met loads of people from around the country and indulged in a fabulous array of delicacies -- hand selecting crab legs, scallops and all kinds of yummy foods from the buffet. There were bunches of waiters. The service was impeccable. I looked up over the ceviche and there upon the server's lapel – ARNOLD! My goodness, how many Arnolds can there be? Was this COINCIDENCE? OF course not, this was my dad, showing up to let me know he was there IN SPIRIT, and paving my way. I do not recall at this moment, but there were 2 or 3 additional SIGNS. One was on the TV. I do not recall exactly what, but I do remember having the TV on while applying my makeup. I got up from the bathroom to go into the bedroom when I saw, the TV showing the credits from the show that had just aired. The first recognition that I noticed was some name, some producer named ARNOLD. What fun and what a secure feeling. Dad was there to WALK with me, throughout the trip.

Psychic Warns Me of a Broken Leg -- Ross Broke His Leg
2012

I was with Burton, my mastermind partner and friend. We set out to enjoy a health fair and metaphysical event at the convention center. Burton decided to meet with ANNIE, the psychic, and after TRULY enjoying what she had to say and gaining respect for her, I decided to give it a try. I paid for the hour. I was not a happy camper at this time in my life, as I had been sad about Armando, yet anticipating going on a HUGE amazing Asian Cruise with Ross.

So excited I was and while chatting with Annie, she was totally right on about where I was emotionally at the present time. We talked for an hour while Burton waited to compare psychic notes with me. ~Smile. At the very end, she warned me, "DO NOT GO DOWN THE GREAT WALL in a toboggan; you're going to break your leg."

"OUCH, THANK YOU!"

I told Ross and he heard me. Of course HE was still going. How often does one go to the Great Wall, with the possibility of going down via toboggan, a chance of a lifetime.

Well, we went to Beijing and our first day there, we went to the Wall -- amazing! I decided to at least take the tram UP, It was about 15 degrees -- middle of February, COLD, and so that was HUGE for me, to swing in 15 degrees high above the land. It was so amazing, wonderful, joyful, thrilling and more. I said to Ross, "Ya know what? I cannot be in Beijing China and NOT toboggan down with you; I'm going!"

We both went down the wall, each in our own little SLED-like contraptions, the kind that we used to take at Raccoon Mountain in Tennessee. It was exhilarating, marvelous and more, I cannot describe. It was an experience that must be FELT; no words exist. Ross saw to it that I was safe and tobogganed behind me - so no one would crash into me.

The Trip was over, TA-DA -- NO broken leg. I wrote Annie, telling her how YES, the trip changed my life. I was now inspired and delighted to wear a COLORFUL wardrobe, as I had been wearing a great deal of black, perhaps my BLACK period. ~Smile. AND I did NOT break my leg; YAY! Mission accomplished!

We returned home on 3/15 and sometime around May 1st, Ross called me from the ER. "Mom, I'm okay, but my toes are facing my calf!"

He broke his ankle, fibula, and a host of other fractures -- NOT good!

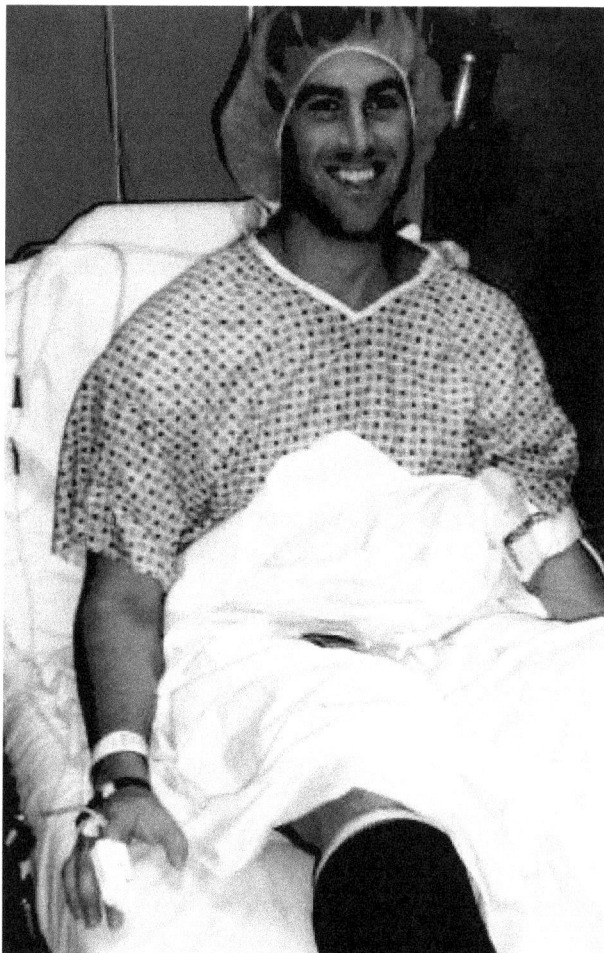

My point, and he does NOT agree, is that there is something symbiotic, suggestive – SOMETHING about HIM breaking his leg/ so to speak and my not doing so. I do not know what. I surely want him to NOT endure, take, and have anything to do with my pain. I do not know what it is; I just know that after that elbow fracture that I had, when he was 7 years old and his expressing how he WISHED he could take my pain away, and then fracturing his own elbow one week later, I believe that we are connected in some realm that I want to DISCONNECT. I totally do not know what it is, but upon this writing I have a thought. It literally just came to me, upon writing.

It is now 9/5/12 and here's what I think. Ross came into this world, as my mom departed. She died suddenly, just days, a week or so, before Ross was born. There was no sadder time in my life. She was wayyyyyyyy too young to die, only 66 years old and I loved her very much. I did not want to be motherless, surely not at this time in my life, having just given birth to my first baby. What a sad time indeed! I used to cry while I would go for walks with Ross. I was deeply mourning and then shortly after my tears began to flow, Ross would begin to cry. I felt so badly, CRYING to this sweet newborn child and so guilty, I would immediately cease crying just as he started.

I do believe on some level, Ross thought that he was taking away MY pain. Literally, if he cried, I would stop. So to me, that was a sensible thought for a newborn. ~Smile. So this continued until I mourned less and less and enjoyed Ross more and more. He was the greatest gift, taking me from my suffering -- my angel of sorts. I even recall Dad and Berniece telling me I was the lucky one, because at least I had this new born, DELICIOUS child. Lest I diverge, so Ross decided on a soul, EARLY level, that if he mimics me, i.e.: crying, he can take MY pain away and re-establish my joy, as in when he told me that he wished he could take my pain away and have the elbow fracture happen to HIM; and it did.

Now so many years later -- decades – I think he heard about me supposedly going to break MY leg and on a subconscious level broke HIS own leg. Who knows? Does he hear the pain I'm in - and decide that if he takes on that pain - that I will cease to suffer - as in him beginning to cry - while I first began crying and that making me stop??? I don't know - All I know is that he injured himself with the elbow fracture and now upon me being told that I was going to break my leg - did he decide to break his??? G_D bless Ross. He is just coming through a most challenging time in his life. Surgery went well; he is well on his way to a complete recovery, AMEN...lots of gifts. I surmise the gifts always come after the dark period.

I personally think the darkness is equivalent to the blessings we are about to receive. ~BIG, BIG FAT SMILE is what I am doing. I am so proud of you, my sweet man child. The tears gather, for I see now how successful you are becoming, how hard you are working, how your life has changed immeasurably over the last several months. I am LOVING this stage of life that you are in. You have courageously and without complaint come through a very dark period -- of little fun, major pain, uncertainty and doubt as to your mobility, health and welfare. It's been probably the HUGEST most difficult time in your life. All of your money gone, as you could not work, girlfriends out the door as you had so little to give, yet here you are, working hard and being financially blessed and sooooooooooooooo much more.

The above, that last statement, I think that the pain is equivalent to the joy that we are about to receive is SOOOOOOOOOOOOOOOOO true in this case and, as to my experience, all of life. Your brother is going through his dark period now -- injury and financial, all kinds of humbling -- and in some respects, I too am traversing a bit of loneliness and uncoupling still. It is this kind of DEMONSTRATION, whoever makes it, that restores my faith, knowing I am ever sooooooooooooooooo grateful. I am totally thrilled for you Ross. G_d bless you and AMEN!

So here I was, listening to Joel Osteen. He was talking about G_D granting FAVOR on you. And it is YOUR time and your victory is NOW.

And I was thinking, "Okay, so where is my biggest prayer at the moment, a wonderful joyful life-long romance? Okay G_d, I have complete faith in you and yet it FEELS like it's taking soooooooooo long. Come on G_d," and all of this was going thru my mind when right at the light at Hillsboro and 95, as I exited, no turn on red, a BIG boat on a trailer went by. My mind was saying, "COME ON G_D! WHEN?"

And the boat's name was "NO RUSH." ~Smile.

Hello G_D, thanks for the sign! Oh how I love this journey. ~Smile.

智 Wisdom 智

Don't Be Impressed With Appearances -- 1978

I was about 26 years old and used to go to the Sporting Club, a gym, in Atlanta. My goodness, I forgot that I was working on my triceps, even then. Still, they are like angel wings...but, I digress.

So, I was at the Sporting Club and lounging at the pool, when I saw this guy pull up in a blue Porsche. Yes, even though I could not care less about cars, I did notice this young man and thought, "WOW, he's surely wealthy."

I sat and sunned and, lo and behold, this very same man came over to sit beside me. NOPE, it was NOT that your momma was hot. It was that he wanted to SELL me -- have me take this debt off of his hands. He came over, introduced himself and said that I could have his Porsche for a mere $479/month -- no strings attached. This was back in 1978. I did not have a clue what he was talking about. I, literally, never even knew about leasing or credit anything. I had purchased my sweet CLEO outright and saved enough to pay $3400. Well, that is not true...my parents split the cost with me. Still I didn't know that you could LEASE a car.

Anyway, the man was in dire straits and needed someone to take over his payments. Never judge ANYONE by what they have or seem to have, flaunt or DRIVE. And remember that MONEY CAN FLY OUT THE WINDOW! That was my mom's advice to me, upon selecting a husband. Money is NOT good criteria. Appearances are not always what they seem to be.

Head AWAY From Life's Storms -- 8/80

I was about 26 years old, living in Atlanta and had these WILD and WONDERFUL older girlfriends -- Gladys and Shirelle.

They were THE most fun, their 'Goyisha' to my Jewish, fun loving to my Careful Nellie and just knew how to laugh, love and have a REALLY good time. I was delighted just having them wanna be friends with ME. They were attractive, could carry their liquor and knew how to party. I loved 'em.

Gladys had a motor boat and we used to go up to Lake Lanier, the big lake, and we would all go water skiing. It was GREAT fun! One day, the three of us were out on the boat when a major storm was approaching. It was getting very black, very dark and I was ready to head for the hills. GLADYS had other plans, turning the boat, hitting the throttle and heading towards the storm. "WHAT ARE YOU DOING?" I hollered with great dismay.

It was noisy. The engine was roaring, "CHECKING OUT THE STORM!"

"PLEASE NO! Go back! GO BACK, PLEASE!"

I was more than scared and Gladys blessedly saw the dismay on my face. "Okay," she responded, "but I've got to pee!"

Shirelle decided she had to, as well. So into the water they went. I, for some G_DLY reason, stayed on board. It amazes me today, knowing how I have visited every restroom in the land, if anyone ever has to pee, it is I! I literally was going to write a funny book called, "Oh the restrooms I've seen." ~Smile.

Well, I did not have to go, so Gladys and Shirelle exited the boat, each with sunglasses and hats on. I sat there, waiting, watching and hoping they would go FAST! I was sitting there when I saw Gladys's hat fly off her head -- FAR gone. Then Shirelle's sunglasses, too, went flying off HER head. I was watching this, not really even noticing that I was getting further and further away from the two of them. The boat was going in one direction, with ME in it, and Shirelle and Gladys were seemingly heading in the opposite direction. HOLY WAKE UP! It finally dawned on me that they were about 40 feet from the boat.

The wind must have moved the boat and there they were -- two little people bandied about by the waves -- and THIS was a LAKE!

Blessedly, I knew how to start the engine, having taught Water Skiing as a child at camp. You never know when your previous skills will come in handy, so start the boat I did! Gladys and Shirelle jumped in. Gladys sped AWAY from the storm and we made it back to land, just full of gratitude for what might have been the end of the three of us.

Blessedly, I stayed in the boat. Those storms in life can surely just POP out at us, coming from nowhere. So today, as I am literally hours away from turning 50 (60) years old, a tear comes to my eye. I am so, so, so, so ultra-grateful to have been somewhat of a Nervous Nellie. I think I ought to think of myself instead as a Wise Woman. AMEN and HALLELUAH! Head away from the storms!

It was rather profound when Andrew told me to LIE about my age and tell people that I am 10 years younger. He was all of 5 years old -- attending my 40th birthday party -- when I became 30!

He said, "Mommy, I think you should lie about your age and be 30 instead of 40!"

And I responded, "Why is that Andrew?"

His answer was, "If you think of yourself as 10 years younger, you'll act 10 years younger, you'll live 10 years longer and I'll have you 10 years longer!"

WOW! Talk about profound...and I did!

Universe is Conspiring to Bless Us -- Blaze – 7/04

I had been hearing news reports about all of the shark sightings locally and it got me a bit concerned, as always...SAFETY MOMMA! So I went home one afternoon and told you boys, VERY seriously, "Boys, there have been lots of shark sightings and I want you to stay out of the ocean!"

Not that we even lived near the ocean -- we were living in Orlando and the closest we were to the Atlantic was a beach named New Smyrna. So, just in case the boys were anywhere near the ocean, STAY AWAY. The responses were, "Mom, don't be ridiculous. The sharks are not going to get us. We'd be close to the shore, if we even went into the ocean."

Back and forth -- I tried to get them to see the seriousness and they tried to show me how they had NO fear! EEERGGGGGGHHHHH! "BOYS!" Fear made the pitch of my voice louder, "Don't look for trouble. If it's all over the news that there have been shark sightings, then STAY away! Swim in a pool!"

I received a perfunctory, "Yes, Mom!" with absolutely NO intention of them listening to me, IF they were to be at the beach.

Oh the fear, love and frustration of being your Mom. All I wanted was your safety and well-being! So, conversation dropped, I know when to STOP nagging. I didn't wanna to turn you off completely. ~Smile. I think it was the very next day, talk about the Universe conspiring to bless US, we were watching the 10 PM News, when all of a sudden there was this photo and report about a child from Longwood -- OUR TOWN. Our ears perked up as we listened to the report that this young man, 15 years old and on the volleyball team at Lake Mary High School – NOW, we were REALLY listening -- was bitten by a shark earlier today. OH MY GOD! BLAZE, BLAZE from Lake MARY -- friends with Ross and Andrew -- Blaze was bitten by a shark out in New Smyrna. I was relieved that he was reported to be okay.

It was a mild bite -- it had not removed his leg, yet even MORE relieved that whatever powers that be made a juxtaposition of the universe, so that MY sons would listen up and NOT swim in the ocean. Yup, they listened. They were humbled. I did not have to spend another moment worrying about your welfare.

GREAT joy recently came to me when Andrew was helping put air in my tires. It was raining and thundering and I offered him an umbrella while he made the effort to fill my tires. "NO MOM! There's lightening! Never put the umbrella up in the lightening! Stay out of harm's way when you hear thunder!"

Oh my happy heart! I am passing the baton – careful, and wise. What a joy loving my sons and hearing THEM tell ME to be careful. I am so, so, so, so, grateful, I can hardly express myself. Thank you Universe for our safety and well-being and for blessing us!

Whenever I Hear Parkland -- 2007

Okay, so it was 2007 and I had been dating and dating. I desired to find REAL true delicious love and so I continued to date all kinds of interesting men and finally came to meet a very lovely man. I think his name was KELSEY. He was totally a gentleman and took me to Houston's upon first meeting. We had a lovely lunch during the week and then each of us went back to work.

He began calling me, texting me and emailing each morning. He was paying me all sorts of attention. He was tall and handsome; I liked him. I had a hot tub at the time and I had a desire to remove it and replace it with an organic garden, as I never used the tub. I might have mentioned it to him and he was more than kind to suggest having HIS workers come to my home and remove it for me. WOW! What a great guy!

He made another date with me for a Thursday evening, but, unfortunately, had to cancel. His son had some school event that required his presence. SURELY, I understood; I love a great parent! We made another date. In between the time we made the date and the date itself I would get GOOD MORNING texts and GOOD NIGHT texts. This was VERY, VERY sweet; he always seemed to be thinking of ME. Unfortunately, he had to cancel this date as well. I started to wonder why he had not been able to get to know me further, even while he was texting me all of these loving warm "hellos."

I sat down and wrote him one evening and asked if he was married? His email response said, "I would never hurt you."

Hmmmmmmmm, that was NOT a response to MY question. Some months later after I ASSUMED that he was married and I never would see him again, I saw him and his wife at the beach. He gave me a look that said KEEP ON WALKING and do not say HELLO to me. I KNEW IT!

Only a week or so after the email, that pretty much confirmed in my mind that Kelsey was a cheater, I met another man. He, too, was from Parkland, where Kelsey was from. Mind you, I was new in town and did not really know the lay of the land.

171

I have heard and learned since, that Parkland is a well-to- do, sleepy family community. Anyway, I met Rick. Rick was a lovely young guy who was friendly and seemed eager to get to know me more. He even went so far as to want to hire me to COACH him. So, while he was interested in 'dating' me, he also wanted coaching. He made arrangements to barter with me. He did clean up and maintenance around my yard and then we hung out and chatted.

We were sitting on the bench in my courtyard, when I noticed a TAN line EVERYWHERE on his hand, except where a wedding band would reside. I immediately asked him, "Rick, are you married?"

With a puppy dog sad smile, he purred. "YES."

I was sooooooooooo surprised! My goodness -- another one from Parkland – and he was married too. END of that story. So, here we were, 2 guys in just a couple of weeks and both were married.

Didn't I tell the universe that I want a single, available and wonderful man to FALL IN LOVE with exclusively? I did. Perhaps, I was being tested.

So, I met a man online. He was an Indian man. This was the first time I ever went out with or would meet an Indian man. He was learned and personable over the emails and phone. While he invited me to a fancy-schmancy dinner first date on a Friday evening, I suggested he come to my ballroom instead. I do not really care about food or big deal, fancy-schmancy, but give me some dancing shoes and I'm yours. ~Smile.

SO, he agreed and was looking forward to meeting me at the ballroom on Friday night at 8 PM. On the way down Lyons Road, I got a call from him. He said he was a little bit lost and could I help him with directions. So, I asked him where he was coming from and he replied, "PARKLAND."

"Are you MARRIED?" I shouted out in an accusatory manner.

"YES," he nervously, somewhat surprised and mousily responded.

"Well then, what the Hell are you doing with me?"

172

He was shocked and gave me some response about how he and his wife have an open marriage and he was merely 'NETWORKING.' PATHETIC!

You bet I was being tested -- and I have surely passed THAT test -- never a married man since, AMEN and Hallelujah! Do these men not know about Karma? Apparently NOT!

The Perfect SAYING for My Recent Relationship – 2011

If a bird falls in love with a fish, WHERE WILL THEY LIVE?

Why Does Lost Love Hurt Soooooooooooo Much? -- 2012

I kept on thinking while in agony, regarding Armando, "Why does it have to hurt soooooooooooooo badly?"

Why would a benevolent G_d make losing love so painful? Here are the reasons, as I continued to think. IF we lost a job, a house or even a dear friend, that hurts for sure. BUT, to lose a BEST FRIEND -- one with whom you shared your life and made so many happy times together -- THAT is the worst kind of pain. And what does that pain do to us? It humbles us. It gets us to SEARCH, to think and to wonder, "What did I do wrong? What could I have done – shoulda, woulda, coulda?"

It gets us to EVOLVE and learn. G_d willing and hopefully, our psyches are willing. SO, now I understand why the pain of the wound is equivalent to the gifts of the joy and vice versa -- perhaps equal to the next love I will find. THIS pain will not be in vain. In addition, I realized that like any other muscle, the heart, when it is torn or torn in shreds, it friggin' HURTS TERRIBLY! Still, like any other muscle, it too will heal and perhaps come back stronger. Love is like a heart muscle. When there is heart disease, it is so painful. Like a broken heart, love gone awry is total DIS-ease.

Pain makes us evolve. Pleasure is joy, comfort and wonderfulness, but not so with pain. Pain grows our souls; it helps to make us evolve into better, more compassionate and humble beings. Surely, my lost loves have grown my soul. I wonder if MY soul is bigger than most, like my TALL body? ~Smile.

On another note -- JUST THINKIN' -- the honeymoon stage is like the deliciousness of having and loving your child. You boys were so, so, so, so, amazingly and dramatically joyful -- like a great honeymoon stage prepares you for the challenges that come, when love is lost and when children become teens. Had we never experienced that deliciousness, I do not think we would endure the difficult times. Pleasure is a foundation -- one on which to build -- for the knowing of how good it can be. Thank you G_d!

Here is what I know. Sometimes you guys mess up, making some choices that I think are not good. I might get annoyed and yet KNOW that my annoyance is an expression of love. Otherwise I would not give a darn.

As William Paul Young wrote in "The Shack," "Emotions are the colors of the soul; they are spectacular and incredible. When you don't feel, the world becomes dull and colorless. Emotions just ARE. They are neither bad nor good; they just exist.

"Most emotions," he continues, "are responses to perception -- what you think is true about a given situation. If your perception is false, then your emotional response to it will be false too. So check your perceptions, and beyond that check the truthfulness of your paradigms -- what you believe. The more you live in the truth, the more your emotions will help you see clearly. But even then, you don't want to trust them more than G_D."

Thoughts -- 2012

I may not be THE best Mom, but I am surely a strong contender for the Mom who loves her sons THE MOST!

Here Are Quotes Boys That I Have Found Immeasurably Helpful Throughout My Life

Life is what's coming, not what was.

The things you cannot control, you bless.

Where God Guides, God Provides.

If I could have done what I should have done, I wouldn't have done what I did.

Ruin is the road to transformation.

The heart has its reasons, that reason doesn't understand. -- Pascal

If you knew better, you'd do better.

If you're always looking in the rear view mirror, you will miss the scenery.

Change the way you look at things and the things you look at will change. -- Dyer

Start looking for solutions, instead of defending your position.

Never be afraid to trust an unknowing future to a knowing G_D.

Be thankful for your mistakes. They will teach you VALUABLE lessons.

Gratitude can turn a negative into a positive.

Find a way to be thankful for your troubles and they will become your blessings.

Advice -- ANYTIME ADVICE

1. Do what makes you like you more. IF you have a choice -- this idea or that -- and you do not know which to pick, do what makes you like yourself the most.

      i.e.: go and workout or indulge in a banana split? WORKOUT, homey boy!

2. You are NOT accountable to something, if you do not know better. Not responsible.

GUILT says YOU know better…and DEFENSE is the progeny of guilt!

A Few Tidbits That I Thought Were
Neat and Interesting

1. Ross and I were in Spain and I was concerned about our next day's plans. Would I have warm enough clothes? Would I have enough sleep, if I was tired? What would we do? I don't recall the exact excursion but I literally fretted my moments in the now for the day we were planning tomorrow. Ross then said, "Mom, let the future Adrian handle all of that and don't worry now."

WOW! What wisdom; what a WISE suggestion. It does always work out and if it doesn't, then you deal with that THEN. I love that idea, "Let the future Adrian..."

2. Dad always IMMENSELY disliked motorcycles. Remember the NO GOOD BIKES? It was when he was depressed and out of my mouth came, "Perhaps you need to ride a motorcycle to get your personal power back?"

It was Thanksgiving 2003. We were separated and Dad would NOT tell us where he was spending the holiday weekend. He was purchasing a motorcycle and taking a riding course. WOW! Was that prophecy or the power of suggestion, LIKE the Jews For Jesus deal? He detested his sister's love for Messianic Judaism and warned her NOT to send us anymore literature.

I mentioned, "Perhaps you will be a Jew For Jesus," and VOILA...only a year later, he became devout. Is that prophecy or the power of suggestion? ~Pondering still.

 # Listen
To Your Gut

Norman and the Necklace -- 2005

So, you might think that I am CERTIFIABLY nuts when I tell you that my mom talks to me or, at least, TALKED to me through a necklace. There is an explanation.

I was newly divorced. You, Ross, were gone and in Tampa and YOU, Andrew, were gone and in military school in Melbourne. I was alone in that great big house on Lucky Lane. It was my mom's yahrzeit and I had a candle lit as well as photo of my mom just beside the candle. I think you boys saw it every year, when I would put the photo of Mom, in the wedding dress from my wedding, next to the lit candle in observance of her passing -- February 15th. I had lit the candle the night before and during the course of the day, while alone in the house, I would talk to her. I still do, of course. It was already evening and I kept hearing her say, "Get Rid of Norman,"

He was the first man that I had met after Daddy and I divorced and I was sort of going out with him. Nothing major, just a nice tall man whose company I was enjoying.

I kept hearing MOM, IRMA, say, "GET RID OF HIM."

She was not speaking out loud, but I heard her in my head. And I responded, "No Mom. I like him. There's no reason to get rid of him."

END of story OR so I thought. All of a sudden while in the kitchen, I was leaning down to pick up something that had dropped on the floor and as I raised my torso back upright, my necklace (the round one with the engraving like a dime with the diamond) caught under the counter. JUST as I was standing straight up, the necklace dislodged from the chain and the round pendant went FLYING across the room. Immediately at the exact second that the necklace broke - I heard IRMA, my mom, in HER voice yelling, "BREAK IT OFF!"

WHOA, easy there, I was taken aback. How odd that the necklace should break and go flying at the same time that mom mentioned BREAK it off. It surely broke off; that is for certain. I spoke up to Mom and reiterated, "NO MOM, there's no reason to break it off. He's a nice guy."

181

Well that was on a Saturday and the next time I saw Norman was on the following Monday AM, when there was a knock at my door at noon. WHO could that be? Why, it was Norman, totally unexpected and totally DRUNK! "What are you doing here and why are you drunk?"

"I lost my job," he responded.

"Well that's no reason to get drunk."

He stayed for a very short while, and yet put a bit of uncertainty and thought into my mind as to what my mom had said a few days prior. Thursday night was the next time I heard from him. I was on the phone with him for about a minute and a half when I asked, "Have you been drinking?"

"Yes," he drunkenly responded.

I never saw him again. THANK YOU MOM. YES, I know you are my angel!

Ned -- House -- 2007

I was searching for my house for a couple of months. I was VERY selective, to the tune of 63 houses, until I found MY CASTLE. Ned was a tad bit challenged, as I understand that is an awful lot of houses to show someone. I honestly do not recall seeing that many, but that is what he said.

I was driving down St. Andrew's one day, never having driven down this street – being new to Boca -- and loved the name of the street, as well as adoring the King Palms, when I just got a FEELING. "NED," I dialed, "my house is on St. Andrew's in Boca. Can you find it?"

Within 2 days he found two houses that fit my description and by weeks end, we had a contract. Oh how I trusted my gut feeling! ~Big Smile.

Listen to Your Gut -- Diane -- 2007

This was a tough decision. Diane had spent literally 20+ hours with me, determined to find the right and perfect investments for my money. I was tired of managing my finances myself. She was a bright young woman and a friend of mine. So we spent several visits determining where to put this money. She came up with mostly mutual funds and gave me every good reason why she selected them. I was all ready to invest with her, but in the shower that morning, I was having a major concern as to giving her the SMALL and LARGE accounts. I had one small account and one large one and was going to give her both accounts to invest.

I recall vividly being under the shower head -- water pounding on me -- while thinking that I could LITERALLY hear my trepidation, that it would be so difficult to tell her. After she spent ALL this time with me, how could I change my mind now? I labored and yet, I felt as though it was MY money and my choice to invest as I saw fit. I just had a feeling that I ought not to give her the big account. I even got clear that if I lost the friendship, it would just have to be such. I felt SUCH pressure; it was as if the pounding of the water was analogous to the pounding of my FEAR to not 'piss her off'.

I called her THAT morning and told her that I could invest the small account and not the large one. I hoped she would not be angry with me. I was listening to my gut. It was really hard. She worked and prepared and spent all this time with me, never pressuring me, yet I HEARD my gut LOUD and CLEAR! She was a total professional and suggested easily that I must listen to myself first and foremost. Whew, talk about timing! I wrote the release and sent the money for her to invest; it arrived within the week. The very following week is when the market started to TANK -- I think in 2008. I lost 1/2 of the value of the small account. I hesitate to even THINK how I would have felt had I NOT listened to my gut and invested and lost 1/2 of the large account. AMEN and HALLELUJAH! LISTEN to that wee, small voice. It is G_D and thus far in MY life...ALWAYS right on!

Scandinavia – 2011 -- and Humility

I hope this is easy to write, as it was such a difficult day -- the second worst day of my life for sure. Losing mom was the MOST difficult.

Armando and I left for Scandinavia. I told him, prior to our departure, that it seemed as if he ought not to go, as he was struggling financially. I do not believe in travel as necessity, but as pure indulgence.

I think his heart was in the best direction, wanting to please me, so I understood. Little did I know that as the doors to the plane closed, his mind said, "I SHOULDN'T BE HERE."

It was too late. We arrived -- good flight to Helsinki, Finland. We found our hotel easily and when it was time to go and sightsee, Armando began walking out of the room. I reminded him to take his passport and documents. He gave me either a 'don't tell me what to do' look and/or an 'I don't need to take it with me' look. "Oh but you do!"

So a bit of a DISCUSSION erupted. Until I finally left the room annoyed and hung out by myself, there was no reasoning. I could have taken them for him, so I have learned -- actually, I had no idea -- how therapeutic and helpful writing this book would be to SEE ME and make ME a healthier person. WOW!

We got back together; all was well, so I will cut to the quick. We spent a couple of days in Finland. There was an awesome church, I recall, built out of a ROCK -- yes, a rather large Rock…very neat. We headed to Stockholm, Sweden. Oh my, what a gorgeous, charming and clean city. We had GREAT lodgings and yet, getting there was so very challenging. Because Armando felt as if he did not have enough money, he insisted we take public transportation. So we did not, once, take a taxi for the 11 visits to and from the airport that we endured. We took buses and subways and wow, did we get lost. Mind you, I was willing to pay, but he was PROUD.

He carried ALL of the luggage and was a perfect gentleman, however, his energy was a bit negative. Perhaps this was understandable, as he SCHLEPPED the two heavy suitcases over cobblestone streets, had our share of getting lost and often going the wrong way on FOOT. I am almost laughing now – sorry, but it was funny. The arrival in Stockholm was literally a comedy of errors. The hotel was on the other side of nowhere. If you lived in the city for 25 years, you would probably never have ventured to where it was that we stayed. Suffice it to say, we walked and walked and walked. We stopped to ask for directions, ended up somewhere where there was a trestle and had no sight of our hotel. Then we became exhausted, stopped people on the streets who did not speak English and asked. "MA RI OTT HOTEL, can you help?"

They pointed here and there and finally, after going in one direction up a huge hill, we came to learn from some amazing looking characters with no teeth and just totally weird-looking, that we were heading in the wrong direction again. The third time, we FINALLY saw the hotel and ARRIVED! I stopped Armando for a hug and joyful celebratory kiss. "We found it and we can one day laugh about this," I said.

His response was, "I don't think it's so funny."

Mind you, he was carrying the luggage. My exhaustion was just the walking. Oh well. I figured his joy would come in time. We enjoyed the city, then headed for Bergen, Norway. It was COLD and rainy, but I endured, with 3 pairs of pants, a sweater and a coat. I had GREAT intention to stay healthy.

Bergen was gorgeous -- a masterpiece of beauty. The yummy salmon that we tasted was not to be had for less than $58/serving, so we decided eating from a grocer would be more our style. We could wait for Outback salmon upon our return, in a week or so. I could tell you about the ugliness that ensued from this city, the hotel patrons not being there when we arrived at midnight and I could also tell you that the bus driver literally waited for us to find the hotel manager. I guess it is all in perspective. I think Armando saw the annoyances as an affront. I have traveled so much, knowing that these things happen. They are still annoying, but here I was, seeing SCANDINAVIA, blessedly!

We headed for Copenhagen – with a very wonderful ice bar, tall Danes, beautiful city and even the little mermaid. While she was surprisingly LITTLE, it was still a thrill. Off to Oslo -- oh my, what a magnificent city -- just gorgeous. It was the latter part of July. We headed to the grocers for our dinners; it was truly an expensive piece of the world. A beer in Denmark was $17. My hot water was $6. I even had my own tea bag!

We finally left for St. Petersburg on the morning of July 22. I was rather proud of us, finding all of the hotels, traveling and seeing the most important parts. It was a challenging trip, with the weather being cold and the food and transportation being absurdly expensive. The bus in one city was $100 one-way to the airport -- the BUS!

We departed from our hotel down the block from City Hall and headed out to the airport at 5:30 PM. We arrived in St. Petersburg at about 12:30 PM. We were so excited to be there. We did TOO much, seeing too many cities in 10 days. We just needed to CHILL in one city and, blessedly, St. Petersburg, Russia was going to be the place. We heard it was 82 degrees and that the currency had a really good exchange rate. We were booked into the Marriott there for 4 nights. We were excited!

We did not have one dinner out. Armando's employee, who was to run his company, had not showed up AT ALL. He was visibly upset, although tried not to show it. There was no romance. It was literally too cold to take my clothes off, because there was no heat in the hotels.

This was summer for the Scandinavians and so no heat necessary. Fifty degrees for them was sandal and swimsuit weather; they were hardy. We did not have great fun, yet it was still thrilling for me. ALL TRAVEL is.

We were excited, thinking of going shopping and all of the indulgences we were about to enjoy...until we arrived at Customs and this HITLERISH man greeted us and pointed to the door. He raised his voice and said, "OUT OF COUNTRY!"

"What? What did he say?"

"OUT OF COUNTRY!"

With that, they led us out of Customs and held us in a waiting area, while a few Russian guards stood there laughing. I looked at them with a ferocity of expression and let them know there was nothing funny about this. I think Armando was afraid I would be locked up by the KGB. Long story shorter, we were shuffled/escorted on to the next plane back to Oslo.

I did go to the head of Customs. This SOB, while eating a sandwich, sipping tea and watching a TV never once looked at me. He just made an arm movement to the sweet interpreter, who felt sorry for us, that we were to leave. She escorted me back to Armando and with thumbs pointed down, I stepped off the escalator and said, "We're not staying in Russia."

I had to at least try to have them allow us in. Our visas apparently were "Out of Order." There was nothing we could do, but leave Russia. This was a new event for my life...after all of this planning and traveling – the shock of literally being REJECTED from a country.

We boarded the plane we arrived on and ANDREW, our flight attendant, was delighted AND surprised to see us back. We told him what had happened as the plane took off -- with Armando giving RUSSIA 'the finger.' OY! We arrived back in Oslo to PANDEMONIUM. The City Hall had just been bombed and there was a terrorist on the loose.

It was challenging enough to not speak the language and not have cell phones, but with a city having just been bombed, it was a shock for them as well. We went from store to store to try and use their phones, literally begging, but getting NO response.

They were stressed I guess, surely not accommodating. I continued to try to call Beth, the travel agent, while Armando went to the Air France counter. We wanted OUT of this city, and fast. We wanted to GO HOME. It was just too challenging and disappointing.

Perhaps I ought to have learned, when Armando and I took the Spiritual Cruise, we might not be the best of travel buddies. Basically, I think as I write this, I knew earlier in the planning that this was just not right. Yet I so wanted to see the world, I used my WILL instead of listening to that small, inner voice. Truly, I had not even remembered how I was NOT listening to my GUT -- knowing that Armando did not have enough time to take off, as well as money to afford such a trip. STILL, I just wanted to go. AHA, so here is another lesson in the title of Willful – Surrender - Let Go - Let G_d and all sorts of lessons in HUMILITY and by LISTENING to that wee, small voice. It surely tells you the wisest info; our jobs are to listen.

Armando came over to me after his discussion with the Air France agent and informed me that the return trip would cost another $3600 – OUCH! Blessedly, I had my credit card and enough credit left. Surely, this was not as we had planned and yet, life often does not go according to OUR plans.

Next thing we knew, we were on a plane to Paris. Beth took care of getting us the tickets. I do not recall exactly how, but she did. We arrived some 7 hours later, first awaiting the flight and then flight time. This was one LONG day. On board, I wanted to share the discussion about what we would do about all of this, but it just seemed to spark Armando's temper, so it seemed better left unsaid. In the meantime, I sat there thinking about where we would sleep and when asked him, he responded something like, "I don't care; I'm sleeping in the airport."

"WHAT?"

I had been flying all day, first rejected from one country, then bombed out from another, there was NO way I was sleeping in some airport! I do not care if I had just come from Tahiti feeling completely relaxed and rested. I just will NOT sleep in an airport; I wanted a BED!

We arrived and as Armando was grabbing the luggage, I waited to go into his bag and get my 5 items. Angrily and pridefully I said, "You're free to go."

And go, he did. Oh my sad, petrified heart! I sat there for a moment and cried my eyes out . I cannot tell you how dramatic and ridiculous I was. I was so ultra-afraid, I became hysterical – and alone in Paris, after traveling since 5:30 AM and in three countries. I am glad THAT is behind me!

I found the Air France office and on some level, figured they would assist me to a hotel, however, NOT! They were caring as I boo-hoo'ed my way into their office, but I just wanted a 'Big Daddy' to take my hand and help situate me. THAT was NOT happening. Instead this kind gal behind the desk wrote out instructions in French, for me to travel -- first on a bus and then on a subway -- to get to my $100/night hotel, instead of staying at the airport hotel for $400/night.

I guess we can do whatever is necessary if we HAVE TO, because as heavy as the luggage was, I found a cart. As exhausted as I was, I calmly checked into the hotel, washed my hair and sang, "I'm gonna wash that man right outta my hair." I arrived back, in ample time, to the airport the next morning, to catch a flight to Miami, AMEN and AMEN! I arrived at the gate, changed my seat, arrived in Miami some 11 hours later and found a taxi to take me home. As far as I was concerned, this was ample reason to no longer continue to date Armando.

I was literally addicted and had a hard time to stop dating him. How pathetic I feel writing this. Yet, for some reason -- perhaps my own self-respect -- now I can see the error of MY ways. No matter how horrible a situation is, there is something to be learned. In this case, I saw the PRIDEFUL me. Instead of asking that he not leave me, I told him he was "free to go." I wonder if I will ever have a man again, that would leave me. I surely hope not. I thought long and hard about how other men would have "HANDLED" me. I guess it is not good to challenge a man like that, but I do not believe a total gentleman and love of 2+ years, would ever leave a woman by herself, alone in a foreign city. Perhaps I am wrong.

Perhaps I ought to present this scenario on the next first date and see what my potential beloved would do! ~Smile. In addition, I surely learned humility and a bit of self-sufficiency. ~Big Smile. Maybe to pack lighter -- surely that is an age old lesson for me.

Another lesson was surely to NOT judge others. I say this because as a 'coach,' I have often had clients tell me that they let their beloved treat them less than well. All this time, I could NOT understand how they took them back, time and time again. Boy, did I get humbled, because I went back with Armando about 2 times after that -- NOT GOOD. Still, I NOW understand why people do such things. It is not because they want to, but it is because it can be rather challenging to give up the love of someone that you have shared your love and life with. While I lost respect for myself, I gained respect for how challenging it was to traverse an intense love.

AND MOST IMPORTANTLY, LISTEN to that wee, small voice. Oh how easy it is to NOT listen. Please Dear G_d, help me to hear you, listen and obey! And so I pray.

What a DEMONSTRATION of listening to my gut this was. Here we were on our first trip to Asia -- Ross and I. We had 8 or 9 ports to visit, a day here, a day there. There was neither a great deal of time nor ability to truly SEE a country, but at least a 'taste.'

And so, the thrill of China, Japan, South Korea, Vietnam, Hong Kong -- even though it is part of China, felt like a city unto itself, Bangkok and Singapore. OH MY G_D, what a trip and with my child! How awesome is that!

We were set to discover another entire continent, just Ross and I. It was very, very exciting in an indescribable way. We arrived in Beijing and went tobogganing down the Great Wall. YUP, you heard me. In the middle of winter, February 15th -- Mom's Yahrzeit -- we traversed history...adventure and MYSTERY at 15 degrees. It was amazing and wonderful!

Our next port, not to make light of Beijing -- just the point -- was Busan, South Korea. Again, it was a wonderful taste of the port -- the containers, the fishery, the fisherwoman -- so much to take in, walking and walking, touring and exploring...all in ONE day.

Next came Nagasaki. OH MY G_D, Japan, I was...we were soooooooooooooo excited, yet it was POURING rain, really, really cold and really, really wet. Our ship held about 3000 persons and about 2950 passengers exited the ship that morning, to see the war memorabilia -- the historical relics from the war. I just had this ominous feeling that NOT only was I majorly challenged with the cold, I had NO idea it would be so cold on board and off. To handle the rain as well, OH MY GOODNESS!

How does one travel across the biggest 'pond,' to have the opportunity of a lifetime to visit JAPAN and stay onboard the ship? That is RIDICULOUS, that is absurd and that would be major guilt -- to not take in the sights, sounds and delicacies of Japan.

It was TUMULTUOUS inside of my body: "I wanna go...I have to go...I'm in Japan. Little Aidan...One day...dress warm...bring your umbrella...don't disappoint Ross...have smarts...stay healthy for the remainder of the 19 more days...be smart...go and see the sights...see Japan. How could you not get off the ship? You came 6,000 miles. You spent a fortune. Get your tuchas off the ship." What a volley of conflict I was internally experiencing.

I tried my darnedest to learn from whatever mistakes I made with Armando and one of them was that I didn't listen to that WEE, SMALL VOICE in my head, heart and gut. I so very much wanna learn my lessons -- BADLY and with diligence! I heard the voice. It resounded, "You don't like to go out in 80 degrees weather, in the rain. Why would you wanna see DEATH memorials in ANYPLACE, in a wet, rainy 25 degrees?"

And so I courageously told Ross that I wasn't going to go, but he could. He decided for a bit that he was going to go and then as he saw the downpour, decided to stay onboard with me. We had a fun time actually watching the window washers onboard and hanging with the other few folks EATING and talking our day away. One by one, the passengers arrived back onboard, one more drenched than the next – cold, shivering, wet -- coming late to dinner after hanging in their showers for an inordinate amount of time to get warm!

During the course of the remainder of the voyage - about 23% of the ship was quarantined - sick as could be - coughing - hacking - a mélange -a cacophony - of coughs and sneezes awakened us daily - literally heard from the next cabin hacking away. They had just begun the trip and only 3 days into its grandeur - had succumbed to rain and cold and sickness all bred from Nagasaki -

Was it worth it? HELL NO. To this day - still healthy and growing healthier everyday - learning from the mold poisoning how blessed my health is - I am so gratified to have listened to that voice.

Ross and I truly fought to stay well. We Lysoled our cabin - we washed our hands literally dozens and dozens of times each day - we lost our dinner mates to being sick - for days at a time..........and we were so so so so ultra-blessed with having listened to the guidance of the universe to remain onboard -

Perhaps even more blessed - I couldn't help but take it a step further - that we were blessed in a way perhaps that we didn't or won't ever fully realize - that we didn't come even CLOSE to any Japanese radiation- who knows.........???

Lesson learned - LISTEN TO THAT VOICE - it will bless you and teach you - it surely did Ross and I..........

 # Prayer

An Answered Prayer – Vanderlyn -- 1994

Talk about DISTRAUGHT, we were VERY. For several years, I received calls about Andrew's behavior. It started in preschool -- Mrs. Breitbeil -- then continued on in Sunday School, Boy Scouts, Church group, Kindergarten and 1st Grade. All along, I listened and HEARD all of these adult educators tell me how poorly my child was behaving. Yet I found him to be a delicious, perfect, precious, adorable child. He was not at all problematic for me...NOT AT ALL!

Then I received a call on a Monday from Ms. Zamora, Andrew's 2nd grade teacher. She had me come into school – AUSTIN, THAT day. Not only was she upset, but also full of anguish. Even with her explanation and my GETTING it, she had to leave me with the words, "He is THE most difficult child," she has ever had in her 16 years of teaching and we will need to do 'something' about that!! My goodness, talk about HURT...upset...not knowing what to do or to whom to go. I still found him rather extra special, quite frankly – sensitive, sweet and while strong-minded, I respected that!

HOLY, what do I do? Of course, I called Melvin and then I set out on a quest to investigate private schools. I found the Brandon School in West Dunwoody, about 11 miles from the house, at a cost of $12K per year.

Classes had a ratio of one teacher to 9 children. We were totally upset, as we had been saving for COLLEGE, money that we thought would be needed in "13th" grade, NOT second grade. In addition, we selected our home, because the bus stopped right down the block and took the little darlings to school. We did not have to drive them. We reserved carpool time for sports, Sunday school and all the rest. Melvin was traveling and I was catering. It was not fitting in with our chosen life style.

Very upsetting, filled with fear, we continued to peruse schools and options in quite an intense, stop drop and roll, do it now manner. Wednesday night was our masterminding night. Rachel, Toni and Donna all came over and Melvin and I joined them at 7pm.

We had our chit-chat time and prayer and masterminding time. Masterminding is when two or more are gathered. We quiet ourselves, recite principles together -- like surrender, gratitude, forgiveness, etc. -- and then we make our "requests" to our partners and to the universe…and G_d.

Of course, mine was a request for Andrew to have us find THE best school for his needs -- one that he would excel in, as well as afford us the ability to still continue on with our plans for him attending college -- WITHOUT going broke. Everyone supported me, as we did in Masterminding and then the next person made their requests.

We hung out and chatted about our options after the session was complete. The girls knew how upset and concerned I was. They reminded me, "Chica, just let it go; hand it over; give it to G_d. Let go, it will all be okay!"

Whew! With a huge sigh, I did just that…best as I could.

The next morning, I received a call from Linda. She introduced herself to be some sort of guidance counselor and, I believe, worked out of several schools in the county. She began her conversation with, "Hello, Mrs. Mallin. I understand Andrew is having some challenges here with Ms. Zamora and I have a suggestion and solution."

"I'm all ears," I said with a smile in my voice.

She told me about a school nearby and how it was ranked number one in Dekalb County. "Oh and by the way," she continued, "it is just 2 miles from Dunwoody West" (where we lived).

"How much does it cost?" I responded.

"Oh, it's free. It's a public school and yet, it has a closed classroom with one teacher, one teacher's aide and 4 students."

"4 students and 2 teachers and it's free and it's two miles from us? Are you serious? Is there a bus that goes there from here?"

"No, I'm afraid not, but there is an after-school program through the' Y' that he can attend, if you have difficulty transporting him home in the mid-day."

The tears well and my body literally shakes NOW -- some 18 years later -- from relief and joy, gratitude and more. I cannot even express my enthusiasm now. It is as amazing to me NOW as it was then. To think that only 2 days later, after making our requests to the universe, our prayers were fulfilled. I do believe, without a doubt in my heart, brain or gut, that there is a connection. She continued on, "It does not have to be a tough transition and perhaps Andrew would like to come for Pizza and a tour, this Friday" she said...some 2 days later.

How amazing was that? How could this be a COINCIDENCE? No way! This entire saga began on a Monday, 2 days spent looking for relief, Masterminding on Wednesday and then an amazing manifestation of answered prayers by that very Friday!

Andrew went with Linda. I didn't go, I just delivered him to her and he visited Vanderlyn and ate PIZZA (good going Linda!). He began attending Vanderlyn that very Monday, one week later from the onset of this challenge. He thrived. He excelled. He was amazing. He was happy. His teachers were happy. Melvin brought him to school every morning on his way to work. It was such a sweet time with his Dad. Then we both picked him up in the afternoon. It was a wonderful time that he had after school. He was loving the sports and, surely, excelling in that realm.

G_d has a plan and for that I am so extremely grateful -- learning every day, still, to let go and let G_d...

Will wonders ever cease? I am still FEELING the BODY 'feels' of the experience I had this morning. Back in high school, I thought MICHAEL FEINSTEIN was adorable. He was one of the 'popular' kids and did not take a second look at me. At the time, I might have even thought he was out of my league. ~Smile.

Well, I attended my 30-year reunion from high school with my husband and MICHAEL was there, CUTE as ever. BUT, I was happily married. This being 2000 and not flirting with Michael, I just made his acquaintance and got his business card. I learned that he was an ALTERNATIVE medicine practitioner and thought, "WOW! We've grown along the same paths...very neat!"

He was still cute and I was still married...end of story.

A few years later and now divorced, I do not recall exactly, but I think I was cleaning out my card file and came across MICHAEL's card. I went to call or email him, but there was no number or address, so I tossed the card. While I would have liked to connect with this man, I could not; so I forgot about it.

Paul Emanuel, a dear friend of mine, was chatting with me one day and I mentioned that I would like to find Michael Feinstein. He gave me a suggestion -- to call Tommy Weihl, another friend and I might have, but do not recall. However, MICHAEL FEINSTEIN remained elusive...forgotten, end of story.

Fast forward a few years and just NOW, only recently, I placed an ONLINE ad -- to flirt and meet men. My posting was about seeking healthy men -- men who are bright, physically healthy, spiritual, financial, emotional, all the AL's! ~Smile. IF they fit that description, they were to please contact me. I posted a photo, too. That was several months ago.

I received an email from a MAN, I think yesterday, and he wrote, "What a great profile. IF ever you get up to Eastern Long Island, it would be fun to meet."

He signed it MICHAEL. He wrote in a PS, "I am VERY into health and practice alternative healthcare and blah-blah-blah."

Oh MY G_D, could this be MICHAEL, from Long Island -- Eastern Long Island -- into Alternative Healthcare?

Could it be? Holy MOTHER -- my heart was racing, my brain was doing flips, and I was living here in Florida -- why would anyone answer my query from ALL the way up there? If it were Michael, would he not have recognized me? I am literally having an OUT OF BODY experience. This is just too amazing. I believe in miracles and yet this is one for the books. I wrote back, "You wouldn't be, by any chance, Michael Feinstein, would you?"

My heart was still palpitating as I awaited a response. Only moments later, did I get it, "Michael Adam Feinstein, how did you know?"

Oh my G_D yes, the universe surely works in magical ways.

I think the story of Lily might well be the most difficult one for me to write. Yet this story is so amazing to me, I can hardly find a clear way to reveal and share it, so that you can hear, feel and understand its significance. Everything I say might sound disjointed even though I labor to be clear. To be sure, it is a woven story.

Many, many years ago, I began attending Unity Church. I first attended due to a painful time in my life...Mom had died and my Dad had changed. I was having a very tough time understanding and handling why my relationship with Dad had gone sour. Unity has taught me a great deal over the years. I was never a religious person – I still do not profess to be. Yet through Unity's teachings, I learned to see situations in a very positive light. I believe there is a gift in everything. What seems good is not always, what seems bad is not always and what seems bad – often, if not always, turns out for the best or for the better.

Week after week, course after course, meeting with like-minded people on a daily or weekly basis had a profound effect on my life. I was loving it, because I was handling emotions and life's unchartered waters better with the skills I was learning. There was a course that Unity offered -- only once per year -- and it was always offered in January and lasted for twelve weeks. It was called the "4T" course. The T's stood for Treasure, Tithing, Talents and ...actually I don't recall the 4th T. It was basically a course on Prosperity, but not only about money. Prosperity is about everything in one's life that can make you grow -- your relationships, your health, your finances and your spirit. You name it! It is all encompassing.

I felt over the years -- perhaps over twenty, attending Unity -- that I did not need this course. I had a fairly prosperous life. My family life, my children, my health and my wealth were all in pretty good stead. So, in all of those years, after reading hundreds of books, attending dozens of lectures, and hearing thousands of sermons, I never felt the need or desire for the course. It was a huge commitment. There was a two-hour per week course with required attendance. Study books had to be purchased and there were homework assignments every week. Still, after continuous weekly announcements that Unity was offering the next 4 T course in January, I decided to take it. I still do not know why I made the decision to take the course.

I was living a pretty good life after the divorce. It had been almost two years since that last rough patch. Here I was settling into South Florida...and all was well. I hadn't a clue why, but it felt right. I felt it was "beshert" -- it was "meant to be".

I started the course, purchasing the $50 worth of study materials and attending the first class. Introductions were made and the first teaching revealed that we were going to select an area of our lives that we wanted to make better, make healthier and to manifest something important – one BIG desire. I had been Masterminding for some twenty-plus years. This course was sounding a bit like that. You speak several thoughts together with partners – for example, "surrender" and "forgiveness" – words that ask for what we wish to manifest. Supposedly, there is more power in prayer when others are praying for or with you. I have found that hugely true. So for our first lecture, our first homework assignment, if I remember correctly, we were to think about what we wanted to manifest in the next twelve weeks and to set an intention.

Just prior to the course, in December, I had just started dating Theo, a counter-intelligence major in the U.S. Army. I was a bit taken with him. He was living in St. Augustine and, thus far, seeing me just on weekends. I don't recall exactly, but knowing me and my love for love, I was more than likely thinking that I would like to manifest something "deliciously" romantic with him.

During the course of the first week of class, I went to the PO box where I had been receiving my mail. Shock of all shocks! In my box, I found a document addressed to me. It was quite heavy -- a large mail envelope. I only read the first paragraph while standing at the PO box. Basically, it said plaintiff Melvin is suing defendant Adrian to overturn their divorce! WHAT? Oh my G_d; Holy S#%t! This was as shocking an experience – by receipt of a paper -- as anything I have ever encountered in my entire life. Not only was I being sued, but by the LAST person on the planet that I ever thought would try to harm me -- your Dad. In my experience, lawsuits are almost always harmful! I cannot tell you...I cannot describe how I feel as my heart is literally beating so FAST, FAST, FAST as I write this. My hands are typing as if I have Parkinson's Disease! I wish I did not have to experience this again as I write this story, but I am literally shaking as I write. It was a horrific experience. I felt so alone and literally within seconds, I thought, "THANK YOU G_D. I KNOW THERE IS A GIFT IN THIS!"

The tears were streaming down my face as I stood at the Post Office. After giving my thanks, I broke down and sobbed, reminding G_d that while I KNEW this was supposed to be a gift, it still felt as s#%tty as anything I can remember feeling, other than when I learned my mom had died. I called Harold.

Harold was my dear friend. He is extraordinary in his ability to see situations in an objective way and NOT get freaked out. He has a really calming influence on me. He has been one of my greatest angels and continues to be. He talked me through my disappointment. I left the post office and I stopped crying. Harold gave me a sense of gratitude as well. He made me realize that if ever I was going to be sued, let it be now and get it over with. At least I think it was something like that...I do not exactly recall what he said. I do not have a clue how the remainder of the day unfolded. Probably, knowing me, I went into OVERDRIVE getting whatever had to be handled done. I recall talking to Theo and being the blessed Angel that he was, he made me feel secure -- as if WE would get through this together. That is all I needed.

I cannot tell you the depth of my feelings. They vacillated between fear, sadness and shock. I was petrified about losing everything and going through life as a bag lady. Do not laugh at me...that was my fear. You will read about it when I get to the LILY story. I was so sad that Melvin would even think to sue me. He was my best friend for most of my adult life. I loved this man and I still do for the magnificence of what we created together. I repeat he WAS my best friend. I felt such fear...such panic...yet I am still standing. I survived it. Suffice it to say the story continued. I think I got carried away (as detailed above), as if I was IN THAT MOMENT. Yet, here I am years later. Thank you G_d! I am writing about it...I am finally able. I decided then that my WISH, my ASK, my INTENTION, was for me to be victorious in this law suit. I even got to the words that I would WIN beyond my wildest dreams. I did the 4T homework -- boy could I go for a cigarette now! To think that I can write all of this stuff -- day after day, armpits DRENCHED, emotions running rampant, OH MY GOODNESS -- I surely would be smoking NOW, had I not quit three decades ago (yes, the desire is still there). Anyway...

Anyway - to continue...I did the homework that week. If I recall correctly, it was to say the affirmation, "I am prosperous beyond my wildest dreams." We were to say it 100 times -- EVERYDAY and OUT LOUD -- Ugh! I so did not like that part of the assignment, but I did it.

Then we were to read one chapter and listen to the CD of that chapter. I am not certain if there was anything else. No matter what, I did it. I spoke to Theo, I spoke to Harold and I spoke to Paul, a local attorney who had just migrated here from Maryland.

Paul's practice was just starting up, although he had practiced law for some 20-plus years prior to moving to Florida. We decided to meet at a hotel nearby. He was in West Palm Beach and was kind enough to drive closer to where I was...he was just very kind. He didn't charge me for the consultation. We talked for over two hours. He told me that his retainer would be $7500 and that he would only spend what the case cost. In other words, whatever the cost, would be what I would pay. If he did not use the entire $7500, the balance would be returned. I told him I would let him know. This was all new to me. I did not see this coming. I did not anticipate a major law suit as being a major expenditure...not at all. I was basically still struggling to get my life back in order. I was living alone in a rental house -- making new friends, dating and keeping up with rental properties up north trying to make a living.

Now this suit...this course...hmm, this course... perhaps there was a reason that I was finally taking the 4T course. The thought had entered my mind.

So I now get advice that it would be wise to seek an attorney from Orlando. In other words, skip Paul and seek someone who was familiar with the courthouse there, where the case was going to be held. I spoke to at least twenty people to get a bit familiar with what I was supposed to do. This case took over my life. There wasn't a pre- or post-dance where I did not think about what was on my plate. It was totally all encompassing and packed with fear!

My faith was not nearly as strong as it is now. It is these experiences in life that, when they turn out okay, grow us. They make us more faithful...you might say, better...especially if you examine them and see just what you are supposed to be learning. I don't believe that they just happen to you. Instead they grow in and develop your soul. You learn from them. They are instructions for the spirit...the soul.

I told Theo that I needed to go up to Orlando and meet with some attorneys up there. Everyone I chatted with told me it would be wise to hire an Orlando attorney. Thank you Paul, but I have got to hire a hometown boy. Paul understood and he even offered to be co-counsel. He said he would look over everything the other attorney would do and ensure it was in my best interest. I had to trust him - he was a decent man. I met him at the ballroom. He just showed up one night and we danced.

Theo knew that I am not the biggest fan of long distance driving, but also knew that I would need to be up in Orlando for several days, since I needed to venture up there and select an attorney. So he offered to drive in tandem with me. This literally shaped my entire life. This lawsuit was not what I would have chosen for myself.

Anyway, we drove up to Orlando, making several stops for coffee (and romance) along the way. It was surely not the most difficult drive, for I had my Theo right there, on the turnpike, next to me. We arrived and I recall checking into some extended stay. He made a business trip out of it and stayed wherever the Army put him.

We were new at romance, and so did not share a room. It was rather a sweet, delicious unfolding, as to our romance. He was being the Hero, helping the damsel in distress. I was the Victim, needing his aid. I know now how often men LOVE that...I do as well. Regardless, it was sweet for the romance. Having him there with me was such a gift. Was it a coincidence that he was so smart, so crazy about me and so willing to assist? I think not.

He drove with me to about five different attorneys, but NOT allowed to go into any one of their offices with me. Because of client/attorney privilege, we thought better of making him a witness. He stayed out in the lobby and did his work. He didn't allow me to feel guilty wasting his time...he wanted to be there.

The next few days were grueling. I literally listened to one of these attorneys talk about his dying wife - and her chemo schedules – while on my dime, charging me up to $250 per hour for the consultation. Another was so arrogant, telling me that HE would make the decisions, that HE was smarter than I was and that because I was so emotional, I could not be counted upon to think logically and objectively...all to the tune of $300/ hour -- NOT FUN. I went to several more attorneys, liking each one less as I went along. I finally found a gal whom I liked. Yet she was too busy to take my case...but not too busy to take my consultation fee of $400 for the two hours we talked.

I was challenged to the max – I would say distraught. But I had THEO there and he was incredibly uplifting...NEW LOVE. Meanwhile the clock was ticking - I had twenty days to...OOPS! I just remembered. Normally, you have twenty days to answer a suit. Being SUED is different from being SERVED. I had only read about the suit from my PO BOX. I had yet to be sued and served papers.

In other words, the twenty-day rule did not begin until the papers were in my hands. Now I had to figure out how to keep those papers OUT OF MY HANDS, until I could at least determine whom my attorney would be!

Ahh! A smart chickadee, I am -- I now remember the doorbell ringing at my home at 6am. I was sound asleep and BANG - BANG - BANG...very unsettling for a single woman to be awakened at that hour...for WHAT REASON? I had a feeling that it was a process server -- one who would say, "Are you Adrian Mallin?"

I would respond, "Yes."

He would hand me papers, telling me that I was being sued. And THEN the clock -- the 20 day clock -- would begin ticking. Once that happened, I would then either need to have an attorney show up in court to answer the suit or I would have to be in Orlando, in this particular judge's chambers, to answer the suit myself. NOT a good idea...I had NO clue what I was doing. I had never been sued before and here I was, three hours away. It was oh so stressful; I am amazed I lived through it! You know how I am with long distance driving...it is just not my forte.

So I stalled. I tried to get the right and perfect attorney FIRST, before time ran out. I recall hearing a process server BANG at my door twice over a period of a week or so - and me not answering. When I thought I had the appropriate attorney, I answered the door. "Hello," I said. "How are you?" I was bright-eyed and bushy-tailed. "I've been waiting for you. YES, I am Adrian Mallin! Thank you!" ~Smile.

So, now I had twenty days. I recall that the twenty days would end on a Friday, so I was honing in on an attorney. I think I only interviewed five in person, the remainder over the phone and all charged me, with one exception...Paul.

This ordeal of searching for an attorney, as previously mentioned, continued. I don't think the process server had ever seen someone so gracious in receiving notice of being sued. I might have been in DEEP KIMCHEE, but I had not lost my sense of joy or humor. THIS was going to be fun, if I could handle it on MY terms.

After about two weeks, I was introduced to a gal by the name of Mercedes. She became my attorney. I sent her the documents, as she requested, along with a check for ten-thousand dollars and a signed document that said if she did not use up the ten-thousand dollars, with time and court costs, phone calls, emails, etc., that it was STILL hers to keep – even if the case could be settled in one day. ERGGGH! UGGGGH! POOH! YUCK! However, I did sign it -- I did -- and attached the check.

It was now Thursday, the day before SOMEONE was to appear in Court. Mercedes had received the check and called me that evening. She told me that she was terribly sorry, but the case was WAY more involved than she had originally thought. She said my ex-husband was not only suing me to overturn the divorce, but was including all kinds of perjury and felony charges that were NOT her expertise. She told me that I could end up in JAIL - and that she was NOT the right attorney for that! OH MY G_D! How could this be happening? I was beyond shocked. What am I going to do? How am I supposed to handle this?

I had to wait to write this story until now, as I am again healthy. Even now, as I write this, my stomach is turning sour. I had NO idea as to the details of the suit. All I knew was fear, because Melvin was going for the jugular. I had no clue that this the man, that I still loved on so many levels, could do something so despicable to me!

Mercedes told me what she had to say and then dismissed me. She would send back the check and GOOD LUCK! END OF STORY. My heart was breaking. How could she?

I called Paul. It was about 7pm. I was crying when I called and told Paul what had happened. I had stayed in touch with him and he knew what was going on -- that I had hired Mercedes. I was crying because she would not be taking the case and because it was to be "Answered" tomorrow. Out of Paul's mouth came the following, "Adrian, I will drive up there tomorrow. I will respond for you. I will not charge you for the drive time, but will charge you while I am investigating Judge C's courtroom and for the time I take to answer the charges. Then you can decide if you want to hire ME or find another attorney after I have answered. Whatever you decide is fine with me!"

I literally had to STOP my writing to call Paul. The emotions I felt were far too intense to continue writing. I had the URGENCY to call and tell him what an ANGEL he was for me. We chatted and reminisced for some time. NOW I am psyched to continue...he recharged my writing just from sharing our experience.

So, the next day, the last day to respond, Paul went to Orlando to answer the suit. OH MY G_D! That kind of gesture -- driving seven hours and jumping through legal hoops -- made it abundantly clear that Paul was the lawyer for me.

The decision was clear. With every fiber of my being, I was certain there was not a better attorney in the land. What a demonstration!

Class continued on Monday and I had made my intention clear -- Paul and I would prevail! I was back in class. Theo was providing joy, Paul was handling my legal strife and 4T was leading me in directions that I never dreamed possible. I did the following week's homework -- saying my "100 times" exercise, "I am prosperous beyond my wildest dreams!"

Attending class week after week, breaking down into small groups to "mastermind" at the end of each class, there were about 40 students, all HANDLING some challenge. That is why we are all here on earth -- to learn, to grow, to achieve, to bless others and to be blessed, allowing it in.

Life calmed down a bit. The hardest piece of this story was getting through the shock -- coming up with a plan and learning that "when you are going through HELL, just keep on going and smile."

Days and weeks passed. Life was okay, except for the occasional little jabs and stabs, yet my life was MUCH more than this suit. I did not want it to be the only piece of my life. I was enjoying a romance with Theo, while trusting Paul to handle the details of the lawsuit. During the course, we learned the lessons weekly -- we tithed, we cleaned the church, we gave back, we shared with our mastermind partners and we tasted prosperity -- in assigned homework lessons.

February, then March arrived. I would tell Paul, after being filled with POSITIVITY, "When we win this suit, I am going to take you on a trip. We are going to celebrate."

He was so logical. I did not see a spiritual bone in his body. Yet, he would, sort of, get onboard with my meanderings. With positivity, he was seriously answering motions and handling all that came up, with me of course.

I had mentioned to you boys, back in December, that I would love for you to find us all a cruise. That I would take us all, but that it was up to you to find us a cruise to Aruba, Barbados or Antigua -- any or all of those islands. I recall you both saying you would, but months passed and you did not do anything about it. Okay, so we will not go… whatever!

One Sunday, Paul came over to my house before dancing that evening. We had to get an entire report of my finances -- every tidbit, every dollar and every asset -- a tough assignment.

I was having an especially hard time coming up with all of the details, partially because it was so hurtful and partially because it was at the request of the opposing attorney and supposedly fair. It was so, so challenging, as I had worked so, so hard for the previous several years -- maintaining life, the rentals and investing money -- WORKING HARD, whereas your dad was not able. He wanted EVERYTHING of mine -- every penny I had earned, every inheritance I had been given – just EVERYTHING! Paul and I were to document every last cent. It was JUST NOT FAIR! However, we got together anyway for him to help me pour through my entire financial life.

We got down to work, with my tax returns and financial statements. While at my dining room table, I showed him my "bathroom books." Of course, you remember those, boys. They led to a significant unfolding in the case. In the meantime, there were several times that I would express what a kind sweet man Melvin had been and Paul would literally remind me that it was Melvin who was SUING me with such artillery, that I could literally go to jail if our case was not proven. I was in such surprise, perhaps denial. I never would have thought things would come to this.

So, here we were -- determined to save my financial life – perusing the bathroom books. We found passages that would prove that the plaintiff KNEW we had real estate. We found writings that proved that Melvin knew about our company. OOPS! BINGO! BINGO! BINGO! We found at least twenty-one documents that proved that Melvin was well-aware of the company we started and well-aware that he created the LLC's -- a term for how we set up the companies – both legally and tax wise.

To make a long story short, we had proof that I was NOT guilty for any of the charges that he had made. We had American Express statements and all kinds of proof that would eventually suggest to Mel and his attorneys that this was about to get ugly! Did they really wish to continue?

Paul and I danced that night, confident in knowing that when Melvin's attorneys saw our proof, they would cave. Meanwhile, there were decisions to be made. Mind you I feel as though I am treading on thin ice here, NOT wanting to disparage Dad and NOT wanting to hurt you boys, yet sharing, as best as I can, how this passage in my life helped me to awaken and further my faith, my destiny, see angels, restore good and live truthfully.

The 4T course continued and on March 29th, only days before the last session of the course, all the homework had been completed. I was seeing its logic and how it was helping me in life. There was a full eclipse of the moon, a somewhat rare occasion, on that day. You would find it in the almanac if you investigate.

Now mind you, Paul and I decided to send Dad's attorney half of the documents of proof we had, with a request to end this suit. They had, I think, ten days to respond. However, they responded rather quickly that they would adhere to the demands Paul was making in order to cancel and no longer go forth with this suit! On that very same day, the day of the eclipse, after the opposing attorney received Paul's notice -- about 6pm in the evening -- I received a call from Paul, "IT'S OVER!"

I said, "What?"

Paul repeated, "IT"S OVER!!!"

I screamed so loud from my office, that in addition to getting a sore throat, my neighbors heard me, wondering if everything was alright! Oh my G_d! It was better than alright. I had WON this case and was to PROSPER beyond my wildest dreams. The details are not important.

The story continues. We went to the last class a day or so later. Amongst the forty or so students, eleven of us had reports of what had occurred during this eclipse of the moon. It was uncanny that so many had had manifestations of their "ask" on that day. We each, one by one, got up in front of the others and shared what had taken place.

I recall a gal whose home had been on the market for seventeen months and who received a signed executed contract. Another gal had a soured relationship with her sibling and had manifested a reconciliation, after a twelve-year silence.

210

There was another man who had had a horrific diagnosis and later learned on that day, that his "supposed serious condition" was misdiagnosed! Then there was me. Elated to the max, I got up, sharing that I had been sued, the case ended and I prevailed "beyond my wildest dreams."

The story continues. It almost sounds made up to me, too, but it is true. I got home from class THAT day and went on the computer to check my email. When I got an email that informed me about a dance cruise – I had never received one before – I knew I must have been on some list. I opened it up and in bold letters it said, "ARUBA - DOMINICA – BARBADOS...dance cruise...December 10 – 17."

I looked up to the heavens and said aloud, "TWO OUTTA THREE AINT BAD! HOLY MOTHER!" This was shocking to me. "OH MY G_D!"

I immediately called Paul. Still crazed and filled with joy, I said, "OKAY PAUL, wanna go on that thank you Cruise with me on December tenth through the seventeenth?"

I had told him that I would take him on a dance trip when we WON the case. He didn't really pay attention to it, as we were deep in the mire of the mess when I mentioned it. NOW, case over, and he listened and asked for a few details. He was so funny - his first remark was, "What happens if I have a girlfriend at that time and cannot go?"

Grinning, I laughed and told him he could get insurance...not to worry. He said okay, so we booked separate rooms. Months later we went on the cruise, dancing our way from San Juan, from where it embarked, to Ft. Lauderdale. While we had a sweet time and it was amazing to have manifested the winning of the suit -- as well as so many other manifestations -- the last one was spectacular as well. Remember the retainer that Paul charged? It was $7500 and refundable, if he did not use it all. He used a portion of it and, almost to the exact penny, there was a balance due me. Paul sent me a check and, would you believe, it was just the amount that it cost to take us on the cruise! END OF STORY. ~Smile...

This piece of my life was amazing emotionally, financially, spiritually, romantically and intellectually, too. While it was happening, and blessedly it was almost as amazing as I have been typing it, what an abundance of signs, faith, angels, destiny, restoration, forgiveness, gratitude and more...WOW, WOW, and then some. There IS a gift in everything!!!

A Gift
In Everything

Chris and Mark - Friday the 13th 1980

I was blessed HUGELY to get a catering job from Mark and Chris - they were friends and Mark worked for the Governor's law firm. He was a very successful attorney - whom I met at my health club -- same club where I met daddy.

They married on the 13th of February, and held their reception at their home in Atlanta - a most wonderful home in a charming neighborhood.

I was totally psyched not only because they were friends, but also because the Governor would be there - and several high profile guests.

I worked like a DOG - was cooking and carrying, cleaning and more, and then two lovely young men came in to assist and help me. They were so amazing - just wanting to help me, like a damsel in distress. I was a bit new at catering and didn't have a clue how much work this job would be. Wow - talk about tired! ~

These wonderful guys carried out garbage - they packaged up left overs - they did mostly cleanup with me and wow - I had such gratitude. I was as exhausted as I was grateful for having their help.

I was also very appreciative - for having borrowed lots and lots of equipment from Rob and Steve - friends that owned Art of Catering. They prepared a great deal of the food for me/ for this job -- and they were just hugely kind to me. Silver platters, chaffeurs, serving utensils, lots of equipment. They neither charged me, nor took an inventory – They just trusted me. We continued a 14 year relationship from this job forward. NICE~!~

The night was nearing its end and most of everything was cleaned up. It had to be 1am and just some garbage to remove, and silver platters and serving pieces to be loaded back into my van.

These guys were so kind and friendly and helped me immeasurably.

They left - I tipped them and then said my goodbyes to Chris and Mark - who were now EXHAUSTED and heading to their first night together as married lovers.

I said goodbye, carried the last load to my van and hopped inside to see that there wasn't ONE piece of equipment - not a chaffeur, not a piece of silverware / NOTHING!!!!!

My stomach skipped a beat - perhaps my heart began to make up for it - and lo and behold - the realization sunk in.................I had been ROBBED!!! Not one iota of equipment and to make matters worse - it was all BORROWED!!! OH MY GOD.........Oh mon dieu - ROBBED.

I went back into the house. Mark called the police and we talked about the guys that HELPED me. "OH dear," Chris said, as she had met them on the Wednesday prior to the wedding and just invited 'em...........she'd literally met 'em on the street while walking her dog.

Oh My GOD!!!!

The police arrived - and just as they were arriving - the phone rang - it was the two guys...........

I told them that the police were heading over and they told me that they knew they'd made a bad choice. I told them I would NOT press charges if they had my STUFF IMMEDIATELY returned to me and they told me they'd be there within 5 minutes!

BIG smile. I got my equipment returned - no charges pressed - and I got THE BIGGEST tip - of MY career~!~!~!~!~!~~!

I have to say - I LOVE Friday the 13th - for me it is a LUCKY day~~

Appearances are not always what they seem to be. There IS a gift in everything!

Theresa and Negative Thinking -- 2000

I was still SMARTING from the pain and hurt that I endured during the end of my friendship with Theresa. There are a few things in life that I will never understand...perhaps upon my death, when I get to Heaven I will come to learn it all. Mom used to say that we will find EVERYTHING out when we arrive -- Kennedy's assassination, OJ (although I already know that one) and so, perhaps, I will learn what happened with Theresa.

She was my VERY best friend and she was more than any friend I could ever have imagined. She would high-tail it from Ashville for a party I was throwing or a surgery I was having. She was like a FANTASTIC Mom! She even came to our home once to visit and take care of you boys while Daddy and I were away – just so that we could get away. Not only did she take care of you guys, but she cleaned my house and purchased nicer dish towels for my arrival home. She was amazing; she was also my hero and, ridiculously, I was somewhat hers. I used to counsel her. I used to be there for her emotionally, whether it was her marriage or her Mom. Together, we had a wonderful and joyful loving relationship. I am grateful for that.

She left her marriage and there were huge 'aftershocks' from that -- from her church, her parents and everyone that knew her. She was involved with her future husband, so there was lots of SCUTTLEBUTT about HER business. I was supportive throughout the entire ordeal, when she disbanded ALL of her friends and they disbanded her. I felt so special. I felt as though she would never leave me nor I her. I took her friendship hugely seriously -- as loyal as they come. I thought that I was going to be a KEEPER.

Moving right along, she and her NEW hubby and kids came for the 2000 Millennium Celebration. I had my typical welcome poem posted for their arrival and everything was planned for the special time our families would enjoy. My entire family LOVED them all. She was your guardian, Boys -- just in case -- and we had a RICH family love. We did things, having adventures that we did not share with most anyone else.

We had all crowded into the sauna -- laughing the entire time, all eight of us and the dog, too – and we would laugh and take photos. I know you remember it well.   It was always a WONDERFUL time with her and this was no different. We played, doing gymnastics on the lawn. It still shocks me as I try to impart the meaning and the richness of our friendship...and the FUN! I am even making light of the intense and HIGHLY joyful relationship we had.

Theresa and I used to write to one another in long-hand -- letters to each other -- for years and years and years. It was a beautiful friendship and we always had a joyful time together. We stood around the front lawn as Melvin helped pack their van for their long voyage home from Orlando to Ashville. Ross took photos of Theresa and I, with our ARMS wrapped around one another. It was HER first time sharing her family -- new hubby and all -- with us...the whole family. It was so joyful and rewarding for her and me, as well. I do not recall the day of the week that they left, but it was the 2nd of January, after the BIG Millennium Celebration. They had stayed with us for about 3 days, going to Disney to celebrate bringing in the year 2000. Theresa was instructed to call me when they arrived home safely, yes, the MOMMA BEAR in me.

I did not hear from her. It was now the next day. They were due home, so I called to find out that all was well. Her son, Timothy, answered the phone. He said they were fine and "Mommy wasn't available."

"Okay Timothy, have her call when she can," I responded.

She did not. I called again, and again, and again, and again, and again. She would not get on the phone. Timothy would tell me he was sorry, but, "MOMMY COULD NOT COME TO THE PHONE!"

I was confused, perplexed, unknowing -- strange feelings, had no clue -- until I received an email the next night that shocked me as only a few shocks in my life, EVER! It said something like, "PLEASE DON"T EVER CALL ME AGAIN AND PLEASE DON'T FORCE ME TO HAVE TO CHANGE MY TELEPHONE NUMBER."

That was it. I was in my office. Do you remember exactly where you were, experiencing the shock, like we all recalled, when Kennedy Died, when OJ made the chase or when Princess Di died. I still feel the GUT punch to my stomach. I read the email again, saw the same thing and then called in Daddy and you boys. Do you guys remember? Of course you do; you too suffered a great loss. I never found out what happened. I went to the SHRINK and speculated about myself being the last vestige of her old life. I could go on and on, but there is no point.

The point was that I cried my heart out, went to a movie the next day to help HEAL my soul and selected "ANGELA'S ASHES." It was reviewed as a gloriously uplifting movie; I thought that would be perfect. I had no clue as to how to process this sadness…NONE! So Melvin and I decided a movie might lift my spirits. I went alone. It was, instead, THE NUMBER ONE DEPRESSING movie I have ever seen. Halfway through and with all of the crying I did, I realized that while DETESTING the movie, it was serving a huge benefit -- helping me to heal. I cried and cried and cried. I have never found it easy to cry and be sad. THIS got it out of me like nothing else could have.

The major gift, which I now see in enduring the sadness, was that I had Melvin and the boys to come home to and be loved. I do not know if I could have endured this without them. It has been difficult getting over romantic love alone and yet, my experience is that G_D sends angels; he sends them when you need them most. There are no accidents that new people will visit your life just when you need them. Thank you, Elaine and Alan. They were my most recent angels upon my most recent sadness.

SO, the days went on…they always do. I learned the magnificence of this betrayal, or call it what you like. It made me go out and make friends. Up until this time, January 2000, I had LITTLE interest in making friends. We had moved to Orlando in '98 and I was completely and utterly content with my friendship with Theresa and having my family. I had my ATLANTA friends and it was just peachy. After this debacle with Theresa, oh my goodness, I could not rush out fast enough to garner a few comrades. ~Smile.

I had to prove to myself that I was likeable or loveable and I did. So THANK you, THERESA for the gift of getting me to grow and make friends.

Are you wondering why the title of this story is "THERESA and NEGATIVE THINKING?" I will explain. It was several months later. I was doing well. Life was good. Friends were in the making and I went to the movies with a friend. It was some Stallone movie and it took place in the snow. There was this amazing, AWESOME woman who handled the cold and mountain climbing. While I had not given THERESA much thought, I did during this movie. My thoughts were unkind. I sat there looking at this adorable blonde in the movie-- and she reminded me of Theresa. She was cute and petite -- an amazing, enduring, resilient athlete – and I could not help but think, "Oh so you think YOU'RE so terrific. Theresa, look at her! You're no big deal!"

Negative thinking or behavior NEVER gets you anywhere, in my experience, other than to a negative place. I clearly had negative feelings. Well, I arrived home that day, and received an email from a friend of mine from Atlanta that seldom wrote to me, the SUBJECT topic was, "IS THAT YOUR FRIEND THERESA WHO IS GOING TO BE ON SURVIVOR?"

My heart dropped. Talk about a gazillion emotions, one being JEALOUSY, this was NOT good. I opened up the email and it read something like, "There's this show on -- Survivor -- with a cute blond gal from Ashville, known as Theresa and I wondered if THAT was YOUR friend Theresa?"

My heart dropped again. Oh my G_D, could that be MY THERESA? YES, she was going to be one of the contestants…oh my jealous heart! Months later, after all of my friends from around the country would write to me and tell me how excited they were for me, having THERESA, my dearest friend be on the show, I could not stand it. I could not watch it and I certainly could not tell anyone that she THREW ME away. It was agony. And then, she won! She won the million dollars! I saw her face on every magazine and news report. Oh my, talk about in my face.

I recall friends telling me their entire TOWN was praying for her because THEY knew someone who knew someone who knew Theresa.

I wonder if they knew how horribly mean it was of her to abandon me and not even tell me why, IF they would have prayed for her? What does it matter? What matters NOW is did I learn anything; did it grow my soul; did it bless me in any way? Of course it did! It makes me wonder how those in Hollywood feel -- when they see their lost, beloved, engaged or succeeding or something revealed in their face. It was, to me, NO ACCIDENT, no coincidence. I still have not figured out all of the emotions, unfoldings and lessons. Yet I have taken much away that has GROWN my soul and taught me. I know that out of adversity come many wonderful gifts. I also believe more than ever that PRAYER works.

Melvin and I got to change our guardians. I got to make local, dear friends. I got to see my humility and humanity. I endured something so terribly difficult, I learned that I can heal. So it fortifies you to endure. What doesn't KILL us, makes us stronger. Amen and thank you, G_D. I surmise there are many gifts here -- of faith, of hope and of angels – and some that I will still gather as the years pass, such as compassion and forgiveness.

 Angels

Angels Just When You NEED 'em...Nellie -- 1970

A reason, a season, a lifetime...

Nellie had surely come into my life for a reason...no doubt.

I was 18 years old and had spent the day at Jones Beach looking rather tan and sexy in my WHITE man-tailored shirt. I was meeting my two guy friends in BROOKLYN. I think I had been to Brooklyn once, but NEVER on my own. It was FAR for me. I had to take the Roslyn Railroad, then change trains in Jamaica and then meet Mark and Manny for a fun evening. I had known them from Camp. I was all dressed and hair in place...jewelry...looking my prettiest! They were older than I and I so enjoyed their parties and company.

I got onto the wrong train and ended up in Bedford Stuyvesant. The neighborhood was so packed with crime -- murders and rapes -- that the telephone company never serviced the phones in the booths, because it was such a crime ridden neighborhood. Sadly, the AT&T workers refused to go to those neighborhoods. As soon as the train stopped and I had to get off, I KNEW I was in the wrong place. All I saw were black men, liquor stores and derelict-looking folk. Bravely, but underneath a bunch afraid, -- as night had fallen -- I walked into the liquor store and asked how I could get to where I was supposed to. The mean-looking man behind the counter did not have 2 seconds for me...end of story. I went out onto the street and looked for a phone booth. I had the dime or the quarter -- I think it was a dime then to make a call and yet NONE of the phones worked. I didn't know what to do. I did not have much money on me, could NOT find a taxi and so, I went back into the train station. I literally tried to flag down police cars that passed and NONE stopped for me.

I was DISTRAUGHT, ignoring all of the looks. I was THE only white person probably in the entire train station. I kid you not and I felt like an eyesore. I was stared at with a knowing that most were thinking, "What is SHE doing here?" and some that were thinking of me like we think of turkey on Thanksgiving, "I can't wait to dig in!"

221

Oh dear, dear! I was so, so, so, so scared and out of my element. Just then, this little old black lady walked by and asked me if I needed help. I burst into tears and told her I was lost. She already knew that. I told her I did not have much money to take lots more trains and all she did was tell me NOT TO WORRY -- that she would help me. She rather looked like SHE could have used help. ~Smile.

Long story short...she put me on THE correct train, helped me with a few dollars and I think saved my life. She even told me that she would go home and call my friends Mark and Manny and tell them exactly where to pick me up -- that I was on my way. I requested her address, to send her the money back and a gift as well. I purchased Estee Lauder cologne, wrapped it up, enclosed a heartfelt letter and sent it a few days later, after a wonderful evening with Mark and Manny. They ended up DRIVING me home to Roslyn, Long Island.

I still have the letter, with the package of perfume, money and note. It was returned to me...there was no Nellie at the address she had given me / No sign of any Nellie and THE package was sent back to me..............no thanks needed.   She was clearly my angel. Thank you and bless you, Nellie! You protected me and sent me on my way to a sweet life -- wayyyyyyyyyyyyyyyy back then!

Vietnam 1978

It was amazing how I LOVED, LOVED, LOVED my visit to Vietnam in February. I loved being with you, Ross, I loved the country, the shopping, the beauty and the people. They were so cute. I took a photo of myself and 5 women. Each one in the photo was a good 18 - 24 inches shorter than I. ~Smile. It was not always joy like that, as I had a major horrible time with a little Vietnamese gal once -- majorly challenging.

I decided to move to Atlanta, leaving New York, and from how this huge move was unfolding, it seemed very BESHERT and BLESSED. Everything was just fitting into place -- to the point where I left New York without a job awaiting me and during the course of my travel down to Atlanta, a job was offered me. I will explain. It was SOOOOOOOOOO MEANT TO BE! I had been working for the Blood Program in New York as a "BLOOD CONSULTANT." It was a fancy name for those of us who recruited corporations to hold blood drives. I liked my job, but just liked the idea of MOVING out of NEW YORK even better. `I tried to leave New York for 4 years. It was too cold, too crowded and too not like how I wanted to spend my adult life. I traveled around the country, much like Melvin and I did, when we knew it was time to leave Atlanta.

However, I was alone, very afraid and EVERY time I would venture to another city, I would GET FAT -- well NOT fat, but I would pack on 10 pounds and hate myself. I ate away the fear and apprehension and would sabotage myself. I did not have what it took to make this huge move as a single gal, or so I thought.

My friends used to tell me to "HANG OUT" at the airport and meet a man from another city who will sweep you off your New York feet and plant you where he lives. Trust me, I might have tried, except that I finally got the courage myself in 1978. I did it! I moved my life and it was no small feat.

I drove my way down over a period of 3 weeks from New York City to Atlanta, Georgia. I made a 2-week stop in Durham, North Carolina, where I would go for REINFORCEMENT for my eating challenges. My GURU, Joe, was there and I decided to spend 2 weeks just fortifying myself, seeing friends and eating healthfully. While there, I received a call from The Red Cross Blood Program in Atlanta. They had heard that I was moving there and contacted me to offer me a job. Talk about faith. I think when you follow your dreams and step out in faith, the good Lord supplies. Here I was, having LEFT NY without a job and finding myself on an airplane from Durham to Atlanta to interview for a job -- a total surprise.

Wanna hear amazing? Something I could not have dreamed of, in my wildest dreams, I interviewed with CHET, a lovely man, and was offered the job. Then he threw in all of my moving expenses as a benefit, as well as 2 weeks in the Ramada Inn, up the block from the Red Cross. I felt like I had died and gone to Heaven. HOLY MOTHER, no job worry any longer and no housing fears for the first 2 weeks. WHAT A SIGN from the universe that I had done the right thing. I was immersed in joy, as I had not had the loveliest of good-byes from my dad. He imparted HUGE guilt to me. His last words, when he said goodbye that morning that I left 54th street in Cleo, my car, were, "I don't know how you could do this to your Mother!"

Holy S&*t! What a rotten person I was and what a send-off that WASN'T! Anyway, back to the joy and YES, I forgive you Dad. I know it was YOUR way of expressing the sadness of me leaving…the tears well. So here I am, getting the green lights, going ahead and flying out of Atlanta back to Durham -- job in hand, moving expenses paid and now heading on down to 'Lanna, GOOOGIA for my next 'chapter'.

I think I am having an out of body experience as I type. I am making the effort in having the reality that all of the above was MY life and here I am, some 35 years later, remembering every last detail of this time. I am so EMOTIONALLY intense at this moment, I cannot imagine this journey any better than how it has been. I am too emotional for words.

There is success, there is fear, there is courage and blessedly, I am able to FINALLY write it all down as if I am living TODAY with a sweeter understanding of all that has occurred in my past. It is an awesome feeling. It just is! I cannot explain it! I want to finish THIS story! I do not know what my hurry is, but 'Hurry' is my writing name these days.

So, where was I in my stream of consciousness? I remember learning that in school. Okay, so, I get to Atlanta and all is well. I check into the Ramada, right there off of 85. I go to work each day and I am grateful beyond 'beyond.' I am doing my walking, eating correctly, doing and utilizing all the skills I learned in Durham -- making a clean break with a new and wonderful life. Chet is pleased and I am learning my way around Atlanta.

Each night I ended up eating in the Ramada coffee shop and most nights, there was this lovely little waitress who had become my friend. Her name was TEENY. She was a mere 80 pounds, if that much and very friendly. One day she offered to have me move in with her. She lived very close to the Red Cross. I was tickled and delighted. I went to see her small apartment in what, I later learned, was the very Spanish and Vietnamese part of town. But I did not care; I was just CERTAIN that this additional piece of the happy puzzle of my life was falling into place. I moved in and, literally, walked to work.

I came home from work one afternoon and while passing the dumpster -- that BIG green, huge dumpster -- I noticed, on top of it, a container that was similar to mine, holding a few pieces of fish and various other edibles. It reminded me TOTALLY of everything that I had put into her freezer. I literally did a double take; it was uncannily similar to MY stuff. I walked into the apartment and looked in the freezer and all of MY stuff was missing. Why, that WAS my stuff. I had NO clue why MY food was perched atop the DUMPSTER. Teeny was not home, so I could not inquire as to what it was doing outside. I figured there was a good reason -- benefit of the doubt thinking.

I went to sleep that night on the sofa, as my bed and belongings had not yet been released from the storage that the movers had secured for me. Teeny was working the night shift.

When she arrived home, I was sound asleep. Awakened by HER PLOPPING down alongside me, sleeping on the couch, I was a bit perplexed, annoyed and CURIOUS as to why she would awaken me. It must have been 2 AM and I had to be at work at 6:30 AM.

I was a bit unnerved; my first thought was that she was a lesbian. I had NO IDEA what to make of this. We talked for a few moments and she let me to go back to sleep.

I did not see her for a few days. Our schedules were totally opposite of one another and yet, it was now Saturday and she was home. She appeared a bit reserved; I figured, perhaps, she was in a LOW mood and I just did my thing. We were not there to be great buddies; I just needed a place that was convenient and she needed an additional source of funds – a perfect liaison, NOT! She sat down at the kitchen table where I was sewing something for repair and she began taking a pin and sticking it in her arm. Yes, you heard me correctly, literally sticking pins in her arms. I was freaked out!

Now I began to worry, as not only was she behaving HUGELY strange, BUT it was becoming extremely cold in the apartment. I was freezing, as it was snowing outside and the temperature had dropped -- a rare, but occasional occurrence in Atlanta. And here, extremely cold, I looked at the thermostat in the apartment and it had been turned WAYYYYYYYY down low. I moved it up to a typical 78 degrees or so and began warming up. Here I was blessedly getting warmer, while outside, the snow was getting deeper.

Well, it literally was turning into the 'BLIZZARD of '78' and here I was, thinking something awry is occurring. I called my mom. She was concerned. I told her all the CRAZY stuff that was going on and she asked me about that lady, MARSHA, whose name I had been given while in Durham. You see, I met THELMA, who was an overweight lady, dieting in Durham. She told me about her daughter and son-in-law, Marsha and Fred, who lived in Atlanta and that I ought to call them and introduce myself. I told my mom about them and my mom told me to call them to see what they said about what was happening. I even gave Mom their telephone number.

I called Marsha and Fred. They were concerned; it seemed VERY weird to be sticking needles in one's arms, as well as the food on the dumpster and the visit in the middle of the night. I gave Marsha Mom's number. Perhaps the storm was unnerving me and making me wise to know that the phones could go out.

I do not recall, other than it was a BAD blizzard. Then I decided to leave the apartment. I slipped and slid my way to the parking lot, got into my car and literally could NOT start the car. The snow was piling up, the ice was forming and the city was turning white.

I do not exactly remember what happened next, but I ended up calling the police. I needed to get out of there, so I made an emergency call. Finally they arrived and actually FELT bad for me. While they told me it would be wise to get out of there, I complained that I had tried and would they please take me to a hotel. They refused, saying it was not their job and that no crime had been committed. Oh my petrified heart!

I do not recall what Teeny was doing when they arrived, but I do recall it annoyed her -- and so BAD got even worse. Here I was wearing my fur coat indoors. Teeny moved the temperature down again, but this time to NOTHING -- NO heat. It was uncomfortable, to say the least. It was scary, cold and I did not have a clue what to do. Here I was in Atlanta, hardly knowing anyone and not knowing whom to reach out to. I called MOM again, to tell her what happened with the police, etc. and I do not recall exactly how it happened, but Teeny cut the phone cord with a garden scissors, so now I was cut off from Mom. Panic! PANIC! Petrified, LITERALLY, to death and leaving the thermostat alone while getting as far away from Teeny as possible, I felt she was like a 'crazy woman.'

I do not recall anything but fear until a short while later when there was a knock at the door -- rather a bang. There were two men -- men I had never seen before. Who were they? I opened the door, welcoming WHOEVER they were. Low and behold, one was Fred, Marsha's husband and the other was Mike, Mike Keone, Fred's across-the-street neighbor in Dunwoody. He worked for the GBI the Georgia Bureau of Investigation -- like the FBI, but state-wide. Because he held that job, he had CHAINS on his car tires. Fred and Marsha had plotted with my mom, knowing that I was in danger, so Fred called Mike. Together, they made the trek through the 'Blizzard of '78...to rescue ME!

Their car was parked in front of the apartment, a ground floor unit that opened directly on those parking spaces that are diagonal. There sat MY immobile car and theirs, equipped with chains, with the motor running. While FRED and MIKE carried my suitcases, TV and whatever else I had in the two-story townhouse, they instructed me to HOLD THE DOOR OPEN, as Teeny would have locked us out.

I stood there holding the door open, watching these two strangers, saviors, walk in and out of the apartment carrying my belongings. We moved -- THEY moved me -- my belongings out into Mike's car, put me in the back seat and we were on our way.

Just like that...I am crying now and I do not think I ever cried as hard while it was all happening. I was stoically shocked just IN the experience, rather than having any perspective to see how ridiculous, scary and horrible it was. To think the blizzard of the decade, LITERALLY, go look it up -- February 4, 1978, and I will never forget, here I was embroiled in this horror.

They drove from Lindberg all the way up to Dunwoody. Several years later, Melvin and I would move into that very neighborhood. Amazing, perhaps, but many years later than THAT, I would go and visit Vietnam. Who woulda thought? We all walked up to the front door of Marsha and Fred's home, where I was met by Marsha and her two young daughters. Wow, would I love to see them now! As I write these stories, I have a major yearning to share with the PLAYERS – the characters in the stories. While I have connected with some, more recently to thank them AGAIN, there are those whose names and addresses I have lost, perhaps I will do my darnedest to find them once this book is complete.

So, as the story continues, I was introduced to them for the very first time and here I was MOVING in with them. Karen and Lisa were the girls' names. They were about 10 and 12 years old, they brought me upstairs and showed me MY room. It was all adorned with pillows, towels and preparations for a LOVING, dear friend/guest and here I was a total stranger. There was a bond there, an alliance from having dieted with their Mom and Granny in Durham. What a gift this family was.

Well, I am of the belief that one ought to never stay in a friend's home for more than a couple of days. Like FISH, you know that saying, they start to stink after a few days. I was there for three weeks, YES, YOU HEARD ME, THREE weeks. I literally went out EVERY morning and every night looking for the right and perfect apartment. While that was easy to find, I had to wait until the month began -- March 1. So Marsha and Fred refused to let me move out to another hotel and to just stay there. I was not in their way. OH MY G_D, OH MY STRESS, OH MY -- challenges to hang and not get in their way.

They could not have been kinder and I could not have been more gracious. Every night I either brought home a dessert, flowers or a bottle of wine -- SOMETHING to show my gratitude and have them NOT hate me for getting in their space. I was so comforted, yet so UNCOMFORTABLE. I do NOT like to wear out my welcome.

Fred, during this time, lost his job as a RICHWAY manager. So the stress was high, surely for them, for me and for the girls. What a time this was. Too funny, while out of work, he decided to build a closet off of the kitchen with his bare hands and so talk about stress!! MARSHA, in the meantime, was THE mildest-mannered, calmest, most collected woman I think I have ever met. Perhaps she just wanted to scream about the noise from Fred -- building and getting dust in her kitchen -- yet polite, calm and mannerly were her middle names.

I went apartment shopping each day and each night. I did my walking and got to work every day at 6:30 AM. Here I was, a NEW RECRUIT. I surely had to prove myself and be all that they thought. They were literally paying for my move, my lodging, etc., and I had a job to perform. I was ON task and yet, the stress was getting to me. I had to be SOOOOOOOOO gentle and that was NOT me, maybe a little. ~Smile. Well, the day came. I found the apartment in the same complex, where some years later -- 4 to be exact – I would meet your dad, fall in love and eventually move up to Dunwoody. Who woulda thought. I moved into Destiny Valley Apartments. In the meantime, Marsha okayed the complex. She was such a gift -- a smart, Yiddisher kop (head). So on March 1, I said my goodbyes, met the movers from storage, as well as drove the multiple trips from Marsha and Fred's and began to create a new dwelling for myself with a new life.

I had to go back to Teeny's, as there were still some belongings there, but I kept getting NO answer when I would call. One day I drove to the apartment complex and went to see the Apartment's complex manager. She greeted me with an, "OH, YOU are ARIEN?"

Hmmmmmmm, how did she know me? That was the name that Teeny had given her, when she informed her that her 'friend' Arien was moving in to take care of her. You see, Teeny had been at Northside Psychiatric Ward after lighting multiple almost-fires in her unit. Her boyfriend at the time, upon her release, was taking care of her until HE abandoned her.

She begged the apartment manager to let her continue to reside there, with the understanding that her friend, Arien, was going to be there to live with her and take care of her.

OH MY G_D, I did not know that. I did not know squat. I literally had a certifiably crazy woman that I was living with, that I had no idea about, WHATSOEVER!

Well, the happy ending is that I got out of there with my life intact, with a little help from a few dear friends. I even knew THEN that they were ANGELS! We continued our friendship for MANY, MANY, years. Another beautiful unfolding of this story is that after Fred lost his job, he and Marsha went into business together. They created a store called 'SOUTHERN LINEN OUTLET.' It was a little hole in the wall on Jimmy Carter Boulevard and so I shopped there to WARDROBE my bed linens and towels etc. They turned this little pitsky store into 13 LINEN SUPERSTORES all over Georgia, until they were bought out by Linens and Things. They became MULTI-MULTI gazillionaires. I will tell you this, not to impress, but rather to share, that we have no clue what G_D has in store for us. What might look BAD, like getting FIRED from a job, can turn out to be just MAGICAL, as it was for Fred and Marsha.

What began as a nightmare for me with Teeny, turned out to provide me with Angels that I still feel blessed by some 35 years later...and so much more. They were the ones that gave me the TIP to purchase a fabulous stock, YES, Home Depot. So, faith, angels, restoration and a trip to Vietnam with a compassionate heart, I remain full of understanding, forgiveness and gratitude.

What a sweet treat! You boys were asked to enter a contest back in 1994 – "Why is your Mommy Special?" And you won! I received a gift certificate for $75 to a neat little jewelry store. Do you remember? Well here is what you said; it is too adorable. I get joy EVERYTIME I read it; you will too!

Ross wrote, "I am nine. I love her so much. My love for her takes up the whole universe, a lot more than that. If there were 30,000 moms in the whole entire world and I had a day with each of them, I would definitely pick her because she loves me that most and I love her the most. She takes me out to the movies, Dave and Busters, bowling, arcade, roller and ice skating. She gives me a good home, bed, food, supplies, and toys, she constantly gives me presents. She gives me a good school, good teacher, and a good brain. She teaches me a lot of helpful stuff too, not just regular subjects but other things that I need even more. She teaches me self-respect and self-discipline. She helps me with balance like not too much television.

She also helps me with my money and bank account. She helps me with my health so I stay healthy and strong. She never forces me to do anything I don't want to do. She gets me a great temple. She helps me with the homework that I get from school and temple. She helps me make great decisions. And you signed it Ross Mallin. OH MY GOODNESS! How amazingly mature, Ross! Can you believe it? And I never forced you to do anything? WOW! What a mom! ~Smile.

Andrew wrote in a bit of broken English, but I shall write it exactly as it was printed in The Times. My mom is speshul because about mothers day -
Dear Mom I love you very very moch (then a heart) I now I love you more then you love (heart) me cuse you are the shon shin of my life. Because you take me to dteos and movis and david busters. I skating that stuf sweemen and all that stuf
You make me so hoppy avry sekind of a sentiermeter. She gives me ice cream to - She loves me - candyand a short that I am weoring right now. And I love all that presents that you gave to me an dyou wont no how much I love you and I rely rely epresheate it. If sunbody took you away from me I wood beet the hell out of the guy - Andrew Mallin age 7.

Could you read it? Can you believe how adorable it was. They surely have warmed my heart, then AND now. Thank you boys; you made being your mom the greatest joy of my life and you continue to do so, AMEN! MUAH!

The Coffee Ground – 1996

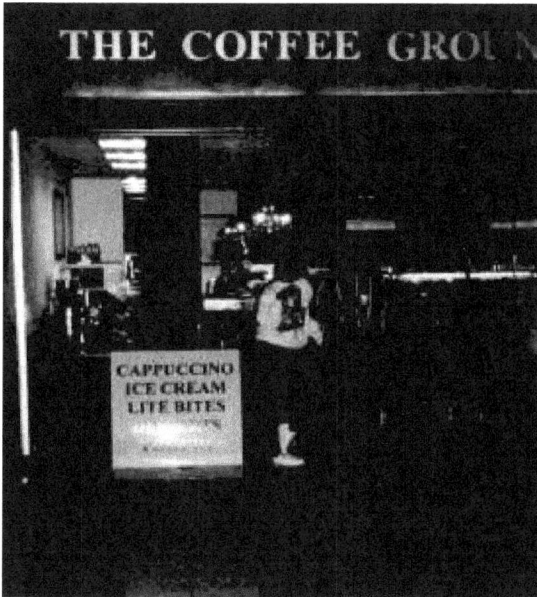

I had just completed my career life as a caterer and had no other business ideas on the horizon. I had gotten to the point where even the BEST nanny could not MOTHER the way that I intended and it was nearly impossible to find a decent, kind and honestly good nanny. It was obvious to me that it was time for me to curtail my business life and get more entrenched in my raising two active sons -- Ross and Andrew. I became the NANNY. I recall MASTERMINDING and praying for the 'right and perfect' nanny - and I'd get the gut feeling that I was SHE. ~Smile.

I hung out with you boys. Every day we would go to the mall, Dave and Busters, swimming…you name it. Although I loved it, I was also in need of something else to stimulate me. Greg, my accountant of 11 years, called me one day and suggested that WE become partners in a coffee house business endeavor. We had discussed the idea greatly as we saw Starbucks having huge successes out in Seattle and figured we could get in on an early trend of coffee drinking.

We got serious and met consistently at Perimeter Mall. We juggled ideas back and forth, with names and specifics for our upcoming venture together. By November, we had worked out a partnership. Greg had been immersed in building Subway stores and ICBY (I Can't Believe It's Yogurt) stores. He had a great 'extra' to offer me...his partner/ as he had been building these stores for a few years, and had found huge success. He had the knowledge of how to build a store down to the finest details. He also knew some excellent contractors and even knew some POWERS that BE - at the mall where we built our store. We had all the essentials at our disposal to parlay this venture into building a GREAT coffee house and getting in early on the coffee wave.

Feeling ever so THRILLED and FLATTERED that he would want ME as his partner, we began by giving our upcoming enterprise a name. I named the store, having been a copywriter at one time, THE COFFEE GROUND. I thought this would be a clever name. We envisioned COFFEE GROUNDS all over the city. This one, the first of its kind, would take place in the Galleria Mall, just across from the movie theatres. What a location! Thrilled to no end, we began planning and worked fastidiously on the colors, designs, tables, chairs, menus and contractors. It was a marvelous learning experience. The only challenge was that it was November/December and Greg, having been an accountant, found less and less time for us to build out the store. It became MY baby and I had LESS of a clue as to how to build a restaurant than how to have a baby. One was natural; one was surely not.

Day after day I would go to the mall. The decisions and build out were becoming more and more expensive and timely. I had major decisions to make. I was handling it well, quite frankly, until I began having to get the construction crew to LISTEN UP. Greg had worked with these guys several times and when I would walk in and mention, "This needs to be green, this needs to be carved, etc., etc.," I would get a blank stare from the owner of the construction company. His name was Richard. I would mention again what needed to be done and I would get no response.

Finally, having to ask Richard if he heard what I was saying, his response was, "I'll talk to the boss," and he would ignore me and surely make it clear he had NO respect for me. I would, on the other hand, try to make it clear that I WAS THE BOSS and that he needed to follow my instructions. Mind you - Greg and I were 50/50 partners - ONE BIG LESSON I LEARNED. ALWAYS be a 51% partner - NEVER the other way around - or else skip partnerships entirely - mine was NOT a good experience and then again - it was THE best business experience I could have ever dreamed of learning - still it hurt.

After each time of complete and utter disrespect -- a litany of calls back and forth to Greg like a whining wife would ensue. Finally, Greg would have to stop what he was doing -- his accounting -- and come to the store location. He would walk in and repeat EXACTLY what I had requested of Richard. Richard would respond, "Yes Boss!" right in front of me -- I guess for effect! Errrrrrrggggggghghhhhh!!!

Then we would have another major decision and I, of course, was handling it all. It was CRUNCH time before taxes, so Greg was hardly available and I would have the exact same situation over and over - telling my hired help what I wanted and needed and each time - Richard made it clear that he had NO respect for me and would NOT take orders from me. I would whine to Greg, be totally frustrated with great angst, and then walk in the door at home and Melvin would want to know all of the details. He was usually HUGELY supportive…TOTALLY, as a matter of fact. Yet, during this 'situation,' he was even MORE frustrated than I was.

I would tell you boys, as well as Dad, a moment by moment explanation and description of my day. While you would mostly comfort me, Daddy would get all HOT UNDER THE COLLAR and literally go through his own frustrations, making it seem as if he were angry with me. Andrew, I recall you once saying to your dad, "Daddy, leave Mommy alone. She just slayed the dragons all day!"

We all had to laugh. Thank you Andrew! Yes, we were all quite frustrated and yet it was what it was.

The store opened In February to a resounding success. The entire movie population came to taste our brews -- Caffeinated, Decaf, Espresso, Latte and all the newest terms and concoctions. We were in our glory and went home exhausted and thrilled. However, we had to make a stop first --late, late, late into the evening. Do you boys remember where we went before heading home? I bet you do not. It was the FIRE STATION.

During the course of the evening, sweet little Andrew wandered off to the Ruby Tuesday restaurant -- right next to us in the mall -- and was lighting matches. Yes, most every restaurant had matches at the counter and our little Andrew decided to experiment. Oh my worried mothering heart. Melvin was mad, I was scared and Ross was tired and wanted to go HOME. No way was I not handling THIS crisis. We decided to take a ride to our local fire precinct. We pulled up and spoke to this fireman who assured ME that Mel was taking the MAN position -- being PISSED at his child. I was taking the nurturing, yet scared position, fearing for his safety and Andrew was creating great chaos. The kind fireman took Andrew aside and had a good chat with him, then sent us all home, to get back to THE COFFEE GROUND early the next morning. It was a huge success. The first dollar hung proudly on the wall.

The following months did NOT go as 'swimmingly.' There were several thefts. My partner was not keeping his agreements, as to being responsible for who would WORK the store. We had hired a manager. He soon became frustrated with taking orders from my partner's son, who was NOT his boss. The dysfunction within the store with its 4 employees and 2 owners was HORRIFIC. I was petrified. I had gotten into this deal with a man I used to go to for wisdom and guidance about finances. Here I was funding a dysfunctional coffee house and much of the dysfunction was due to him. I had no one to go to.

I even had a panic attack -- my one and only in my entire life. My heart was racing as I lay in bed, thinking about the $100,000 plus that Greg and I were responsible for, if we were to break our 3-year lease. Perhaps your dad remembers when I called him at work and suggested that we move to Mexico...and quick.

(TOO FUNNY -- while editing and rereading / I'm now LAUGHING - and yet at the time - it was NOT funny!) I could not imagine having to pay that kind of money to the mall, when we had worked so hard. Here we were about to lose EVERYTHING that we had worked for, because others were irresponsible. It was NOT fair.

Daddy came home. I so clearly remember. He was sitting on the bed, while I was crying and breathing heavily, telling me, "We are NOT having to move to Mexico."

I swear, I was so crazed that I would have, rather than give up $100,000 plus! Oh my goodness…desperate measures…NOW rather comical. I kept pouring money into the shop and it was NOT doing well -- a consideration I had NEVER even thought of. All we did while building the store was 'count the money' we would soon be making. Little did I know, in a VERY humbling way, this was going to become a HUGE failure. I do not believe I ever failed at anything, which I had poured my heart and soul into, and I surely did such with this enterprise. It got to the point where I was finally forced to see a business broker and sell my shares of the business. I was no longer going to put forth another nickel into this venture.

My partner, blessedly, when he saw that I meant business, decided to BUY me out. YIPPEE! HALLELUAH! -- and then some! I drove a HARD bargain and fortunately I can say I got EVERY penny back from my investment -- YIPPEE again -- and not a nickel less. While it took two years to cash his checks, I got it ALL back and then some. On a lighter note, I put into the contract that I would be entitled to ALL THE FROZEN yogurt, sugary and sugar free, that I wanted during the "LIFE OF THE STORE."

I used to go to the Coffee Ground on my own while you boys were in school and sometimes make the trip with the two of you. We would go with huge plastic containers and fill one with regular yogurt and one for MOMMY, with the sugar-free. We walked into the store and received all kinds of dirty looks. Then, I proceeded to go behind the COUNTER, that I had purchased and built, and retrieve yogurt from the machines and then WALK out. What a treat that was!

That lasted for almost 6 months, until the store went under. Yes, it closed -- end of story -- OR SO I THOUGHT! Here it was, 6 months later. I received a call from Richard, the owner of the construction firm. He shared with me that I had an unpaid bill totaling about $10,000 and he wanted his money! What? What $10,000? He told me that certain bills were not paid and that THIS was my share -- still owing. Shocked, to say the least, I had a most unsettled sleepless night. This was 6 months later.

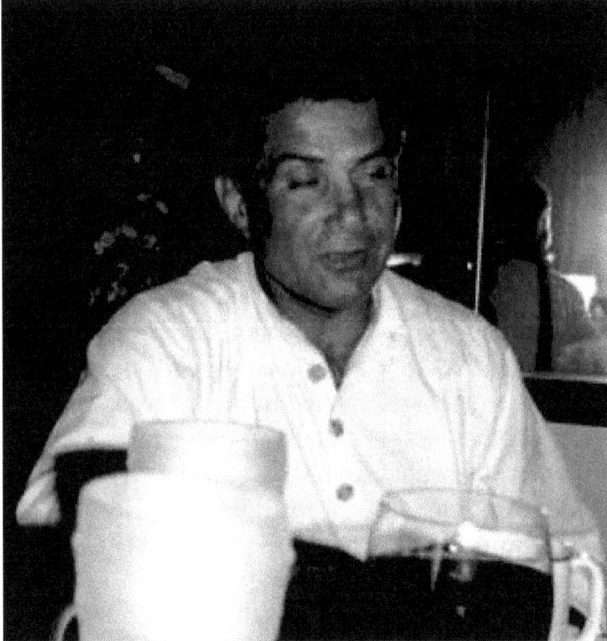

Looking back - I'd have to say that Richard was bullying me! I went to sleep that night, prayed hugely and asked G_d to tell me -- WHOM to call...what to do. I mentioned in my prayer that I would be grateful to awaken in the AM with the right and perfect person in my mind, to call to help me. I awakened the next morning with the name John -- my dear friend, whom I had met at Toastmasters. He, at one time, owned Cheese and Steak Restaurants throughout the entire country. He was a millionaire and then some -- an Israeli guy -- and had become our family friend. He was brilliant beyond brilliant!

So I gave John a call. I was rather upset and John listened to my every word and fear. He suggested that we make an appointment to meet Richard at The Galleria, as soon as I could schedule it. I called Richard and told him that I wanted to meet and discuss this bill. He was more than available to meet with me. I first met with John (oh, how my heart is still singing about our meeting -- THANK YOU JOHN!). John and I discussed the situation for 15 minutes before Richard was to appear and John told me to basically sit and be still -- to just let HIM take care of it!

WOW! I loved THAT BIG Daddy feeling – LOTS! ~Smile. I introduced the two of them. John was introduced as my consultant/business manager. He and Richard were quite cordial. Oh how I will never forget, they began chatting about building, housing and family. I sat there smiling for the most part leisurely, while the two of them were becoming FAST friends. 10 minutes…15 minutes…30 minutes and they were still 'shooting the sh%$!' I began getting a tad bit impatient. I THOUGHT we were going to figure out how to get rid of this bogus charge and here I was, listening to these GOOD OLE BOYS having a merry time bonding.

I started to squirm, but I kept my mouth shut. I was almost ready to GET THIS MEETING STARTED! I was becoming more and more uncomfortable, as I felt like an intruder on a GREAT joyful conversation between Richard and John. STILL, I kept my mouth shut. About 40 minutes later (what seemed like a lifetime), John said, "Okay, so I understand you did some work for Adrian and that you've not been paid."

I could see the joy on Richard's face. He had won John over and NOW he was FINALLY going to get paid. I sat there thinking, "WHAT THE HELL IS GOING ON?"

The next thing I know, John says to Richard, "Okay, I hear you. Just give me the construction work records and we can surely work this out."

Dumbfounded, Richard said, "What records?"

Very kindly John answered, "You know, the hourly records for the plumber, the electricians, the build outs and the carpentry -- the daily work records."

Stammering and stuttering, Richard shyly mentioned that he had no records of that kind. "Not to worry," replied John.

Here I am thinking, "WHY THE HELL NOT TO WORRY! GET 'EM!"

Richard, on the other hand, was taking a major sigh of relief, when John brings out the big guns, "Well, of course you have the bank account records specifically for the Coffee Ground. Let me see those."

Now Richard was really squirming, "I only had ONE bank account for all HIS business." He was referring to Greg - as he'd built out the Subway and ICBY stores.

"WHAT?" John now was coming in for the kill. "One bank account? Are you telling me you did all your business with ALL of Greg's stores thru ONE account? Do you mean to tell me that you didn't create a bank account strictly for the Coffee Ground?"

John, escalating his voice, was transforming from Jekyll to Hyde. Now I'm seeing some action and beginning to LOVE every moment of it! This was better than Super Bowl Sunday, tied in the last quarter with 2 minutes to go and your team on the 10 yard line, possibly making the winning touchdown. Hey boys, how do you like my analogy? I sort of do NOT have a clue what I am talking about when it comes to FOOTBALL, but I know that YOU know! ~Smile. So, Richard was really feeling the intense heat now! I was literally watching him sweat. John is taking the team over the finish line and just getting started! I was just sitting there watching this amazing and brilliant master go in for checkmate, while keeping MY mouth 100% shut -- not bad for YOUR mom! ~Smile.

John, now stating in a rather authoritative and commanding voice, "YOU EITHER GET ME THE WORK RECORDS and BANK ACCOUNT HISTORY or cease any and all contact with my client! Do you understand me?"

With that, he literally SLAMMED his hand down on the table! I jumped, but only meagerly, compared to the jumping up and down AFTER the meeting was over. Richard excused himself and walked away with his tail between his legs. John preened like a peacock making a feathery mating call. I had pep and energy in my step, as if I had won the lottery!

I basically had, in so many respects. I no longer was going to be bullied, I was NOT going to be $10,000 poorer and I was befriended by a kind, benevolent soul. Thank you G_d for my faith, as well as the Angel that you sent to me! Wow! What a joyful unfolding – "It ain't over 'til it's over!" Never put a period where a comma belongs...UNTIL now!

As an aside boys - I am rereading right now - and I had to laugh out loud - I almost want to insist that we read this one together. It IS such a litany of emotions - I was laughing and rooting for John - while ending the story with Tears in my eyes - oh G_D - life is good - thank you G_D. I wonder IF I will ever have perfect faith - I doubt it - and yet all things are possible with G_D. How looking back on this MOST NIGHTMARISH business situation in my entire life - taught me more lessons - I cannot even begin to express. I am thrilled beyond my wildest imaginings to consider that these stories might well uplift your souls / even though you will have your own trials and tribulations - G_D BLESS YOU BOTH - thank you for letting me share~

One of the Sweetest Gifts I Have Ever Received -- Andrew --
2001 -- Angel JOY

This gift has been on my desk for some 12 years; my how time flies. It is faded and a bit ragged, even rusty where the staple is. Might you remember it Andrew? You wrote it back in 2001, in celebration of my 49th birthday. I will quote what you wrote, as it will have a different meaning from when you wrote it at 13 years of age.

It is a compilation of 29 pages written on the back of scratch paper that you had, with the logo "A Memo From Andrew Mallin." You WROTE me a birthday gift, of course you remember; it was a synopsis of MY life as your mom. I am more than proud and more than grateful to share what you wrote, for it means sooooooooooo much to me. I will cry as I type.

I love you. I hope you enjoy this and Happy 39th birthday. Love, Andrew (cutiebatooch).

I meant
39th year

ha ha ha
ha ha
ha ha ha
ha ha
ha

It is titled 1st Hour. You were born and there was no turning back. You were named Adrian Meyer Mallin (the baby).

1st Year. You were leaning how to walk and how to whine when you wanted something. You were getting the gist of life. Wake up, cry have breakfast take a nap be changed and so on (the infant).

3rd Year. You could walk. You were learning how to be potty trained and not do in your diaper. You could talk. Sometimes you'd mumble but your mommy and daddy would understand. Everything you saw you had to touch or put in your mouth (the young'un).

5th year. You could walk and even run. You were getting ready for pre-school. You wanted all the Barbie's and all the teddy bears. You got pictures taken of you. To be put on the New York Taxi cabs (the young child).

8th Year. You started 2nd grade. You also started homework. You loved it. You also started allowance. You were wondering who ever invented this was a genius (the child).

10th year. You started the 4th grade. This is when you needed the cool shoes. Awesome backpack and the new addition of Barbie and Ken (the double digits).

12th year. You started sixth grade. This is when you went home, threw all the Barbie's in the attic and pulled out the basketballs, baseball mitts, and the chewing gum (the kid).

13th year. This is when you moved the sports stuff to the side, put the telephone on your desk and talked to your girlfriends about the cute boys you saw at school (the teenager).

15th Year (going on 21). This is when your hormones start changing and your so-called body starts changing. This is when you ask Daddy for twenty bucks, because you want to go to the mall with your friends (the teen).

17th Year. This is when you get your driver's license. You are now the junior in High School. You think you are the princess of the world (the curfew breaker).

18th Year. This year you graduate from High School. You own a car and you have a fine looking boyfriend. Now you think you're a queen of the world (the teenster).

20th Year. Now you are wondering what college you want to go to. What career you want, what kind of man you want, but you still are cheering inside that your teen years are over (the go-getter).

21st Year. You now are in college seeing your folks only a month, maybe less. You're maturing and seeing what it's like on your own. You are learning lessons out the wazoo (yin-yang) (the maturing process).

24th Year. You are now a graduate not only from high school, but college as well. You now know what you want, why you want and you also own your own place (the entrepreneur).

28th Year. Now your 20's are almost over and you are thinking these years went so fast you're amazed. You have a great car and a great job -- A Catered Affair – and then you think, but not a great man. Well, you have boyfriends but no one that's really special (the lady).

30th Year. You meet someone really special, you introduce your parents to him and a few months later, he gets down on one knee and asks you to marry him and you accept (the bride).

31st Year. You are very happy you have a great job, your husband, Melvin Mallin has a great job, but then you think you want a baby (the dynamic duo).

31st year, 11 months and 2 weeks. Your mom dies. You now really are on your own. You are really sad, but you live every day one at a time (the matured).

32nd year. You have your very first baby. It's a boy. You name him Ross Isaac Mallin. You now are a mother of 1. You have accomplished, really, your main goal in life (the mother).

33rd year. You now have a husband that loves you, a happy healthy baby and a beautiful condo. But you feel as if you haven't accomplished something. Then it hits you, you want another baby (the goal accomplisher).

34th Year. Now you have brought another little boy into your life and the world. You named him Andrew Brett Mallin (the mommy of 2 boys).

35th year. You now live in a house that you and your partner worked for, for many years. You live in now Dunwoody West (the mom).

40th Year. Now you are 40 and a mother of an 8 year old and a mother of a 6 year old. Your husband throws a huge birthday party at 828 Misty Lane (the thinker).

43rd Year. You are now hearing from your kids that they want a dog. So we go and get a little cute shi tzu and we named her Jazzy (mommy at her best).

45th Year. Well you are now a mom. You are a full time mom. You do a bunch. Daddy is doing pretty well in his new insurance business (the Cajun boogeyer)

46th Year. Down in Atlanta Georgia, the schools are getting worse by worse so we decide to move to a better location, Then we think, hey let's make Mommy happy and move to Florida (hectic moving year).

49th Year. Now Mom has done two bar mitzvahs, got married, graduated college and had two baby boys and a billion more thinks. Now both of her kids are going to be in high school. You are a success (life coach).

I meant 39th Year. Ha-ha-ha. Ha-ha. Ha-ha-ha. Ha-ha. Ha.

What can I say? Words cannot express the love and joy and heartfelt awe that I felt then and feel now, as well as many days that I just see this treasure upon my desk. What a walk down memory lane and all through the eyes of my child. Such love poured out of you, Andrew and such clarity at, I believe, 13 years old. How extraordinary to take the time to write my biography, every word was as it appears on this treasure. I am so blessed.

Both you and your brother have a deep admiration and adoration for one another. I cannot share the heart that swells inside my chest at this moment. Having these two sons makes everyday a gift; you guys know that. I used to say that MY idea of success is when my sons are grown and have something amazing happen to them and they each think, "I gotta tell Mom!"

Well, you two have done it and I am, perhaps, THE most grateful mom that I have the capacity to be. Amen and Hallelujah! Thank you G_D!

Every decision is a good decision. It is indecision that keeps you STUCK. Andrew was 17 years old at the time. He is my baby. And like most teens, he, too, was sleeping until 3 PM on the weekends and during the week, had a heck of a time awakening on time to get to school.

He was often late for class and very stuck in a mode of NON-PRODUCTIVITY. Time and time again, he was forced to take a taxi to Lake Mary High School, as he missed the bus. This was the consequence -- of course, he paid for the cab, our thinking that he would learn to be ON TIME.

He took pleasure out of doing nothing – studying and being responsible, as little as possible. Something had to give. My decision was to enroll him in military school for his senior year. Melvin was depressed and not available to help me make the decision. It was THE hardest decision I have ever had to make.

Moving cross-country, divorcing after 23 years of marriage, having elective surgeries that were necessary, were all EASY decisions to make compared to THIS one. My eldest son Ross -- do you remember? You told me, "Andrew would hate you forever, until his LAST BREATH, if I took senior year away from him at Lake Mary."

Twenty-thousand dollars was no small change either. Still, my gut gnawed at me NIGHT after NIGHT agonizing whether or not to send him. Just the thought of perversity and child predators -- every mother's nightmare. Andrew was still only 5'8" and so I had one hard time sending MY baby to military school and it kept me awake at night.

G_D always intervenes. Here I was having a chat with my girlfriend Barbara, I will never forget. I was sitting on the stairs that were split, with both sides leading up to the loft upstairs. Melvin and I were separated. Ross was in college in Tampa and Andrew was out -- it was a Saturday night. I was on the phone with Barbara. I was beginning to pace back and forth, as we were discussing my dilemma. "What do I do with him , Barbara?"

My dear friend and an awesome good mom herself said, "Adrian, parenting is NOT for sissies. If you're a sissy Adrian, go get a puppy."

I heard her. My decision was made. And now all I had to do was APPLY it - THAT would be easier than the indecision.

Do you recall threatening to run away Andrew? I told you GOOD LUCK – GO!" While in my heart - I was packed with fear. Another job description for a good mom - was NEVER let em see you with that fear......smile.

Oh my G_d, Oh my G_d! What a strong confident face I put on for that one. Six days after, Andrew was enrolled and delivered to Florida Military Air. He called me at 5:30 AM. "Mom, I feel like such a man...thank you!"

GLORY BE!

248

Ellen and the Boynton Beach Condo – 2005

So, here it is 2005, before I even moved to South Florida and I was having LOTS of these "coincidences." No they are not coincidences/ rather they are extraordinary experiences, all guided by loving angels above, I BELIEVE.

There are so many, that I have come to study them. I learned that Albert Einstein said that they are the norm. Something else he said about miracles is that they are commonplace. Perhaps it is in our perspective. All I know is that they happen often and always provide me with joy. One of the ingredients is being truthful. Another is being self-aware and another is surrendering to a higher power.

I once went to a psychic with your dad (remember, I am writing this for my sons), across the street from where we lived -- at Brad's house in Atlanta. Remember his son, Michael? Anyway, the psychic told me that I am a truth teller, the likes of which is RARE and that, at times, it is a blessing and at other times it can be a curse. Still, it is a personality trait somewhat before its time.

Daddy stood there and gave me that look like, "See, I've always told you Adrian. I KNEW IT!"

Anyway, I came to learn this that day and so it is. Shocking (actually when he came to distrust me after the divorce -- I think it was Ava, but he allowed it)! ANYWAY, I got carried away! ~Smile.

So, here I am, having visited GOLD COAST, my ballroom now, and I loved, loved, loved it! I took 2 or 3 trips to South Florida while separated. It was my greatest joy during a very somber time. I wouldn't normally have driven down -- HUGE for me (you know how I am about long distance driving) -- but the dancing was so extraordinary. I would get away from my sadness. I would stay in a hotel or motel and stay for a week or sometimes even stayed for 2 weeks. TALK ABOUT ESCAPE!

I made a couple of friends along the way. Here I was sitting at a restaurant with a friend in Boynton Beach, literally in the midst of discussing where I ought to stay for my next visit.

We were BRAIN STORMING, trying to save me some money. I hadn't yet decided to move down here. SO, the eggs arrived as the phone rang and it was this gal that I met and liked from dancing. She began to tell me that she had a friend from UP NORTH -- New York, I believe -- and this friend's parents had recently died, so they had this condo in Boynton Beach...and it was empty.

Her friend was concerned about leaving the condo unoccupied until they could sell it. Ellen continued to share with me how her friend would love to have someone come in, flush the toilets and make sure no bugs came -- basic maintenance. Because she did not know anyone in the complex, she mentioned to Ellen that if Ellen knew someone that might want to live there, she would be thrilled for them to do so and maintain her deceased parents' home. Ellen thought of me!

OH MY GOODNESS! Eggs be damned -- let 'em get cold -- this was AMAZING. So I continued to chat with Ellen (visualize me looking at my friend JOHN, with whom I was dining and trying to get him to understand what is happening...he was paying RAPT attention), "So Ellen, if I hear you correctly, you wanna give her my number, have her send me a set of keys and have me visit there to stay for free whenever I come, flush a few toilets and make sure the place is safe and sound? Is that correct?"

"Yes, maybe stay a week or two and then come back every month or two. Make sure all is well," reported Ellen.

Had I died and gone to Heaven? Was this heaven on earth? Was I blessed or what? OH MY G_D, amazing huh? ~Smile.

SO, I spent the first visit, living in a marvelously well-kept condo, right near the Turnpike -- a breeze down the highway to the Gold Coast.

I was allowed to have friends there. I took excellent care, flushing a few toilets here and there. ~Smile. AND, I basically had a place to reside until I moved down to South Florida. I stayed there after I made the decision to move. It was my home base while I would go out with the realtors during the day and dance at night.

I am so blessed -- I was so blessed. The interesting part is that while I was aware and did know how lucky I was, I was IN the situation, so I truly did not realize, until writing these stories -- writing 'em while reading 'em through your eyes -- how awesomely, amazingly I was blessed. Could it be that G_d was paving my path? OF COURSE! No doubt, that was just one more miracle, a joyful direction that I was being led to. "G_D BLESS my sons -- as I know you are -- and give them the ability to KNOW how fortunate they are, while they are ..me too! Thank you G_d!"

Clearly One of My Greatest Angels -- Ava -- 2006

Perhaps I think out of the box...............perhaps my thinking is evolutionary - the BIG picture.

Daddy met AVA and seemed to be happy - I want him to be happy. I loved him. That will never fade. Quite honestly he always had a THING for redheads.

As much as Ava behaved cordially when I went to introduce myself one day at Dance Orlando - I knew in the recesses - not too far - that she looked at me with Dis EASE. I had been married to your dad for a good 2 decades plus - and in stature - stood very congruently and eloquently in tandem with him.

The day daddy and I came to an agreement - AFTER divorce - how we would split up the money -- he and I not only hugged after a 4 hour cordial meeting at the Hilton /Altamonte Springs - but we kissed. Nothing romantic - just with feeling and gratitude / another step in our unfolding - finally achieved. We were both so happy - and as he got on his motorcycle - he told me that he'd have HIS attorneys draw up the agreement - as he'd already paid a retainer. He was just being kind.

I left the Hilton - headed for Tampa and you, Ross - and was excited to share the good news with You and Theo - and all of the 'angels' that I enlisted in prayer with me. PRAYERS ANSWERED!!!!

252

I arrived some hours later in Tampa - sooooooooooooooooooooo excited - and then went on the computer - almost dusk - to find an email from your dad. It said something like - " All bets are off - I want this house and that - this amount of money - the rent - your inheritances - EVERYTHING!!"

At least that's what I read when I read it - shock of all shocks - oh my devastated world. FINALLY we had come to an agreement - we could go forth into our own separate worlds with LESS baggage - and now that was clearly about to change.

In another story - more details will unfold and yet - shortly after this trauma - there was THE LAWSUIT - where dad sued me to 'overturn' the divorce.

I've not met ONE person who ever heard of such a thing - and yet - it is when one of the parties (spouses) in a marriage seek to change the course of the divorce and begin all over - usually for a financial purpose.

I recall daddy once telling me that he would "NEVER SUE ME". Verbatim. And here that's exactly what he chose to do. Being that no one that I've spoken with has ever heard of such a legal suit -- I wonder how dad came up with the idea? Hmmmmmmm.

Surely - I'll never know - as we do not talk any longer - and while I have reached out multiple times to communicate - I always receive an ill spirited response that says - there will be no communication with my husband.

As I'm typing this - I am beginning to get uncomfortable - my book is NOT a HE SAID / SHE SAID........and I see it drifting in that direction - perhaps you are uncomfortable as well - allegiances are tricky -

So - with that said - this is a story that unfolded in my life - to show me that what seems like an 'enemy' if you will - or an adversary - can sometimes turn out to be an angel in one's life. I believe Ava is one of my greatest angels.

You know the outcome of the legal suit - While it was horrific / on so many levels - betrayal - trust - force - unkindness and more - it turns out to have blessed me financially in ways that I could not have dreamed of - for that I thank Ava - And while it was NOT her intention - on a deeper level - I do believe that it will bless her as well - in some way - as it was God's plan.

When there was an occasion of her speaking poorly of me to you boys - YOU have no idea - how that too blessed me. For a mom - such as myself - to observe her children - disallowing betrayal and 'having my back' - that spoke volumes of your love for me. How else might such an outpouring of loyalty arise?? That too, blessed me immeasurably in ways that I never even imagined.

All I can say - is that I have been reminded of one of the verses of the bible. It's something like "GOD makes your enemies the footstools to your good."

Anyway - I am prospered financially and lovingly by what seemed like an enemy and instead it has RICHLY blessed me. Amen and God Bless you Ava.

Laurie and the Ear Nose and Throat Doctor -- 2006

Too funny -- those that know me well know that there is something about my life that seems pleasantly orchestrated. It is so obviously clear that so many delicious, wonderful manifestations happen to me. Why, I wonder...well, I have an idea why and I will share.

It is just my GUT feeling. I am NOT complaining here, just stating the truth. I have lost most all of those that I have loved in my lifetime -- Mom, Dad, Aunt Ida, Ricky, Uncle Harold, Lily, Nanny -- Grandma, Uncle Greg, Aunt Jeanie, Ray, Linette, Fred and more.

Please know that my sons are my greatest gifts and blessings. I BELIEVE that there is a G_D - inside each of us and there are Earthly Angels and G_dly Angels. I believe that my 'above' relatives and friends that I have lost have become my G_DLY Angels. So, being that there are so many of them UP THERE and basically no family down here to love, I feel as if they are ORCHESTRATING my life in magnificent ways. It is NOT all peaches and cream. I seem to STRUGGLE almost each and every holiday. It was LONELY on July 4th. Everyone was scurrying through their work to get home and begin to barbeque and party with their families and loved ones. I was alone. Surely it is WAYYYYYYYYYYYYYYYYYYYYYYY easier if I am married or have a significant boyfriend. I did not recently and still do not.

ANYWAY, I seem to observe that those who have families HERE, on this plane of reality, are content during their birthdays, Christmas and other family holiday gatherings. I am alone and sometimes that is okay...sometimes it is lonely.

It seems as if for the remainder of the year, the angels are creating so many NEAT and amazing manifestations for my life, what others might call COINCIDENCE.

I recall dating after divorce. I had a wide range of men that I met and went out on dates with. It was almost ridiculous in a GREAT way how so many seemed to be there for me, just when I needed them.

I realized through Laurie's eyes. I would tell her that here I was, out on a date with a man -- of course separate cars -- when MY car broke down and LO and BEHOLD, he was a mechanic. I recall sitting in the parking lot of Wal-Mart, while he opened the hood and ran into the store, and came out and repaired what was wrong with my car. WOW! That was fabulous. Not long after, I was out with Harold. My tooth was cracked or some such malady and lo and behold, HAROLD was a dentist. Anyone that knows me knows that my teeth are my nemesis. Blessedly, Harold had me go into a CVS and purchase some kind of grip, a remedy, until I could get to a dentist…blessed to have been with the dentist. ~Smile.

I continued to have these experiences and one day, I mentioned to Laurie that I had been suffering from a sore throat and achy ears. She said, "Why I'm surprised you don't have a date with an Ear Nose and Throat man."

We laughed. It astounds me that these occurrences are surely MORE than just coincidence. Why would they constantly occur? Am I just more aware of them? I think not…well, maybe to a degree. I think it is my loved ones above who are paving my way and blessing me along the journey! I would have to say, I have no doubt.

Levent -- My Angel Who Helped Me Heal From Mold Poisoning 2007

Life was moseying along when I came down with MOLD poisoning. Funny how Andrew tells me, "MOM, you get the WEIRDEST diseases!"

And he's correct. Who has ever heard of FROZEN SHOULDER? I surely did not. Anyway, there was MOLD in the FLORIDA home I was living in. It was a rental and no matter how healthy you are, MOLD can have its way with you. It surely did with me.

Levent contacted me through a dating site and we met. He was a sweet, smart, loveable guy. I had all sorts of limitations. My energy was very minimal.

I was not my dancing, exercising self...NOT AT ALL. And yet, Levent and I found things to do to help to heal me, as well as have fun. He clearly was my Angel.

Much of what we did was find courses to learn about gaining energy after illness. I remember us making this FERMENTED concoction. It was a bit odd and I do not believe I could have made it without his expertise. He was smart and he cared. We made sure that I was getting the best and latest remedies.

I had my first major European trip scheduled over MOTHER's DAY with Ross. I was feeling rather HORRIBLE, yet Ross and I were so excited. We had never gone away together, just the two of us. I could not cancel, although I probably should have. ALWAYS take insurance for the big trips! To this day, we have YUCKY memories about how less than WONDERFUL the trip to Europe was. Still it was for the two of us and the memories are still poignant. We are both totally grateful to have gone together. While we were in Prague, Budapest and Vienna, I would get calls from Levent to share with me what was going on with the progress of my new home. I had FINALLY found a home that I could move into and get out of the moldy house.

It was all happening around the same time as my trip abroad. And who would handle the contractors building a new kitchen and the floor man putting in wooden floors? Levent...he volunteered. He was SMART, he knew exactly what I wanted and he handled all of the renovations during my absence. He would call me from the States and share the progress. He was an ANGEL!

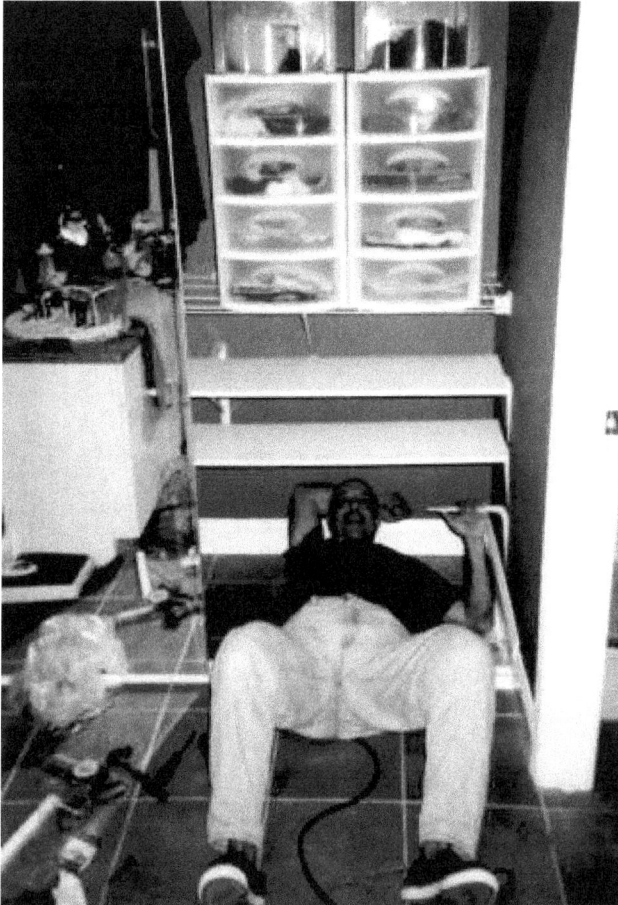

I will never forget when it came time to take title. He came here and cleaned, doing everything a man could ever do to be helpful, loving and kind to me. I was hardly walking through Hungary. It was soooooooooooo challenging. I recall walking down a large avenue, somewhat crying to Ross about how I could hardly move. I had NO energy and Ross said, "Mom, you're 50 years old. Perhaps that's what happens when you get older. You'll be okay."

Oh my G_d! I recall 80 and 90 year olds at the ballroom. They could dance, dance, dance and here I was, hardly able to move. Just when I needed an Angel, Levent was there. I will be forever grateful and beyond. G_D does provide.

John Being My Angel When I Tore My Rotator Cuff -- '08

I became ill with the mold poisoning and many months later - I realized that I was enduring a SOUL passage, FEELING what it must have felt like to be on Melvin's journey. Yes, we might well be divorced, actually have NOTHING to do with one another and yet/still, he is/was my soul mate -- ONE OF THEM.

So, I lie there thinking, day after day, I had NO company; I had no ability to talk on the phone, as it HURT when I spoke. I watched TV and detested it, I read or got up, on occasion, and did my chores. It seemed a huge task just bringing in groceries and maneuvering that ONE step up into the house. I recall lying in the bed, having to go to the restroom, and my brain saying, "Adrian, GET UP OUT OF THIS BED AND GO TO THE BATHROOM OR YOU WILL PEE IN THE BED. NOW GET!"

I surely thought I was going to die. I almost had no doubts. With all of the solitude, I realized that my journey was now giving me the same GROWTH and hurdles that Melvin's journey gave him during his depression. He had NO children around. They were in military school and college. His wife, ME, was out and about trying to keep up with life, managing the real estate and providing myself with joy through ballroom dancing.

I was totally responsible while he was ill, but NOT there for him enough, like sweet companionship, etc. So NOW I HAD A TASTE of that. Surely, this was a lesson to be learned.

No kids were around. Ross and Andrew did not know the severity of my health. Melvin was LONG gone. My friends were kind and emailed me, but literally provided no companionship, as I could not talk. I could not have visitors. Like everything else, I grew to handle it.

I began thinking of Melvin's reality while he was depressed and felt as if mine mimicked his, but in another city, another circumstance. I got a MAJOR taste of the aloneness, etc. I also thought about how long his lasted for…at least 20 months. I also realized that I needed this time to process, cry, realize and FEEL the loss of my marriage. I had earlier danced it away.

We would never be grandparents to OUR grandchildren together. We would never bury one another and lie side by side -- that would never happen. While I prefer not to say NEVER any longer, this was a far reach to ever think that this love could be rekindled .

I literally felt our souls separate -- another story. Anyway, I finally was beginning to feel a bit better. I was eating more and getting out of the house more. The mold had been PARTIALLY removed and I realized that each time I was away from the house, it was healing. I was gaining energy, the beginning of the end of the worst part of the illness. I ended up finding better health through a lecture at Hippocrates, a wellness center.

Along with moving out of the moldy house, it was suggested to me to eat SPROUTS -- LIVE food. So I did, day after day. I did anything and everything I could to regain my health. I went back to the ballroom. I felt a bit like myself again, with much more energy. I had moved and just being out of the sick environment, I was healing rapidly. And, the sprouts were significant in giving me energy. I began dancing again, little by little. Then, ONE night while dancing the foxtrot with Kevin, a fabulous foxtrot dancer (we moved through the ballroom like Fred and Ginger), we were just passing the mirrored post near the restrooms, when QUILQUE, swquack, I felt something tear in my right shoulder. I continued dancing. It hurt for the next few days AND weeks.

I finally sought remedy, but it was THE WRONG KIND. It hurt me more. The point of the story is that I tore my rotator cuff, unbeknownst to me, and once again had to curtail my dancing. Dancing was a way to NOT feel my feelings. Apparently, I needed more time to grieve, to feel the loss of the marriage and future that we had mapped out and FEEL, FEEL, FEEL, without avoiding the grieving part of renewal and loss. I have only learned recently how to FEEL the pain and not mask it with overeating or dancing -- just to embrace, cry and FEEL it. It was HARD. Actually, I never felt the sadness until the injuries and mold forced me to. Ballroom masked all semblance of pain. It is better to grieve when it is appropriate, rather than wait. As I have learned, your body WILL feel what it is meant to feel, ONE WAY OR ANOTHER.

I had lots of time on my hands to just lie there. I realized that I was getting a GOOD taste of Melvin's journey. I do believe our souls have always been connected, regardless of if we speak, see or have anything to do with one another. Interesting, is it not, that he was an insurance man, yet struggled, while I became one and basically did not like it. Still, I tasted HIS journey. Even more interesting is that he was a GIFT salesman. Lo and behold, when I was placed in my volunteer capacity, where did the Boca Raton Hospital place me? … In the GIFT shop. There were at least 100 other voluntary posts, yet they chose me for GIFTS! Coincidence? I think not.

Anyway, I healed more and more, returned with the torn rotator cuff and almost NO ONE wanted to dance with me. My "follow" arm was injured and even the instructors were not comfortable leading me with my left arm. Then I met John, a BIG, tall guy from Nigeria and what an amazing Dancer! He is one of the best. He took a liking to me and each week I would summons the energy to dance all evening with John…with my 3 working limbs. I would rest the torn cuff of my right arm on his chest. I had a ball. I was dancing and he was ultra-protective. We did this for almost 8 months. Finally, I was told by P/T that my arm was as healed as was possible, so now I just needed to take good care of it and basically go back to normal. YAY! YIPPEE! I was elated.

I went to the ballroom, excited to tell John. However, he had something he had to share with me that very evening. "Adrian," he said, "I've just met someone and she doesn't want me to dance with anyone else, so I'm going to have to no longer dance with you. I'm sorry."

OH MY SWEET DEAR G_D! Talk about a reason, a season or a lifetime. Was this a coincidence? I think not! I think the ANGELS gave me JOHN, my sweet friend/Angel to comfort me, dance with me and give me solace during a hard time. There's always an angel that G_D sends to help us through the storms. Watch and see. Thank you G_D and Thank you JOHN! You were my sweet, sweet, FABULOUS dancing Angel.

Getting to the Port in China -- 2/12

Ross and I arrived in Beijing. We had NO idea how challenging it would be to understand and be understood. MOST people that were native BEIJINGER's – (~Smile) I do not know if that is a word -- but most of them did not speak OUR language, NOT a word.

We had places to go, things to see and, of course, did our best to spend as little as we had to, to get where we needed to get to. IN other words, we could have taken the hotel shuttle to the cruise ship for $150 per person; it was a 4-hour, lengthy ride OR we could take the subway, the taxi, the train and then the taxi again for $50, for the two of us. We opted for the inexpensive route, NOT ONLY for $ sake, but WAYYYYYYYYYYYYYYYY more interesting and exciting than a bus full of Americans -- everything we were already used to. We are adventurers.

SO, Ross and I decided for HIM to figure out how to get there. He had more patience than I, in discussing the highways and byways with the concierge at our Marriott. I sat and waited for him, thinking it would be about 10 minutes until he would come over to me and share what they told him. It was more like an hour! I sat and sat and sat and could not understand why it was SOOOOOOOOOOOOOOOOOOOOO involved, yet I learned that it was the language barrier, even at the Marriott.

Finally he came over, a tad bit nervous. He confessed that it was a bit intricate how we would get to the port on that Monday morning. He explained that we had to take a subway to a certain stop, all of this with our luggage, which HE pulled...then, a taxi to the TRAIN station, then the train to the end of the line and then, finally, another taxi to the ship. They had moved the disembarkation port to a new port and Beth had warned us to make SURE we would get to the correct port. It was a bit intense, and we did not even realize just how intense it was going to be, as we were communicating with educated Marriott employees.

The people we would meet along the way were part of the 18 million city dwellers that lived around Beijing. Most had never SEEN an English speaking person, let alone spoke English.

At first we thought during our stay there, that the people were a bit rude, mean and unfriendly, as we would stop them in the streets, ask directions and they literally did not even blink at us...they just walked right past us. WOW! Then, FINALLY, we realized that they did not have a clue as to what we were saying to them and they were busy on their way to work, their homes, and their lives.

Well, we got all dressed up, in hats and gloves. It was 30 degrees out, as we headed out of the hotel, bill paid and on our way to the CRUISE ship. The meat of our trip, a toboggan down the Great China Wall, made our stay in Beijing VERY complete!

We embarked at 11 AM set out for the port, having to be onboard at 4 PM -- LOTS of time. WE got on the subway easily, We had already been there before when visiting Tiananmen Square -- just typing that name and recalling having been there is PURE JOY! Then we exited and found a taxi easily – one to transport us to the train. Once ticketed and onboard, Ross expressed concern that we basically did not have a clue as to where we were heading -- where the train was going and we were heading -- far out SOMEWHERE. He was clearly nervous. For some reason, I was quite calm. I think gratitude for NOT breaking my leg in Beijing was keeping me cool and calm, as well as knowing that if we missed the ship, we would find a way to deal with it. I was just grateful and in Ross' care.

The reason I mention breaking my leg is that a week before we TRIPPED off to Beijing, I had seen a psychic with Burton and she WARNED me very clearly NOT to take the toboggan down the Great Wall. She said I was going to break my leg. UH OH! I listened and decided NO way, I am not going down the great wall. NO THING, NO adventure would be worth a broken leg. Ross and I arrived at the Great Wall. It did not look so ominous, so I went and, VOILA, TA DA, and TOUCHE, no broken leg! AMEN and Hallelujah! The train ride to the port was downhill...no biggie.

Anyway, Ross was a bit apprehensive. So, we settled ourselves in the luxury kind of seating, he on one side of the aisle and I on the other. We gave one another looks as to HOPE that we were heading in the correct direction. He took a chance and asked the young gal next to him IF she spoke English?

"YES, she responded eloquently, "I am a translator. How may I help you?"

Oh my goodness, a translator! WOW! "Well, we're heading to the XYZ port (I don't recall the name) and we're wondering if we are going in the correct direction?"

Not only did she assure us that we were traveling accordingly, but she offered to get us a taxi and bargain with the driver, to try to get us the best price. She was totally kind. Actually, I think she had a CRUSH on Ross! ~Smile.

We gathered our luggage, exited the train and she walked with us to our destination. She found a driver, spoke back and forth and back and forth. We recognized an amount that she was vying for, as well as "SHE-SHE," which we knew meant "THANK YOU." Within minutes we were on our way to the taxi that would take us to the ship. We were driving and driving and driving. It was an hour plus ride and as we passed the signs for PORT, both Ross and I looked at one another with apprehension. Uh oh, perhaps we were going the wrong way. We had PASSED the signs.

After TRYING to have a dialogue with the driver, which was NOT GOING TO HAPPEN, we just let go and prayed for the best. We sat back, a tad bit nervous, yet I was so, so certain that if the angels had planted that interpreter in the middle of nowhere, we surely were not going to be FORSAKEN NOW on our way to the port. We arrived within plenty of time for disembarkation. What a sweet sweet trip. Our angels were among us!

Just last evening, I was meeting a lovely man for dinner at Capital Grille. It was such a nice evening. We talked about this very book and I told him how my life was EXTRAORDINARY. I explained that I was so blessed on how life works for me at times. He said, "Surely these 'stories' sound like more than just coincidence."

Our conversation turned to my frustration for having lost a story during the course of the day -- merely hours before I met him. I was soooooooooooo bummed out. Well, referring back to the story "Laurie and the ENT doctor," you will experience, as we speak, what I mean.

GUESS what Paul does for a living? He is a DATA RECOVERY expert and here, I had lost data. Only LESS than the exciting unfolding of this experience is that he could not locate my story this AM although he was kind enough to spend the time trying. Still, I found it awesome, just that the universe put us together. Maybe we are meant for something other than data recovery -- date recovery perhaps? ~Smile.

And NOW - four months later - Paul and I have become very good friends and lo and behold - guess who has become the EDITOR of this book? Paul was just so very talented - that I literally / seriously LITERALLY - begged him to help me with his expertise in editing and grammar. There are literally NO accidents -

Did I have ANY idea back in July - when Paul and I met - that one day he would become such a significant person in my life?? It is truly amazing - we never know who we're going to meet - and we never know how our 'stories' will unfold. Just KNOW KNOW KNOW. Believe that G_d has a plan and 'HE" is always orchestrating our lives for our highest good. Each time I even read my own stories - my faith and belief renews. Thank you G_d - and thank you Paul!!~

How Do the Angels Work -- 2012

I guess all of these stories have had me ANCHORED, pleasantly to spirit, for the last month or so as I type away. Here is how I think it works and why.

I have always been told that when we pray with the Master Mind, to be SPECIFIC. In other words, if you want to lose weight, ask to lose weight. But make certain that we ask specifically to lose it in a HEALTHY way, as we could lose a limb. Ten pounds would be an answered prayer, just NOT the way we want it. In our asking, it is as if there are "order takers" and they just listen to what we ask for. They make no judgments -- no ask/request is too big or too small. They are just manifestations that are requested of the angels. In other words, okay, here goes. There are angels here on earth, our friends or strangers who assist us most unexpectedly. These are our earthly angels. When they do something to bless us, it is usually that they know exactly what we want or need, i.e.: someone comes and changes your tire or a friend takes care of you.

Then there are Heavenly Angels and it is as if they are UP there, TOTALLY non-judgmental. They give us what we ask for. We do have free will. It is NOT G_D who says, "DO this to her/him!"

It is we who choose. So THEY, the heavenly angels, are listening for us to tell them what we want or need. Do you think it is coincidence when we find the partner that is so perfect for us? Of course not. It is DIVINE, divine being anything heavenly. When we get specific and CALL IT IN, call in all of those qualities, is that coincidence? Of course not. So the Angels are ready, willing, able and eager to serve. We just need to have FAITH that they are listening and have faith that they are sending us what we ask for, as well as know that there are three responses from these Angels and GOD. One is YES and you get your desire. One is NOT NOW and you have to wait. Remember GOD's timing, it might take some time to ready you or your partner that is so perfect for you. The third response is I HAVE SOMETHING BETTER IN STORE FOR YOU.

The idea is to have faith that they are bringing our desire to us. We have to let go and trust them, like when we plant seeds and cannot see what is happening to them under the earth. We just have to trust that they are growing and will sprout eventually, in THEIR own time. Along the way, we usually do NOT get what we want every time we make a request and, therein, we are learning patience, faith and all the lessons that we have come here to learn.

So, share with the angels what it is you seek and be prepared to receive it, be specific and let GOD/ANGELS know when they are getting close to your desire. It is as if it is a blue print and you have had the first run-thru and want to have a "little more of this, a little less of that, refigure this part, etc."

My friends laugh when I request a love/romantic partner and God sends me one. I get back to Him/The Angels the next day, saying YES, he was wonderful and I need a little more of this, a little less of that, until FINALLY, the right and perfect partner comes to me. Then we do the earthly partnership and I have either been blessed by what I requested and received or learn a new lesson.

Put in your Affirmation/Order, because GOD and the Angels, just like us, LOVE gratitude. I truly believe that the right and perfect partner for me is so awesome, such a fine creature of G_d's creation. So it might take time to find this, perfect for me, man. Whatever the reason, it is G_D's timing and I am faithful to know that G_D is working alongside the Angels ON MY FILE. ~Smile.

Thank You G_d -- Thank You for the Flowers -- 11/8/12

Wow, truth is stranger than fiction! GET THIS! I was having a perfectly easy, flowing day -- gym in the morning and walking done by noon -- a day with time to tie all the loose ends, return calls and just FLOW. Mind you, Mercury is in Retrograde and so who knows what lurks behind the planets at this time?

Paul came over and we were editing the book, making plans as to this book and he continued to teach me computer tasks -- A GREAT DAY!

Rick arrived. He is the gentleman that I selected to repair the POPCORN ceiling that had a major leak last April. He was a tad bit late, but no problem! I was home and he was very communicative, telling me his whereabouts and when I could expect him.

The day was superb; actually, it still is. What an amazing ANGEL Rick turned out to be. I was saying goodbye to Paul, literally walking into my kitchen when I heard SOMETHING. It sounded like water and as I entered the kitchen, not TOUCHING the sink, the faucet started pouring out water -- gushing water! OH MY G_D, OH MY G_D! HELP! My sink! I did not even turn it on! It is leaking! HELP! OH MY G_D!

Paul came running and Rick got off of his 14-foot ladder and ran into the kitchen to immediately get on his hands and knees to go under the sink and shut off the water valve, WHICH WOULD NOT SHUT OFF! Water was still pouring out, so in seconds, he zipped OUTSIDE and shut off the main water valve. The three of us stood there in disbelief pondering the fate of this faucet -- a Price-Pfister, which recently had two pieces replaced in the last 3 months and NOW THIS! Long story short -- the drama was still happening -- I called PF for a new faucet cylinder. At least the water was mostly down the drain, rather than making a total mess. Amen to that!

The part is on its way, perhaps in 5-7 days. I could not get it over-night. In response to me asking 3 times, "ARE YOU SURE I CANNOT HAVE WATER FOR MAYBE A WEEK IN MY KITCHEN?"

Rick told me, "Yup, I'm sure!"

I know not to ask again. I CAUGHT myself THIS time, as I have, in the past, asked a dozen times, asking until I get the answer I want to hear…not gonna happen! Oh my, I am getting it! ~Smile.

Anyway, Rick went to the store to get valves, etc. and, lo and behold, he returned with a bouquet of flowers for me. Not being flirtatious, he just saw a guy on the exit ramp selling flowers and while he was stopped for a light, he thought, "Adrian's having a hard day…why not?"

WOW, WOW, WOW! Is this a story of an ANGEL or what? I am so blessed, so grateful and so amazed. What kind of timing would have this amazingly talented contractor here JUST when I needed him? How blessed I am! Thank you G_d for Rick, his help and thank you for the flowers. ~Smile.

I Was My Own Toilet Angel -- 8/12

I am so proud of myself. You might have heard me screaming today, "THANK YOU EKA and THANK YOU G_D."

I might have well shouted, "THANK YOU ADRIAN."

Eka arrived at about 11 AM to do repairs. Ever since Armando, there have been FEWER repairs. Amen and Hallelujah!

Well, this one needed Eka to come out and repair the faucet. It took him 5 minutes and to repair the garage light, another 10 minutes. My goodness, how thrilled I am. Armando tried to repair it and time and time again, it did not work. I have literally been arriving home in the dark and not having a light to see where my keys are to enter the house…NOT good. He repaired the kitchen drawer that had too many utensils, making the bottom of the door drop out from under.

Just as he completed the jobs, he inquired how my beloved master toilet was behaving. It was a major nuisance and he put tender loving care into it last time and, FINALLY, it was fixed. It is one of those quiet old fashioned ones that does not regulate how much water comes out, so it is better than the newer brands.

The only challenge is that after the cleaning ladies were here, there was a residue that was DISGUSTING and HORRIBLE. It looked AWFUL and I was BLAMING them. I scrubbed, Cloroxed and did EVERYTHING I could think of to get this GUNK off. It seemed as if it was just scratched and could not come clean. I was willing to PAINT it, dry it out and put some kind of porcelain paint on it, but all of the authorities that I asked said NOPE, it would not work.

SO, EKA took a look at it. I blamed the cleaning girls again. ~Smile. He said NO, that is calcium, lime and other chemicals. He told me what to get, what to do with it and then, what the maintenance would be. I listened INTENTLY. Normally, I would only give him half an ear and ask HIM to do it. I have always been SEEMINGLY blessed with others DOING stuff for me, yet today was different. I was even MORE blessed. He told ME what to do and I left for Walgreens immediately.

I was able to get the two items at Walgreens, not having to go to Home Depot…YAY! I came home and with a VERY busy day and not lots of time, became TOTALLY unfocused on my day at hand and decided to hang with the toilet and do my miracle. ~Smile. I was on all fours, taking out the water, turning the water valve -- new to me – rinsing, emptying, and finally, setting the chemicals upon the stain.

Blessedly, I had the wash cloths and the equipment, or so I thought. I was instructed to use a bristle brush and, so excited that I had one, when going to use it, it would not fit down the toilet tunnel. IS that a real name, or did I just coin it? ~Smile. "Toilet Tunnel."

Anyway, unprepared, I scrubbed, with rubber gloves, the entire tunnel, over and over and over again, seeing VERY little success. The STUFF was ground on so majorly, that I figured it would NOT work. Still, I continued scrubbing, now sitting and trying NOT to breathe in the chemicals. All of a sudden, BIG chunks of CRUD came loose. It was WORKING! YAY! Ta Da! I continued scrubbing and within the hour, most all of the crud was unhinged. I went into the other bathroom and got rid of the ring around the toilet. Oh my IMMEDIATE GRATIFICATION heart, what a treat. Back to the master and MORE came loose.

WELL, here I am, hours later with a PERFECTLY clean, shiny, gorgeous white porcelain bowl. The rags have all been cleaned on the HOTTEST of hot cycles. And I think I ought to do the advertising for this product. I doubt there has ever been a happier consumer. I called EKA to ask him if any of his clients have ever told him that they LOVED HIM. "NO, "he responded.

Well NOW they have! "I LOVE YOU EKA!"

I could hear a big smile on his face. He then told me that the reason I am soooooooooo, soooooooooooooooo elated and happy is because I DID IT MYSELF! TOUCHE, TA DA, Hallelujah and AMEN, he is 100% correct! I loved being my own toilet angel! It looks GORGEOUS. Do you need to go to the restroom? Use mine! ~Smile.

My greatest "Healing Angel," Barry

My dearest friend and Angel, Elaine

My wonderful mastermind partner Burton

My greatest Accomplishments

My dear friend and Angel, Rick

My dearest Chicago friend Beth

Our States Trips by Adrian Meyer Mallin – 1990

This speech is a challenge - all I know is to relax
Yet I'll share my vacation with you, now that I'm back.

You would think there was romance but it was a bust,
Only a wee glimmer of camaraderie certainly no lust!

We began our journey on the 18th of June,
You'd think we had packed for a trip to the moon.

We took umbrellas and sweaters and a VCR-TV,
We prepared for it all - except the work it would be -

You see Ross is 6 and Andrew is 4
They're a handful to care for - to keep civil for sure.

We arrived first in Denver and picked up the van -
We had maps, books, and trip tiks and a well-made plan.

There was joy in our hearts and a smile on our face
Yet 6 hours' drive to New Mexico - put exhaustion in its place.

But - then we could sleep - no alarm to go 'RING'......
Until 6am the next morning when Ross decided to sing!

Melvin and I could have killed him or disowned him for certain.....
Our eyelids, our bones, our backs, they were hurtin' -

So the vacation - it started - we were in for a shock
There was bathing and food prep and kids who talked back.

Thought with Taos, Santa Fe, Albuquerque and more
We began to get acclimated and our spirits did soar!

We saw mountains and gorges and nature at its best -
Our hearts beat with joy - as we'd ventured out West.

The sights they were awesome and the animals sublime
There is an art to traveling and we'd taken the time! ~

We continued thru Durango and to Utah as well -
We danced in the streets at the Square Dance Festival.

We visited the Tabernacle and the Great Salt Lake
Yuckked up with chemicals but still no mistake~

For we played Duck Duck Goose and we tasted the salt -
We preferred the Coors brewery tour and the taste of good malt.

We drove around curves and scary winding road........
I let go and surrendered for God to carry our load.

We found ourselves in Idaho before the Great Bear Lake
It was breath giving and magnificent what scenery it did make.

We're sick of peanut butter and the rolls we ate each day
Yes I wouldn't change one iota of this trip in any way!

It was scenic and majestic and family at its best -
We fell in love with America with heartfelt zest!

We even got to Wyoming and saw buffalo and sheep
They were grazing around the greenery while Andrew looked for
Bo Peep.

We continued back thru Colorado to Glenwood Springs we went
We celebrated our anniversary and made festive plans for the
event.

You see we hired a babysitter and finally got savvy and smart
We ate superb food, we went for a walk and tended to affairs of
the heart! ~

So our 9th anniversary - it was EVERYTHING great
A break from the boys and time to REALLY celebrate ~

For our trip was almost over and we had 2 days to go -
We swam in the hot springs and went to the best rodeo.

We then headed for Aspen and more beauty galore -
The drive provided us with an unbelievable scenic tour.

We watched a symphony rehearse for that night -
It was magical and marvelous and so delicate and light.

We packed up and drove back to Denver next day
And recounted the blessings we'd had along the way.

It was God's country and we played our part.......
In creating family dreams and this traveling art.

And so now I can relax - it is so great to be home
My own bed - this Toastmaster's group - no more motels to
roam.

My speech tonight and this poetry creation
Have for me added joy to this wondrous vacation.

And so as I close just remember the start
It's just the BEGINNING to this traveling art!!! ~

About the Author – **Adrian Meyer Mallin**

"THEY" say - "Those that are Religious - are afraid of going to Hell - and those that are Spiritual have already been to Hell".

I'd have to say that while I dedicate this book to my Sons, Ross and Andrew - it is the soul journey that I had with my Dad, Arnold - that GLUED me to this spiritual path. Thank you, Dad.

I've always listened to my heart - my mantra was TO THINE OWN SELF BE TRUE. And once figuring out 'my own self' - the rest is a piece of cake. Smile.

My definition of success has always been - - - - when my sons are grown and something WONDERFUL happens in their lives - they will say -" I GOTTA CALL MOM!!"   And when they do that - and they have - - - - -I will be continuously living a successful life! ~

Other successes came in the form of owning my own businesses for most of my adult life - always my own creations - made up businesses. I've tasted foods, countries, businesses, friends and loves from all over the world. I guess I set out to Taste it All~

I reside now - in Boca Raton, Florida after having been born in New York. I moved my life to Atlanta, Georgia, married and birthed my sons - detoured to Orlando for a divorce after 23 years of marriage and became a ballroom dancer - HUGE JOY!!~ Life is good and then you DANCE!!!!~

Ms. Mallin can be reached at YoadrianM@aol.com.

Thanks

I actually do not know how to express my thanks here. It seems so trite to say "words are not enough." And yet, for the first time while writing this 'book'........I am at a loss for words. That's a place I seldom find myself. ~Smile.

This book has been an escape TO LOVE. I have ADORED each and every moment of recalling these stories and seeing them all in a different light then when they were happening and taking place. Some, I fretted and labored over - some I had no faith and total fear from within and so from THIS perspective, looking back, I am grateful first and foremost to my newer vision. I do believe that as I see the world - the world becomes what I think and see.

My mom and so many since, have very often told me, "You think too much." And for that I say - "too much for you - it serves me." I THINK I have a most wonderful life and for that I can say Thank You to my parents, to those that I have loved and have loved me, to my sons for selecting me as their mom, to Joe Kertesz and Durham for helping me to grow healthier, and to all of the ANGELS that I've shared about in this book.

I want to give THE MOST SPECIAL book thanks to Paul Gettleman. I might have been able to WRITE this without him - I surely could not have produced this final product without him. My mom used to tell me that there is NOTHING I cannot do. Well, Mom - I could NOT have made this book the way that Paul spent hours and hours, days and days, meeting after meeting, and patience after patience. He made dealing with me seem sooooooooooooooo easy - and so DON'T LAUGH boys - he was/is a champ!!!!! ~Smile. I must add that he spent his time coming over to my office - never feigned inconvenience, never got annoyed, just did a creative, integrity-packed job and I cannot express the thanks that I feel!!!!

I received blessed generous help editing from Mike Solomon - my brother that I never had. Joe Aronstein gave editing a shot - thank you Joe. And there were multiple others that offered and yet it is PAUL that followed thru and helped me in completing this 'work of heart' that I have labored over for almost a decade and it finally came THRU me in July. It has been like a birth - and I loved THAT process as well.

Thanks to Raymond - you were the first that requested I send you a story or two and then you shared how it "made your day better."   I received countless accolades from countless people that wanted to hear more about faith and angels, surrender and signs. Thank you all. I have so enjoyed this process and have learned how much I like to sit and just write whatever my heart thinks. I've loved it - even watching my sons watch me being so happy not only with DANCE but with writing as well. Smile.

Last but not least - 'we' had the joyful pleasure on this Christmas morning of having my dear friend Olivia Fullerton come over and take photos of Ross and Andrew and me. She was such fun - she is a photographer/creative director and yet more so a generous friend who's expertise and company we so enjoyed.

THANK YOU GOD for all of these joyful, loving and angelic souls that you have sent to me!!!!!~   I am thankful beyond beyond...............0xAdrian

www.ingramcontent.com/pod-product-compliance
Lightning Source LLC
LaVergne TN
LVHW051452080426
835509LV00017B/1741